Education, Student Rights, and the *Charter*

Selected Titles From Purich Publishing Ltd.

Aboriginal Law: Cases, Materials, and Commentary by Thomas Isaac. Second edition, 1999, paper, 640 pages, bibliography, $45.00

The Cypress Hills: The Land and Its People by Walter Hildebrandt and Brian Hubner. 1994, paper, 136 pages, maps, photographs, bibliography, index, $16.50

The Dynamics of Native Politics: The Alberta Metis Experience by Joe Sawchuk. 1998, paper, 192 pages, bibliography, index, $26.00

In Palliser's Triangle: Living in the Grasslands, 1850–1930 by Barry Potyondi. 1995, paper, 144 pages, map, photographs, bibliography, index, $18.50

Indigenous Peoples of the World: An Introduction to Their Past, Present, and Future by Brian Goehring. 1993, paper, 80 pages, maps, bibliography, index, $15.50

Justice in Aboriginal Communities: Sentencing Alternatives by Ross Gordon Green. 1998, paper, 192 pages, map, photographs, index, $27.00

Municipalities and Canadian Law: Defining the Authority of Local Governments by Felix Hoehn. 1996, paper, 400 pages, index, $39.00

Tom Three Persons: Legend of an Indian Cowboy by Hugh Dempsey. 1997, paper, map, photographs, index, $19.50

Urban Indian Reserves: Forging New Relationships in Saskatchewan edited by F. Laurie Barron and Joseph Garcea. 1999, paper, maps, photographs, index, $36.50

Mail orders: add $4.50 shipping and handling for the first title and 50 cents for each additional title. Canadian orders, unless exempt, must also add 7% GST (our registration 867199973) to the order.

Purich Publishing Ltd.
Box 23032, Market Mall Postal Outlet
Saskatoon, SK, Canada, S7J 5H3
Telephone: (306) 373-5311; facsimile: (306) 373-5315
E-mail: purich@sk.sympatico.ca

For more information on these titles, visit our web site at
www3.sk.sympatico.ca/purich

Education, Student Rights, and the *Charter*

Ailsa M. Watkinson

Purich Publishing Ltd.
Saskatoon, Saskatchewan
Canada

All inquiries and orders regarding this publication should be addressed to

Purich Publishing Ltd.
Box 23032, Market Mall Postal Outlet
Saskatoon, SK, Canada, S7J 5H3
Tel: (306) 373-5311; facsimile: (306) 373-5315
www3.sk.sympatico.ca/purich

Canadian Cataloguing in Publication Data

Watkinson, Ailsa M. (Ailsa Margaret).

    Education, student rights and the Charter

    Includes index.
    ISBN 1-895830-13-3

1. Students--Legal status, laws, etc.--Canada.
2. Canada. Canadian Charter of Rights and Freedoms.
I. Title

KE3835.W38 1999   344.71'079   C99-920157-3
KF4150.W38 1999

Editing, design, and layout by Page Wood Publishing Services, Saskatoon
Index by Geri Rowlatt, Victoria
Cover design by NEXT Communications, Inc., Saskatoon
Printed in Canada by Printcrafters, Winnipeg
Printed on acid-free paper

The publisher acknowledges the financial assistance of the Cultural Industries Development Fund, Saskatchewan Municipal Affairs, Culture and Housing, towards the publication of this book.

Table of Contents

Acknowledgements

I wish to acknowledge and thank the Law Foundation of Saskatchewan and the Children's Advocate of Saskatchewan for their financial support, which assisted in the writing and researching of this book.

There were many others who provided support and assistance to me while I was undertaking this task. First of all, thank you Don Purich, my publisher, for your encouragement, guidance, and patience. It was a pleasure working with you. Thank you Jane Billinghurst, my editor, for your diligence and thoroughness. Thank you also to Ken Norman, Professor of Law, University of Saskatchewan, for your review of and comments on the book's content and interpretation. And a special thank-you to all friends and relatives, in particular to Carol Schick, Yvonne Peters, and Allan Wickstrom, who listened to me thinking out loud while I was immersed in research and writing. And while many people assisted me with this book, all judgements, opinions, and errors are mine.

This book is dedicated with love to Allan, Sheldon, Jeffrey, and David

Introduction

Human rights legislation has taken a prominent role in Canadian education over the last decade. The catalyst has been the inclusion of the *Canadian Charter of Rights and Freedoms*[1] in Canada's Constitution. Prior to the repatriation of the Constitution in 1982, provincial legislatures had exclusive jurisdiction over education. Section 93 of the *Constitution Act, 1867* allowed provincial governments to "make laws in relation to Education,"[2] although it restricted their authority to interfere with the rights of religious minorities in denominational schools.

Provincial supremacy "in matters of education" has been limited by the entrenchment of the *Canadian Charter of Rights and Freedoms* in the Constitution. Laws affecting education and the policies and practices of school officials must abide by the rights and freedoms enunciated in the *Charter* and in other human rights legislation. Education—including departments of education, school boards, and school authorities—falls within the authority of the provincial legislatures and is therefore subject to the *Charter*.[3] This means that provincial governments and school boards, while still able to provide direction through laws and policies, must ensure that the rights and freedoms set out in the *Charter* are protected. If they do not protect the rights and freedoms of students and staff, their laws, policies, and practices may be subject to *Charter* challenges.[4]

The *Charter,* along with other human rights statutes—including the recently adopted international *Convention on the Rights of the Child*[5]—is a powerful ally of those subjected to the rules of government, since it provides protection from the sometimes arbitrary, limiting, and excessive policies of decision-makers. If any law or policy is inconsistent with the *Charter*, section 52 rules the law or

---

1   *Canadian Charter of Rights and Freedoms*, Part 1 of the *Constitution Act, 1982,* being Schedule B to the *Canada Act 1982* (U.K.), 1982, c. 11.
2   *Constitution Acts, 1867–1975* (No. 2), s. 93.
3   See s. 32 of the *Charter, supra* note 1.
4   See, for example, *Lutes v. Board of Education of Prairie View School Division No. 74* (1992), 101 Sask. R. 232 (the court ruled that students can expect the right to freedom of speech while in school); *Zylberberg et al. v. Sudbury Board of Education* (1988), 29 O.A.C. 23 (Ont. C.A.) (the court ruled that school prayer was unconstitutional), and *Canadian Civil Liberties Association v. Ontario (Minister of Education)* (1990), 71 O.R. (2d) 341 (Ont. C.A.) (the court ruled that religious practices in school interfered with students' religious freedoms).
5   *Convention on the Rights of the Child,* U.N. Doc. A/RES/44/25 (1989).

policy to be of no force or effect.[6] Not only do school boards and provincial governments face the prospect of having their policies and practices ruled unconstitutional, the *Charter* includes the right to sue for the loss of one's constitutional rights.[7] Over the past ten years a number of important cases have demonstrated the *Charter*'s impact on the role of educational decision-makers.[8] Students, parents, and their advocates have used and will continue to use the *Charter* to challenge the decisions of educators. As legal scholar Wayne MacKay noted:

> The Charter will provide a vehicle for parents and others to ask for a hearing and, in the Charter world of education, educators will have to allow this. The rather select club of educational policy-makers will be opened up to a number of new voices. In that respect the Charter may be a democratizing influence.[9]

Researchers from the University of Alberta recently conducted a study to determine how familiar educators in the four western provinces of Canada were with legal rights in education and to identify the attitudes and values of these

---

6   *Supra* note 1, s. 52. In 1982, for example, the Quebec Supreme Court ruled that part 8 of the *Quebec Charter of the French Language,* otherwise known as *Bill 101,* was inconsistent with s. 23 of the *Charter of Rights and Freedoms,* which guarantees the right of English-speaking parents to have their children instructed in English. Part 8 of *Bill 101* stated that instruction in kindergarten classes and in the elementary and secondary schools in the province of Quebec is to be in French. The decision ruled that the sections contained in part 8 of *Bill 101* were of no force or effect because of the inconsistency.

7   *Doe v. Metropolitan Toronto (Municipality) Commissioners of Police* (1998), 39 O.R. (3d) 487. The case involved a Toronto woman who was raped by a serial rapist. She alleged that the police did not warn her that she was a potential rape victim because of their stereotypical belief that women would become hysterical and scare off the rapist. She successfully sued the police because she was denied equal protection of the law under s. 7 and s. 15 of the *Charter.* She was awarded $220,364.22 in general damages, special damages to date, and future costs. See also, Ken Cooper-Stevenson, "Tort Theory for the Charter Damages Remedy" (1988) 52:1 Sask. L.R. 1.

8   *Jones v. The Queen,* [1986] 2 S.C.R. 284; *Zylberberg et al. v. Sudbury Board of Education,* (1989), 29 O.A.C. 23 (Ont. C.A.); *Russow v. British Columbia (A.G.)* (1989), 35 B.C.L.R. (2d) 29 (S.C.); *Mahe v. Alberta,* [1990] 1 S.C.R. 342; *Canadian Civil Liberties Association v. Ontario (Minister of Education)* (1990), 71 O.R. (2d) 341 (Ont. C.A.); *R. v. Keegstra,* [1990] 3 S.C.R. 697; *Manitoba Association for Rights and Liberties Inc. v. Manitoba (Minister of Education)* (1992), 5 W.W.R. 749 (Man Q.B.); *Central Okanagan School District No. 23 v. Renaud,* [1992] 2 S.C.R. 970; *Eaton v. Brant County Board of Education,* [1997] 1 S.C.R. 241.

9   A. Wayne MacKay, "The Judicial Role in Educational Policy-Making: Promise or Threat?" (1988–1989) 1 Education Law Journal 127 at 148.

educators about legal rights in education.[10] The study found that "few educators in the Western provinces have a firm grasp of the law as it pertains to rights in education."[11] The study also found that educators did not support the mainstreaming of students with disabilities or the abolition of corporal punishment. They were, however, willing to "provide selective support for particular rights, generally in those areas which don't appear to impact directly on their own operations in their classrooms or schools."[12] An earlier American study on the attitudes of educators towards student and teacher civil rights had found that educators were more conservative about the application of civil liberties to students than the courts were.[13] The authors of the Canadian study concluded:

> We should be concerned that educators' level of knowledge of rights is as low [as] this study showed. Until educators acquire a more accurate knowledge of the individual's and group's constitutional and statutory rights regarding education, efforts to develop attitudes supportive of human rights and the *Charter* will likely be less successful than public policy makers might wish.[14]

How educators view student rights may influence how much they know about them. A 1990 study questioned teachers, principals, superintendents, department of education officials, and school board trustees about the rights of students and their parents. The study reported that, among other things, 98 percent of the respondents believed that principals should have the right to choose the appropriate punishment for students, 79 percent said that corporal punishment can be justified, and 66 percent agreed that school authorities should have the right to refuse a parent's request for the admission of a learning disabled child into a regular program.[15] These attitudes are becoming increasingly unacceptable, and, if they persist, they can lead to conflicts between parents and school officials and between school officials and students. These attitudes are contrary to the changing philosophy surrounding public education in which students are seen

---

10 Frank Peters & Craig Montgomerie, "Educators' Knowledge of Rights" (1998) 23 Canadian Journal of Education 29; Frank Peters & Craig Montgomerie, "Educators' Attitudes Towards Rights" (May 1994) The Canadian Association for the Practical Study of Law in Education (CAPSLE), Saskatoon, Saskatchewan.
11 "Educators' Knowledge," *ibid.* at 43.
12 "Educators' Attitudes," *supra* note 10 at 17.
13 J. Menacker & E. Pascalla, "What Attitudes Do Educators Have About Student and Teacher Civil Rights?" (1984) 19 Urban Education 115.
14 "Educators' Knowledge," *supra* note 10 at 45.
15 J.J. Bergen, N.P. Gour, & B.W. Prichard, "Perceptions of School Authorities Regarding the Rights and Freedoms of Students and Parents" (1990) 29:4 The Canadian Administrator 1.

as persons in their own right and not as property to be cultivated.[16] The *Charter* is not going to go away and the more students learn about their rights, the more they are going to pressure officials in departments of education and schools to consider these rights.

It is clear, however, that acquiring knowledge of the law, an important step on its own, is not enough. A change of attitude is also required. A change in attitude requires those who have the power to effect change to engage in reflective thinking. According to John Dewey, a renowned educational philosopher, reflection begins "when old institutions break down: when invasions from without and inventions and innovations from within radically alter the course of life."[17] The invasion from without is the *Charter;* the inventions and innovations from within are increasing student demands for respect of their rights, parent intervention, and changing educational philosophy.

According to Dewey, reflective thinking requires open-mindedness, responsibility, and whole-heartedness.[18] Open-mindedness is the "active desire to listen to more sides than one; to give heed to the facts from whatever source they come; to give full attention to alternative possibilities; and to recognize the possibility of error even in the beliefs that are dearest to us."[19] Educational scholar Vicki Kubler LaBoskey describes open-mindedness as an attitude that enables educators to question all assumptions and rationales, to become experts at alternative points of view, and to see things from the students' point of view.[20] Responsibility is the consideration of long-range goals as well as immediate issues. The reflective educator feels "responsible for helping to fashion a more equitable and humane tomorrow."[21] Whole-heartedness is the strength to move beyond abstract notions and put ideals into practice. It is a willingness to take risks and act despite the fear of being criticized, of disturbing tradition, and of making changes.[22]

---

16 Amy Gutmann, *Democratic Education* (Princeton: Princeton University Press, 1987); Jesse Goodman, *Elementary Schooling for Critical Democracy* (Albany: State University of New York Press, 1992); see also *The Adaptive Dimension in Core Curriculum* (Regina: Saskatchewan Education, 1992) for a discussion of the philosophical changes in education.

17 John Dewey, *The Theory of the Moral Life* (New York: Irvington, 1980) at 30.

18 *Ibid.* at 30–33.

19 *Ibid.* at 30.

20 Vicki Kubler LaBoskey, *Development of Reflective Practice: A Study of Preservice Teachers* (New York: Teachers College, 1994) at 13.

21 *Ibid.*

22 J. Goodman, "Using a Methods Course to Promote Reflection and Inquiry Among Preservice Teachers," in B.R. Tabachnick & K.M. Zeichner, eds., *Issues and Practices in Inquiry-Oriented Teacher Education* (London: Falmer, 1991) at 61.

In 1995, students told the ombudsman for British Columbia that they wanted educators and other government agencies to "respect us, listen to us, inform us, go to bat for us, involve us and don't give up on us."[23] The educators who satisfy the students' criteria are reflective educators. They are able to put themselves "into the shoes" of another, to understand the context of another's circumstances and experiences, and to bring about change. The entrenchment of the *Charter* in the Canadian Constitution has led to a pressure for reform in education. Officials and educators who have both an intellectual and an empathic understanding of student rights will be able to respond effectively to this pressure.

This book examines recent court decisions that have an impact on education. To formulate policies that fulfill the criteria of the *Canadian Charter of Rights and Freedoms*, educational decision-makers need to understand the legal rights of students and the philosophy that guides the courts' interpretation of these rights. The text relates cases to sections of the *Charter* and discusses the philosophy behind each judicial decision. This information will help educational decision-makers formulate school policies that will satisfy the requirements of human rights legislation today.

---

23 *Fair Schools* (Victoria: Office of the Ombudsman, 1995) at 41.

Chapter 1 ■
Human Rights Legislation

Federal and Provincial Human Rights Legislation

As recently as the early twentieth century, many federal and provincial laws in Canada condoned discrimination. For example, women were not eligible to hold public office until they were recognized as "persons" in 1930,[1] and legislation denied Asians, North American Indians, and women the vote,[2] and restricted the employment and business opportunities of Asians.[3]

The first human rights legislation to be passed in Canada was Ontario's 1944 *Racial Discrimination Act,* which prohibited the publication or display of signs, symbols, or other representations expressing racial or religious discrimination.[4] This was followed by Saskatchewan's *Bill of Rights Act*[5] in 1947. The Saskatchewan legislation was more expansive than Ontario's, since it included protection of the fundamental freedoms of speech, press, assembly, religion, and association, and it prohibited discrimination with respect to education, accommodation, employment, and business enterprises. Other provinces soon drafted similar legislation. Enforcement of these early human rights acts was through penal sanctions. The establishment of human rights commissions began

---

1   *Henrietta Muir Edwards v. Attorney General for Canada*, [1930] A.C. 124 (P.C.).

2   Most women were given the vote around 1916 to 1922, but it was not until 1940 that Quebec women gained the right to vote. Status Indians and Asian Canadians had to wait until after World War II; South Asian and Chinese Canadians were not enfranchised until 1947; Japanese Canadians gained the right to vote in 1949; and, in 1960, Status Indians were given the right to vote. For a full discussion of discrimination before the enactment of human rights legislation, see Walter Tarnopolsky & William Pentney, *Discrimination and the Law: Including Equality Rights Under the Charter* (Scarborough: Carswell, 1985) c. 1. See also, Alvin Finkel, *History of the Canadian Peoples: 1867–The Present* (Toronto: Copp Clark Pitman, 1993).

3   *Qwong-Wing v. The King* (1914), 49 S.C.R. 440.

4   *Racial Discrimination Act*, S.O. 1944, c. 35.

5   *Saskatchewan Bill of Rights Act*, S.S. 1947, c. 35. In 1979 the *Saskatchewan Bill of Rights Act,* along with other human rights legislation, was codified into the current *Saskatchewan Human Rights Code*. Chap. S-24.1, S.S. as amended.

in Ontario in 1961, followed by Nova Scotia in 1967. Eventually all provinces and territories created their own human rights commissions, whose duty it was to administer and enforce their respective human rights legislation.[6]

Provincial human rights legislation varies across Canada but generally it protects all citizens from discrimination in education, employment, accommodation, and places customarily open to the public. The *Saskatchewan Human Rights Code* and the *Quebec Charter of Rights and Freedoms* specifically address the right to an education without discrimination. Other provinces protect a student's right to a non-discriminatory education under the sections of their legislation that prohibit discrimination in the provision of services or facilities offered to the public.

In a 1992 case heard before a board of inquiry in New Brunswick, the board considered whether education in public schools was a service. The complainant (the person filing a complaint of discrimination with the provincial human rights commission) alleged that the school board had violated the *New Brunswick Human Rights Act* by discriminating against him and his children in the provision of accommodation, services, or facilities on the basis of religion and ancestry.[7] The relevant section of the act reads as follows:

> 5(1) No person, directly or indirectly, alone or with another, by himself or by the interposition of another, shall
>
> (a) deny to any person or class of persons any accommodation, services or facilities available to the public, or
>
> (b) discriminate against any person or class of persons with respect of any accommodation, services or facilities available to the public,
>
> because of race, colour, religion, national origin, ancestry, place of origin, age, physical disability, mental disability, marital status or sex.[8]

The board of inquiry ruled that section 5 applied to the provision of public education. The board took its direction from the New Brunswick Court of Appeal, which had ruled earlier that public education falls within the purview of services and facilities as stated in section 5 of the *Human Rights Act*. The Court of Appeal said that "to hold otherwise would . . . frustrate the legislative intent of the *Human*

---

6   See Tarnopolsky, *supra* note 2.

7   *Attis v. New Brunswick School District No. 15* (1992), 15 C.H.R.R. D/339 (Board of Inquiry). The board of inquiry agreed with a parent who believed that the board of education had discriminated against him and his children by failing to take appropriate action in the case of Mr. Ross, a teacher who made racist and bigoted statements in writing and in public regarding Jewish people and members of other minority groups. The case was appealed to the Supreme Court, who upheld the decision. See *Ross v. School District No. 15,* [1996] 1 S.C.R. 825.

8   *Human Rights Act,* R.S.N.B. 1973, c. H-11.

Rights Act . . . and amount to a rejection of the broad purposive approach to the interpretation of anti-discrimination legislation adopted by the Supreme Court."[9] The principle has been and will continue to be applied to other jurisdictions that have similar legislation. Thus it appears safe to say that every provincial and territorial human rights act prohibits discrimination in education that occurs due to stereotypical beliefs in the capabilities and worth of certain protected classes of persons.

In 1960, the first major federal human rights legislation was passed. The *Canadian Bill of Rights*[10] was widely attributed to the efforts of then–prime minister John G. Diefenbaker. It proved to be ineffective partly because it was a federal statute and of no consequence in provincial matters and partly because it lacked an enforcement agency. But perhaps the most important reason it was not effective was that it was given a restricted interpretation in the courts.

One well-known example of the Supreme Court's cautious interpretation of the *Bill of Rights* is the case of an Indian woman, Ms. Lavell, who unsuccessfully argued that the section of the *Indian Act*[11] that caused Indian women to lose their Indian status when they married non-Indian men violated section 1(b) of the act.[12] Indian men who married non-Indian women did not lose their status and in fact their non-Indian wives gained Indian status. Lavell argued that Indian women were discriminated against by reason of their sex and that they were not being treated equally before the law. The court, however, ruled that the law had been administered equally because all Indian women were treated in the same manner.[13]

In 1980, the federal government enacted the *Canadian Human Rights Act,*[14] which protects Canadian citizens from discrimination in employment and in the provision of public services provided by federal agencies such as railways, banks, the Royal Canadian Mounted Police, and all departments of the federal government.

The Supreme Court of Canada has made it clear that provincial and federal

---

9   *Attis, supra* note 7, quoting with approval from *New Brunswick School District No. 15 v. New Brunswick (Human Rights Board of Inquiry)* (1989), 10 C.H.R.R. D/6426 at D/6431. The New Brunswick Court of Appeal set aside a Court of Queen's Bench ruling that quashed the application of the human rights board of inquiry to hear the complaint of Mr. Attis. In its ruling, the Court of Appeal found that the Court of Queen's Bench had erred in finding that education was not a public service.

10 *Canadian Bill of Rights*, R.S.C. 1970, App. III.

11 *Indian Act,* R.S.C. 1970, c. 1-6, s. 12(1)(b).

12 Section 1(b) of the *Canadian Bill of Rights, supra* note 10, reads as follows: "1. It is hereby recognized and declared that in Canada there have existed and shall continue to exist without discrimination by reason of race, national origin, colour, religion or sex, the following human rights and fundamental freedoms, namely . . . (b) the right of the individual to equality before the law and the protection of the law."

13 *A.G. of Canada v. Lavell,* [1974] S.C.R. 1349 at 1366.

14 *The Canadian Human Rights Act,* R.S.C. 1985, c. H-6.

human rights legislation is to be given a broad and liberal interpretation rather than a narrow "black letter of the law" interpretation. The Supreme Court described the broad approach to the interpretation of human rights legislation by stating:

> The accepted rules of construction are flexible enough to enable the Court to recognize in the construction of a human rights code the special nature and purpose of the enactment . . . and give to it an interpretation which will advance its broad purposes. Legislation of this type is of a special nature, not quite constitutional but certainly more than the ordinary—and it is for the courts to seek out its purpose and give it effect.[15]

The overall purpose of human rights legislation is to foster respect and security for all members of society. The Supreme Court affirmed that "[h]uman rights legislation is of a special nature and declares public policy regarding matters of general concern."[16] The plain meaning of the words is important and so are the rights enunciated within the words. The Supreme Court stated that since the intent of human rights legislation is to give rise to individual rights of vital importance, "[w]e should not search for ways and means to minimize those rights and to enfeeble their proper impact."[17] Thus, according to the Supreme Court of Canada, to ensure that the intent of human rights legislation is realized—that is, the valuing of all people regardless of their sex, religion, or sexual orientation—rigid and formal interpretations of the law are to be avoided. Human

---

15 *Ontario Human Rights Commission and O'Malley v. Simpson-Sears Ltd.*, [1985] 2 S.C.R. 536 at 546–47. This case is considered a landmark decision in defining adverse impact discrimination. The complainant, a member of the Seventh Day Adventist Church, was required to work Friday evenings and Saturdays as a condition of her employment. Her religion required strict observance of the Sabbath from sundown Friday to sundown Saturday. The court ruled that the application of business rules to everyone can discriminate if the rule affects a class of person adversely.

16 *Winnipeg School Division No. 1 v. Craton*, [1985] 2 S.C.R. 150 at 156. The complainant, a teacher, successfully argued that the mandatory retirement provision of her collective agreement, which forced her to retire at age sixty-five, discriminated against her on the basis of her age.

17 *Action Travail des Femmes v. Canadian National Railway Company*, [1987] 1 S.C.R. 1114 at 1134. The Supreme Court upheld a federal human rights tribunal's decision, which imposed an affirmative action plan on CNR. The case was heard under the *Canadian Human Rights Act*. The court ruled that an affirmative action remedy was an appropriate remedy in cases of systemic discrimination. Employment equity is designed to work in three ways: first, to counter the cumulative effects of systemic discrimination; second, to place disadvantaged group members into the workplace to prove their abilities; and third, to develop a "critical mass" of the previously excluded groups so as to positively influence organizational culture.

rights legislation is "not to be treated as another ordinary law of general application. It should be recognized for what it is, a fundamental law."[18]

Every province has a human rights commission, whose mandate it is to investigate, and wherever possible to resolve, complaints of discrimination. A person in Alberta or Ontario who believes he has been refused educational opportunities because of his sex or colour would file a complaint with Alberta's or Ontario's Human Rights Commission. A person who believes she has been denied a job with a bank because of her sex or colour would file a complaint with the Canadian Human Rights Commission. It all depends on whether the individual or group who it is believed has caused the discrimination falls under provincial jurisdiction (such as education) or federal jurisdiction (such as banks). Human rights laws apply to the private as well as the public sphere. For example, privately owned recreation facilities such as golf courses, skating rinks, or fitness centres must ensure their services are provided to every member of the public without discrimination.

The purpose of human rights legislation is not to punish wrongdoers but to prevent discrimination.[19] Remedies are designed to counter the impact of discriminatory practices, including discriminatory practices that were never intended to cause discrimination.[20] For example, remedies may include financial compensation for the loss of a job because of one's sex or age. Remedies may also include compensation for the humiliation and embarrassment caused by the discrimination or the imposition of an employment or education equity plan to counter the impact of discrimination.[21]

Canadian Charter of Rights and Freedoms

On April 17, 1982, when Canada's Constitution was repatriated from the British parliament, the *Canadian Charter of Rights and Freedoms* was included in the Constitution. The inclusion of the *Charter* in Canada's Constitution cannot be understated. It meant that for the first time in Canadian history fundamental freedoms and equality rights had constitutional status. As part of the supreme law of Canada, the *Charter* trumps all provincial, territorial, and federal legislation that conflicts with the rights and freedoms it protects.

Prior to the enactment of the *Charter*, there was much speculation about its scope. People wondered whether it would bind private as well as public actions, and whether it would address only written laws or whether it would also affect common law and government policies and guidelines. Over the past decade and

---

18 *Insurance Corporation of British Columbia v. Heerspink*, [1982] 2 S.C.R. 145 at 158.

19 *Action Travail des Femmes*, *supra* note 17.

20 *Simpson-Sears*, *supra* note 15.

21 *Action Travail des Femmes*, *supra* note 17.

a half, many of these questions have been answered.

Scope

Section 32 of the *Charter* states:

> 32(1) This Charter applies
>
> (a) to the Parliament and government of Canada in respect of all matters within the authority of Parliament including all matters relating to the Yukon Territory and Northwest Territories; and
>
> (b) to the legislature and government of each province in respect of all matters within the authority of the legislature of each province.[22]

The *Charter* is seen as a shield against the actions or inaction of governments and their agents. It was generally believed that it did not interfere with private actions. However, recent Supreme Court decisions have ruled that the *Charter* regulates private individuals, businesses, and institutions if they are under governmental control or if they function as an aspect of government.[23]

Interpretation

The Canadian Constitution is a special breed of law. It is not an act of Parliament, nor is it an act of the legislature. It is the "Supreme Law of Canada"[24] and, as such, can be amended only by resolutions of the Senate and the House of Commons and by resolutions of the legislative assemblies of at least two-thirds of the provinces comprising at least 50 percent of the population.[25] The supremacy of the Constitution, coupled with the difficulty of amendment, makes its interpretation a matter of national interest.

Whenever a court is asked to decide on a constitutional matter, the court's decision provides new insight into how the Constitution is to be interpreted. Since 1982, when the *Charter* came into effect, the courts have dealt with literally

---

22 *Canadian Charter of Rights and Freedoms,* Part 1 of the *Constitution Act, 1982,* being Schedule B to the *Canada Act 1982* (U.K.), 1982, c. 11, s. 32.

23 *R. v. Carosella,* [1997] 1 S.C.R. 80. The *Charter* reaches into agencies that are provided with government funding, such as sexual-assault crisis centres. In this case, notes taken by a social worker concerning a sexual assault were requested by the defence. The notes had been destroyed. The Supreme Court, in a split decision, found that the destruction of the notes breached the accused's rights under s. 7; *Eldridge v. British Columbia (Attorney General),* [1997] 3 S.C.R. 624. The case considered whether a decision concerning health care was subject to *Charter* scrutiny when the decision was made by a subordinate authority and not the legislation itself. The court said that in order for the *Charter* to apply, the entity must be found to be implementing a specific governmental policy or program.

24 *Charter, supra* note 22, s. 52.

25 *Ibid.* at s. 38.

hundreds of *Charter* cases. The most important decisions are those issued by the Supreme Court of Canada, the court of last resort, simply because its decisions are the final decisions.

One well-respected legal scholar has described the evolution of legal reasoning and decision-making as awkward:

> These fundamental conceptions once attained, form the starting point from which are derived new consequences, which, at first tentative and groping, gain by reiteration a new permanence and certainty. In the end, they become accepted themselves as fundamental and axiomatic. So it is with the growth from precedent to precedent.[26]

Two of the most important messages to come from the Supreme Court through its decisions are that the *Charter,* like other human rights legislation, will be given a broad interpretation and that its application will be interpreted in the context of the situation under review.

Two of the first three *Charter* cases considered by the Supreme Court of Canada referred to a metaphor used by Lord Sankey in 1930 to describe *The British North America Act:*

> *The British North America Act* planted in Canada a living tree capable of growth and expansion within its natural limits. The object of the Act was to grant a constitution to Canada. . . . [I]t is certainly not their [Lordships'] desire . . . to cut down the provisions of the Act by a narrow and technical construction, but rather to give it a large and liberal interpretation.[27]

The analogy of a constitution as a living tree is not only poetic but also appropriate. It places a unique caveat on interpreting the Constitution, as compared with other laws, in that the interpretation of the Constitution is to be broad enough to allow for growth and changing circumstances.

Enforcement

Enshrined in the *Charter* is a section that provides for a remedy whenever a person's rights or freedoms have been infringed. Section 24 states:

---

26 B. Cardoza, *The Nature of the Judicial Process* (1921), quoted in Joseph Beckham & Terrence Leas, "The Legal Research Dissertation: Methodology and Procedures" (1990) 25 NOLPE 1 at 23.

27 *Edwards v. Attorney-General for Canada*, [1930] A.C. 124 at 136. This case was a landmark equality decision for women. The Government of Canada asked the court, "Does the word 'Persons' in the British North America Act, 1867 include female persons?" The judicial committee of the Privy Council ruled that it did.

24(1) Anyone whose rights or freedoms, as guaranteed by this *Charter,* have been infringed or denied may apply to a court of competent jurisdiction to obtain such remedy as the court considers appropriate and just in the circumstances.

(2) Where, in proceedings under subsection (1), a court concludes that evidence was obtained in a manner that infringed or denied any rights or freedoms guaranteed by this *Charter,* the evidence shall be excluded if it is established that, having regard to all the circumstances, the admission of it in the proceedings would bring the administration of justice into disrepute.[28]

Defensive remedies are usually used to guard against unconstitutional laws or government actions. They arise in cases when the accused argues that a law or practice violates his or her rights. When granting a defensive remedy, the court tells the government what it can or cannot do. The Provincial Court of Alberta (Youth Division) granted a defensive remedy in the case of a student who was charged with theft after he and several accomplices admitted to taking $65 from their teacher's purse.[29] The judge in this case dismissed the theft charge because the school principal and the teacher did not advise the youths of their constitutional rights under section 10 of the *Charter,* which states that everyone who is detained or arrested has to be informed of his or her right to a lawyer. The charges were dismissed because the student's constitutional rights had been infringed. The court said:

> To allow the admission of the evidence obtained by the school principal who would no doubt have been unaware of these legal requirements would allow the state to avoid the need to respect the rights of this young person where its own agents are ignorant of the law. I am of the view that such a result would bring the administration of justice into disrepute and accordingly, the evidence of the principal and the accomplices must be excluded under section 24 of the *Charter.*[30]

Defensive remedies are not the only remedies available under section 24. Damages can be awarded, not only to compensate for losses suffered as a result of an infringement of a constitutional right, but also to redress the infringement of the right itself.[31]

The *Charter* also allows courts to have laws or policies declared invalid. Section 52 of the *Charter* permits courts to rule that a law or regulation is of no force or effect if it violates the *Charter*'s goal. It states:

---

28 *Charter, supra* note 22, s. 24.

29 *R. v. H.* (1985), 43 Alta. L.R. (2d) 250 (Provincial Court, Youth Division). The decision was ultimately overturned for reasons not related to the *Charter.*

30 *Ibid.* at 260.

31 M.L. Pilkington, "Damages As a Remedy for Infringement of the Canadian Charter of Rights and Freedoms" (1984) 62 Can. Bar Rev. 517 at 536.

52(1) The Constitution of Canada is the supreme law of Canada, and any law that is inconsistent with the provisions of the Constitution is, to the extent of the inconsistency, of no force or effect.[32]

The courts are empowered to rule that actions or even school programs that infringe on the constitutional rights of students are of no force or effect and must be discontinued. For example, the Ontario Court of Appeal ruled that legislation that provided for religious studies in school violated the *Charter* provision that guarantees religious freedom because religious studies are a form of indoctrination into the Christian faith.[33] As a result, the section of the act and its accompanying regulations were ruled of no force or effect.

The Supreme Court clarified the scope of section 52 by saying:

Depending on the circumstances, a court may simply strike down, it may strike down and temporarily suspend the declaration of invalidity, or it may resort to the techniques of "reading down" or "reading in."[34]

"Reading down"—or severance—is used by the courts so as to interfere as little as possible with the laws adopted by the legislatures. It is used "when only part of a statute or provision violates the *Constitution*, it is common sense that only the offending portion should be declared to be of no force or effect, and the rest should be spared."[35]

The courts must distinguish between the need to read or strike down by first

defining carefully the extent of the inconsistency between the statute in question and the requirements of the *Constitution*, and then declare inoperative (a) the inconsistent portion, and (b) such part of the remainder of which it cannot be safely assumed that the legislature would have enacted it without the inconsistent portion.[36]

The inconsistency is usually something improperly included in the statute that can be severed and struck down. For example, in 1988 the Ontario Court of Appeal ruled that the *Ontario Education Act*,[37] under section 28(1) of its

---

32 *Charter, supra* note 22, s. 52.

33 *Canadian Civil Liberties Association v. Ontario (Minister of Education)* (1990), 71 O.R. (2d) 341 (Ont. C.A.).

34 *Schachter v. Canada et al.*, [1992] 2 S.C.R. 679 at 695. Mr. Schachter successfully applied for a declaration that unemployment insurance benefits should be payable to natural fathers who stayed home to look after babies on the same basis as benefits were payable to adoptive parents. Mr. Schachter alleged discrimination contrary to s. 15 of the *Charter*.

35 *Ibid.* at 697.

36 *Ibid.*

37 *Education Act*, R.S.O. 1980, c. 129.

regulations—which required that public schools be opened or closed each school day with a reading of the Scripture or other suitable readings and the reciting of the Lord's Prayer—was unconstitutional. The remedy in that case was to read down that section only.[38]

By comparison, "reading in" identifies when something has been improperly excluded. The Supreme Court ruled on this matter in the case of Mr. Schachter, a recent father. Mr. Schachter successfully applied for a declaration that unemployment insurance benefits should be payable to natural fathers who stayed home to look after babies on the same basis as benefits were payable to adoptive parents. Mr. Schachter alleged discrimination contrary to section 15 of the *Charter*. The Supreme Court said when the inconsistency is identified as exclusion,

> the logical result of declaring inoperative that inconsistency may be to include the excluded group within the statutory scheme. . . . [T]hat has the effect of extending the reach of the statute by way of reading in rather than reading down.[39]

Thus natural fathers who stay home to look after their children are to be treated the same as fathers who adopt.

To illustrate the need for "reading in," the Supreme Court made reference to a Nova Scotia case where a challenge had been made to a welfare benefit that was available to single mothers but not to single fathers. The situation was found to have violated section 15, the equality section of the *Charter*. The lower court in that case believed that it could not extend the benefit and that the only course available was to nullify the benefits to single mothers. The Supreme Court said:

> [T]he irony of this result is obvious. . . . The nullification of benefits to single mothers does not sit well with the overall purpose of section 15 of the *Charter* and for section 15 to have such a result clearly amounts to "equality with a vengeance."[40]

Under section 52, the courts may also "read up." This option was used in a case involving the exclusion of common-law spouses to insurance benefits. Mr. Miron was injured in a car accident in 1987. Neither the owner of the car nor the driver was insured. As a result of the accident, Mr. Miron could no longer work.

---

38 *Zylberberg et al. v. Sudbury Board of Education* (1988), 29 O.A.C. 23 (Ont. C.A.).

39 *Schachter, supra* note 34 at 698.

40 *Ibid.* at 701–02, referring to the case of *Nova Scotia v. Phillips* (1986), 34 D.L.R. (4th) 633 (N.S.C.A.), in which the Nova Scotia Supreme Court overturned a lower court decision that ruled a section to the *Family Benefit Act* of no force or effect because it provided benefits to single mothers but not to single fathers. The effect of the lower court decision was to remove benefits for everyone—thus, "equality with a vengeance."

Mr. Miron made a claim for accident benefits for loss of income and damages under his common-law spouse's insurance policy. The policy extended benefits to the "spouse" of the policyholder but denied Mr. Miron benefits because he and his common-law spouse were not married.[41] In 1990 the *Insurance Act* governing the insurance policy was amended to include common-law spouses. The case was heard by the Supreme Court in 1995. It reasoned that in such cases it was appropriate to "read up" the earlier statute to the terms legislated in 1990. The result of "reading up" in these circumstances would be "to cure an injustice which might otherwise go unremedied."[42]

The most common type of remedies available under the *Charter* are those mentioned above, but some individuals have used the *Charter* to sue for damages. Jane Doe is one example.[43] Jane Doe was sexually assaulted and raped by a serial rapist. Police knew at the time Jane Doe was raped that the serial rapist's victims were single, white women who occupied second- and third-floor balcony apartments within a district of Toronto. However, police decided not to notify potential victims, partly because they believed such a notification "would cause hysteria on the part of the women and would alert the suspect to flee and not to engage in further criminal activity."[44] Jane Doe brought action against the police department, alleging, among other things, that her right to security of the person under section 7 and her right to equal protection of the law under section 15 and section 28 had been violated by the police. Her suit was vigorously challenged by the Toronto Metropolitan Police Force.[45]

Although few students in Canada have sued school officials breaching *Charter* rights, students in the United States have sued school officials for breaching human rights legislation. In 1991 the Minnesota Department of Human Rights ordered a school division to pay a student $15,000 U.S. after the school division was found to have violated the state's sexual harassment clause. Sexually explicit graffiti about the student had been written on the walls of the boys' washroom

---

41 *Miron v. Trudel*, [1995] 2 S.C.R. 418.

42 *Ibid.* at 510.

43 *Doe v. Metropolitan Toronto (Municipality) Commissioners of Police*, [1998] 39 O.R. (3d) 487. Ms. Doe successfully argued that the actions or inactions of the Toronto Police Force in failing to warn women of a serial rapist violated her *Charter* rights under s. 7 and s. 15. Evidence showed that the police did not warn her of the serial rapist.

44 *Jane Doe v. Board of Commissioners of Police for the Municipality of Metropolitan Toronto* (1989), 58 D.L.R. (4th) 396 at 400 (H.C.).

45 For a discussion of the implications arising from the case, see Mayo Moran, "Case Comment: *Jane Doe v. Board of Commissioners of Police for the Municipality of Metropolitan Toronto*" (1993) 6 C.J.W.L. 491. See also Michelle Lansberg, "Police Owe Explanation to Jane Doe" *The [Toronto] Star* (12 July 1998) A2. For a personal account of the story of Jane Doe, see Kim Pittaway, "Woman of the Year: Who Is Jane Doe?" *Chatelaine* (January 1999) 36.

and had been left there for eighteen months, despite the student's request to have it removed.[46] In 1992, the Saskatchewan Court of Queen's Bench ruled that limiting a student's right to freedom of expression violated his *Charter* right, and allowed the student to proceed with an action for damages for infringement of his fundamental freedom as guaranteed by the *Charter*.[47]

Limitations and Exemptions

The rights outlined in the *Charter* are not absolute. Some of them may be subjected to limitations or even removed completely. Section 1 of the *Charter* allows the rights and freedoms to be limited if the limits are reasonable; section 33 gives governments the option of overriding some of the rights and freedoms as long as they expressly declare, by legislation, their intention to do so.

Section 1 of the *Charter* states:

> 1. The *Canadian Charter of Rights and Freedoms* guarantees the rights and freedoms set out in it subject only to such reasonable limits prescribed by law as can be demonstrably justified in a free and democratic society.[48]

The importance of this section cannot be underestimated. Every *Charter* analysis involves a two-stage process. First, the courts must decide whether a challenged law limits a guaranteed right. At this stage the onus of proving that an alleged breach of the *Charter* has occurred due to the actions of the government or its agent is placed upon the individual challenging the law or government action. If the court agrees that the challenged law limits a guaranteed right, it moves to the second stage, which is to determine whether the limit upon the right can be justified under section 1. The onus of proof shifts to the government or its agent seeking to uphold the limitation. The government or its agent must show that the limit is a reasonable one and can be "demonstrably justified in a free and democratic society."[49] It must do this in the context of a legal system that, in the words of former Justice Wilson, is committed "to uphold[ing] the rights and freedoms set out in . . . the Charter."[50]

---

46   Susan Strauss, *Sexual Harassment and Teens* (Minneapolis: Free Spirit, 1992).

47   *Lutes v. Board of Education of Prairie View School Division No. 74* (1992), 101 Sask. R. 232.

48   *Charter, supra* note 22, s. 1.

49   *Ibid.*

50   *Singh v. M.E.I.,* [1985] 1 S.C.R. 177 at 218. For a more recent interpretation of s. 1, see *Vriend v. Alberta,* [1998] 1 S.C.R. 493, in which the Supreme Court found that the exclusion of sexual orientation from Alberta's *Individual's Rights Protection Act* infringed s. 15 of the *Charter* and could not be justified under s. 1. See also *Rosenberg v. Canada (Attorney General),* [1998] 38 O.R. (3d) 577 at para. 22. The Ontario Court of Appeal ruled that the section of the *Income Tax Act* that permits the

Another important section in the *Charter* that may be used to encroach upon guaranteed rights is section 33(1), which states:

> 33(1) Parliament or the legislature of a province may expressly declare in an Act of Parliament or of the legislature, as the case may be, that the Act or a provision thereof shall operate notwithstanding a provision included in section 2 or sections 7 to 15 of this *Charter*.[51]

Section 33 also stipulates that a declaration made under section 33(1) expires after five years unless it is reenacted for another five years by Parliament or the legislature.

Section 33 is referred to as the "notwithstanding clause" or the "override clause." It empowers the federal and provincial governments to take away fundamental rights. It was drafted as a compromise between the premiers to achieve agreement on repatriating Canada's Constitution. Section 33 caused quite a stir in many circles, but Jean Chrétien, then the Canadian minister of justice, downplayed its importance when he introduced it to the House of Commons. He said:

> The agreement signed by the Prime Minister and nine premiers does not emasculate the *Charter*. Democratic rights, fundamental freedoms, mobility rights, legal rights, equality rights and language rights are all enshrined in the Constitution and apply across the land.
>
> . . .
>
> What the premiers and the Prime Minister agreed to is a safety valve which is unlikely ever to be used except in non-controversial circumstances by parliament or legislatures to override certain sections of the *Charter.* The purpose of an override clause is to provide the flexibility that is required to ensure that legislatures, rather than judges, have the final say on important matters of public policy.[52]

It was generally believed that the political fallout from using section 33 would be so embarrassing that governments would rarely, if ever, use it. The Quebec government, however, has used it by passing a bill exempting all of their laws, where applicable, from the provisions of section 2 and sections 7 to 15 of the *Charter*.[53] On January 30, 1986, the government of Saskatchewan passed *Bill 144,* a law

---

registration of a private pension plan with Revenue Canada only if the plan restricts survivor benefits to spouses of the opposite sex, thus excluding same-sex survivors, discriminates on the basis of sexual orientation and cannot be justified under s. 1. Justice Abella's discussion of s. 1 relied heavily on the earlier decision in *Vriend.*

51 *Charter, supra* note 22, s. 33(1).
52 Canada House of Commons Debates, 20 November 1981 at 13042.
53 *Act Respecting the Constitution Act*, 1982 (S.Q. 1982, c. 21, ss. 1, 2, 5, 6, 7).

ordering its striking government workers back to work. To ensure the bill's safety from any constitutional challenge, the government invoked section 33.[54]

Application to Education

Public education is established by provincial statutes,[55] all children and youth are compelled by law to attend school, and public education is funded by public money. The effect is that the *Charter*'s net falls over the actions, policies, and decisions of departments of education, school boards, and school administrators,[56] as well as over curricula[57] and pedagogical theories.[58] The Supreme Court has also made it clear that independent or private schools that exercise delegated governmental power or are otherwise responsible for the implementation of government policy, such as providing a public education, are bound by the *Charter*.[59] The rationale, the court said, is obvious: "Governments should not be permitted to evade their Charter responsibilities by implementing policy through the vehicle of private arrangements."[60]

Convention on the Rights of the Child

Human rights legislation seeks to protect vulnerable members of our society. Children are vulnerable members of our society because they are politically disenfranchised and because they are often powerless in relation to their parents and other adults. Historically children have been considered chattel and as such

---

54 *Bill 144,* 4th Sess., 20th Leg. Sask. 1985–86. See Donna Greschner & Ken Norman, "The Courts and Section 33" (1987) 12 Queen's L. J. 155, where it is argued that s. 33 ought only to be used to overturn a decision of the courts and not prospectively to preclude a dialogue between the legislative and the judicial branches of government.

55 For example, see *British Columbia School Act*, S.B.C. 1989, c. 61; *Alberta School Act*, S.A. 1988, c. S-31; *Saskatchewan Education Act,* R.S.S. 1978, c. E-0.1; *Manitoba Public School Act*, R.S.M. 1987, c. P-250; *Ontario Education Act*, R.S.O. 1980, c. 129; *New Brunswick School Act*, R.S.N.B. 1973, c. S-5.

56 *R. v. M. (M.R.),* [1998] 3 S.C.R. 393 at para. 25. See, for example, the *Ontario English Teachers Assn. v. Essex County Roman Catholic Separate School Board* (1987), 58 O.R. (2d) 545 (Div. Ct.), which ruled that the *Charter* applies to the actions of school boards; *Lewis v. Burnaby School District No. 41* (1992), 71 B.C.L.R. (2d) 183 (B.C.S.C.), which ruled that the *Charter* applies to a provincially mandated retirement age for teachers.

57 *Canadian Civil Liberties Assn., supra* note 33. Curriculum is considered government conduct authorized by regulation.

58 *Eaton v. Brant (County) Board of Education* (1995), 22 O.R. (3d) 1. The decision was overturned by the Supreme Court on other issues in *Eaton v. Board of Education of Brant County,* [1997] 1 S.C.R. 241.

59 *Eldridge, supra* note 23.

60 *Ibid*. at 658.

have been and continue to be subjected to an authoritarian and paternalistic relationship with their parents and other adults.

On November 20, 1989, the United Nations General Assembly unanimously adopted the *Convention on the Rights of the Child,* which came into force on September 2, 1990.[61] The convention provides a societal vision of children's rights in which the status of children has "evolved from economically valued property to emotionally valued, vulnerable, and emerging persons."[62] The convention has received overwhelming support all over the world. Within a year of its ratification, ninety-four countries had become state parties to the convention, including Canada. No other human rights treaty has ever been ratified by so many countries so quickly.[63]

The *Convention on the Rights of the Child* is an international law, which means that states that have ratified the convention (referred to as State Parties) must review their laws to make sure they are in line with the forty-one articles of the convention. Stephen J. Troope, dean of law at McGill University, noted that "although the *Convention* will not apply automatically in Canada unless it is 'incorporated' into national law, Canadian courts have been inclined to interpret Canadian legislative and administrative actions in the light of Canada's international obligations."[64] This point was clearly made by Chief Justice Lamer in an address to the International Commission of Jurists.[65] International documents, he said, inform the interpretation Canadian courts have given to the *Charter.*[66] The Supreme Court has cited at least one of the six international human rights treaties in twenty-two *Charter* cases, three of which made reference to the *Convention on the Rights of the Child.*[67]

Chief Justice Lamer said the rationale for relying on international human rights law as an aid to *Charter* interpretation are threefold. First, the *Charter* gives "effect to Canada's international legal obligations, and should therefore be interpreted in a way that conforms to those obligations."[68] Second, international

---

61 *Convention on the Rights of the Child,* U.N. Doc. A/RES/44/25 (1989).

62 Cynthia Price Cohen, Stuart N. Hart, & Susan M. Kosloske, "The UN Convention on the Rights of the Child: Developing an Information Model to Computerize the Monitoring of Treaty Compliance" (1992) 14 Human Rights Quarterly 216 at 220.

63 *Ibid.*

64 Stephen J. Troope, "The Convention on the Rights of the Child: Implications for Canada," in Michael Freeman, ed., *Children's Rights: A Comparative Perspective* (Dartmouth: Brookfield, 1996) 33 at 39. See, for example, *R. v. Keegstra,* [1990] 3 S.C.R. 697.

65 Antonio Lamer C.J.C., *Address by the Right Honourable Antonio Lamer, P.C. Chief Justice of Canada* (Address to the International Commission of Jurists, 27 August 1997) [unpublished].

66 *Ibid.* at 1.

67 *Ibid.*

68 *Ibid.*

human rights treaties "serve as a benchmark against which to measure the protection provided by *Charter* rights."[69] Finally, "Canada's international human rights obligations are relevant to *Charter* interpretation because they reflect the values of free and democratic societies."[70] International human rights laws, including the *Convention on the Rights of the Child,* are a reflection of "what it means to live in a free and democratic society."[71]

The convention protects the economic, social, cultural, civil, political, and humanitarian rights of the child. It recognizes that a child needs freedom to develop his or her intellectual, moral, and spiritual capacities, and that the ability to develop these capacities depends on a healthy and safe environment; access to medical care; minimum standards of food, clothing, and shelter; and protection from all forms of exploitation. The convention affirms the obligation of the state to help children develop their capacities. Every five years, State Parties to the convention must report on the measures they have adopted to recognize the rights of children. The reports are made to the Committee on the Rights of the Child, which is the monitoring body of the convention. The reports are to include detailed accounts of the state's record in upholding each of the forty-one substantive articles. If a signatory to the convention fails to comply with these articles, the state is answerable to the international community.

Application to Education

Article 28 recognizes the right of the child to an education. It states:

1. State Parties recognize the right of the child to education and with a view to achieving this right progressively and on the basis of equal opportunity, they shall, in particular:
(a) Make primary education compulsory and available free to all;
(b) Encourage the development of different forms of secondary education, including general and vocational education, make them available and accessible to every child, and take appropriate measures such as the introduction of free education and offering financial assistance in case of need;
(c) Make higher education accessible to all on the basis of capacity by every appropriate means;
(d) Make educational and vocational information and guidance available and accessible to all children;
(e) Take measures to encourage regular attendance at schools and the reduction of drop-out rates.
2. State Parties shall take all appropriate measures to ensure that school discipline is administered in a manner consistent with the child's human dignity and conformity with the present Convention.

---

69 *Ibid.*
70 *Ibid.*
71 *Ibid.*

3. State Parties shall promote and encourage international co-operation in matters relating to education, in particular with a view to contributing to the elimination of ignorance and illiteracy throughout the world and facilitating access to scientific and technical knowledge and modern teaching methods. In this regard, particular account shall be taken of the needs of the developing countries.[72]

Article 29 provides direction on the education of the child. It states:

1. State Parties agree that the education of the child shall be directed to:
(a) The development of the child's personality, talents and mental and physical abilities to their fullest potential;
(b) The development of respect for human rights and fundamental freedoms, and for the principles enshrined in the Charter of the United Nations;
(c) The development of respect for the child's parents, his or her own cultural identity, language and values, for the national values of the country in which the child is living, the country from which he or she may originate and for civilizations different from his or her own;
(d) The preparation of the child for responsible life in a free society, in the spirit of understanding, peace, tolerance, equality of sexes, and friendship among all peoples, ethnic, national and religious groups and persons of indigenous origin;
(e) The development of respect for the natural environment.[73]

Of particular interest is section 1(d), which calls upon educators to prepare students to live in a free society that recognizes and respects the rights of all citizens.

Canada made its first report to the Committee on the Rights of the Child in May 1995. In its response to Canada's report, the committee noted a number of "principal subjects of concern," including the need "to effectively prevent and combat all forms of corporal punishment and ill-treatment of children in school or in institutions where children may be placed."[74] The committee urged the Government of Canada to review legislation that allows "corporal punishment of children by parents, in school and in institutions where children may be placed"[75] The committee also expressed concern for increased suicide rates among Canadian youth, increased child poverty,[76] and the problems facing children from "vulnerable and disadvantaged groups, such as aboriginal children, with regard to the enjoyment of their fundamental rights, including access to housing and

---

72 *Ibid.*, art. 28.
73 *Ibid.,* art. 29.
74 U.N. CRC 9th Sess., 233rd Mtg., U.N. Doc. CRC/C/15 Add. 37 (1995) [Concluding Observations of the Committee on the Rights of the Child. Canada] at 3.
75 *Ibid.* at 5.
76 *Ibid.* at 3.

education."[77] Under the heading Positive Factors, the committee noted with satisfaction "the general strength of the protection of human rights, particularly children's rights through the *Canadian Charter of Rights and Freedoms*."[78]

Conclusion

The history of human rights legislation in Canada began in earnest after World War II. The legislation has expanded in its scope and effect over a fifty-year period at the provincial, federal, and international levels. Perhaps the most significant change for Canadians came in 1982 with the entrenchment of the *Charter of Rights and Freedoms* in Canada's Constitution. For the first time in Canada's history equality rights and fundamental freedoms were given constitutional status. Nineteen eighty-nine saw a change at the international level with the United Nations' adoption of the *Convention on the Rights of the Child*. The impact of the *Convention on the Rights of the Child* has already been felt by the magnitude of its international support. Its impact on the everyday lives of children throughout the world will be worth watching.

---

77   *Ibid*. at 4.
78   *Ibid*. at 2.

Chapter 2 ■
Caring and Contextuality[1]

Educational policy-making, once considered the exclusive domain of provincial governments, is now governed by the *Charter of Rights and Freedoms,* the touchstone against which all federal and provincial government policies are to be measured. The purpose of the *Charter* is to ensure that "Canadian society is free and democratic."[2] A truly free society is one that accommodates diversity, aims at equality, and is "founded in respect for the inherent dignity and the inviolable rights of the human person."[3] With this as a guiding principle, the *Charter* has been interpreted to mean that it will protect the rights of those who historically have been disadvantaged[4] and the courts will provide a voice for those excluded from equal participation in society.[5] The underlying democratic principles and values that the *Charter* protects are human dignity, social justice, equality, respect for differences, and the accommodation of a wide array of beliefs.[6]

With the *Charter* firmly entrenched in the Constitution, the most compelling factor in advancing the rights of Canadian citizens is the courts' interpretation of this fundamental legislation. In decisions made in the late 1980s and early 1990s, the Supreme Court has directed that human rights legislation is to be given a broad and liberal interpretation, that rigid and formal interpretations are to be avoided, and that, when interpreting the rights of individuals, decision-makers must become familiar with the context of the individual's circumstances, reflect on those circumstances, and then come to a decision. This way of thinking is based on an ethic of care and the idea of contextuality.

The Ethic of Care

Carol Gilligan, a psychologist and education professor and current chair of Harvard's Gender Studies Program, has written and researched extensively on

---

1 This chapter is a revised edition of an earlier article, "Equality, Empathy and the Administration of Education" (1994) 5:3 Education and Law Journal 273.
2 *R. v. Oakes,* [1986] 1 S.C.R. 103 at 136.
3 *R. v. Big M Drug Mart Ltd.,* [1985] 1 S.C.R. at 336.
4 *Andrews v. Law Society of British Columbia,* [1989] 1 S.C.R. 143 at 154.
5 *R. v. Holmes,* [1988] 1 S.C.R. 914 at 993.
6 *Oakes, supra* note 2.

two moral orientations,[7] which she refers to as the ethic of care and the ethic of justice.[8] She developed her theory of two moral orientations in response to Lawrence Kohlberg's theory of moral development.[9] Kohlberg was a professor of developmental psychology and moral education at Harvard. His theory proceeds from the familiar premise that everyone should be treated the same and that to treat people differently is unfair.[10] Gilligan calls this the justice perspective. In contrast, the care perspective is based on the premise that hurting others is to be avoided. Adherents of the ethic of care argue that treating oneself and others with equal respect is the mainstay of relationships, and that it is vital to listen to others and to build and sustain trust.

The justice perspective proceeds from the premise that everyone should be treated the same regardless of circumstances; the ethic of care is drawn from a contextual understanding of the circumstances of another. Each of these orientations perceives self differently. Educational researcher Nona Lyons has shown that those who describe the self as separate from others tend towards the ethic of justice.[11] They value autonomy and view relationships as contractual. For adherents of the ethic of justice, relationships are necessary primarily because of the mutual benefit each party derives from them, and they are based on reciprocity and grounded in duty and obligation.[12] In contrast, adherents of the ethic of care perceive the self as connected to others. According to Gilligan, the ethic of care "reflects a cumulative knowledge of human relationships [and]

---

7   Carol Gilligan, *In A Different Voice: Psychological Theory and Women's Development,* (Cambridge: Harvard University Press, 1982).

8   The ethic of care is also referred to as the care orientation and the care perspective. The ethic of justice is sometimes referred to as the justice orientation and the justice perspective.

9   Kohlberg's theory of moral development consists of six sequences within three levels. The pre-conventional level (stages 1 and 2) confronts moral dilemmas with an "egocentric understanding of fairness based on individual needs." This develops upward in a hierarchical progression to the conventional level (stages 3 and 4). At this level, "a conception of fairness is anchored in the shared conventions of societal agreements." The post-conventional level (stages 5 and 6) culminates in principled moral reasoning that demonstrates an "understanding of fairness that rests on the free standing logic of equality and reciprocity." Lawrence Kohlberg, *The Philosophy of Moral Development: Moral Stages and the Idea of Justice* (San Francisco: Harper and Row, 1981) cited in Gilligan, *supra* note 7 at 27.

10   Kohlberg, *ibid.*

11   Nona Plessner Lyons, "Two Perspectives: On Self, Relationships and Morality," in Carol Gilligan, Janie Victoria Ward, & Jill McLean Taylor, eds., *Mapping the Moral Domain: A Contribution of Women's Thinking to Psychological Theory and Education* (Cambridge: Harvard University Press, 1988) 21 at 26.

12   *Ibid.*

evolves around a central insight, that self and other are interdependent."[13] The ethic of care is, in Gilligan's words, "an activity of relationship, of seeing and responding to need, taking care of the world by sustaining the web of connection so that no one is left alone."[14] The ethic of care recognizes the importance of connection between one's self and others and is centred in the need for compassion.

The contrast between these two moral orientations can be seen in how individuals perceive moral problems. When individuals operate within a justice perspective, the focus is on competing rights; within the care perspective, individuals focus on conflicting responsibilities. The ethic of justice, in Gilligan's words, is "formal and abstract. . . . [T]he conception of morality as fairness ties moral development to the understanding of rights and rules"; the ethic of care "requires for its resolution a mode of thinking that is contextual and narrative,"[15] and it centres on an understanding of responsibility and relationships. The care orientation is based on the assumption that human nature is co-operative rather than competitive, connected to others rather than autonomous, inclusive rather than individualistic, and caring rather than egotistical.

The ethic of care includes an ability to empathize, that is to say, an ability to take the role of "the particular other" rather than "the generalized other."[16] Adam Smith, best known for his capitalist economic writings, was also a professor of moral philosophy at the University of Glasgow. In 1759 he wrote the *Theory of Moral Sentiments* in which he described sympathetic understanding, or as he termed it "our fellow-feeling for the misery of others," and its role in our moral life as

> [placing] ourselves in his situation, . . . enduring all the same torments, we enter as it were into his world, and become in some measure [the same person with] him, and thence form some idea of his sensations, and even feel something which, though weaker in degree, is not altogether unlike them. His agonies, when they are thus brought home to ourselves, when we have thus adopted and made them our own, begin at last to affect us, and we then tremble and shudder at the thought of what he feels.[17]

---

13 Gilligan, *supra* note 7 at 74.

14 *Ibid.* at 62.

15 *Ibid.* at 19.

16 *Ibid.* at 11. See also Seyla Benhabib, "The Generalized and the Concrete Other," in Eva Feder Kittay & Diana T. Meyers, eds., *Women and Moral Theory* (New Jersey: Rowman & Littlefield, 1987) at 154.

17 A. Smith, *The Theory of Moral Sentiments* (Edinburgh: A. Kincaid & J. Bell, 1971) at 2–5.

Caring and Contextuality in the Law

Former Supreme Court judges have identified passion and humanity as elements that have been absent from legal decision-making. The former United States Supreme Court judge Justice Brennen said passion is "any mental faculty which is not reason, narrowly defined,"[18] and which is essential to good thinking and judging. He defined passion as "the range of emotional and intuitive responses to a given set of facts or arguments, responses which often speed into our consciousness far ahead of the lumbering syllogisms of reason."[19] Passion, he said, includes personal subjective vision, emotions, intuition and imagination, understanding, love, hatred, empathy, and "all purely personal, irrational, and emotional elements which escape calculation."[20] Former Justice Wilson of the Supreme Court of Canada has called for "a new humanity,"[21] one that requires judges "to enter the skin of the litigant and make his or her experiences part of your experiences and only when you have done that, to judge."[22]

Historically legal matters appear to be the antithesis of caring and empathy. As legal scholar Lynn Henderson writes, the formalistic discourse of law "provides refuge from empathy. . . . [It] can block empathic understanding and moral choice."[23] Feelings are denied legitimacy under the guise of the "rationality" of the rule of law. Law is considered the epitome of the ethic of justice. Lady justice is portrayed as blind, unmoved by the sight of an individual's circumstance, thus ensuring that the rule of law (which holds that all people, regardless of their circumstances, are to be treated the same) will remain sacrosanct.

Henderson advocates the use of empathic narratives to break through the legalistic armour. She describes an empathic narrative as "descriptions of concrete human situations and their meanings to the person affected in the context of their lives. It is contextual, descriptive, and affective narrative, although it need not be 'emotional' in the pejorative sense of overwrought. It is, instead, the telling of the stories of persons and human meanings, not abstractions."[24] Using the case of *Brown v. Board of Education,*[25] Henderson illustrates the impact of the narrative on judicial decision-making. In arguing the case of *Brown,* Thurgood

---

18 Martha Minnow & E.V. Spelman, "Passion for Justice" (1988) 10 Cardoza Law Review 37.

19 *Ibid.* at 39.

20 *Ibid.* at 40.

21 Madame Justice Bertha Wilson, "Will Women Judges Really Make a Difference?" The Fourth Annual Barbara Betcherman Memorial Lecture, Osgoode Hall Law School, York University, 8 February 1990, at 22–23.

22 *Ibid.* at 22.

23 Lynn Henderson, "Legality and Empathy" (1987) 85 Michigan Law Review 1574 at 1590.

24 *Ibid.* at 1592.

25 *Brown v. Board of Education,* 347 U.S. 483 (1954).

Marshall,[26] legal counsel for the NAACP (National Association for the Advancement of Colored People), repeatedly turned to the experience of segregation—its pain, its harm, its evil—and to the irrationality of racism:[27]

> [S]egregation deterred the development [of black children's personalities]. . . . [I]t denies them full opportunity for democratic social development. . . . [I]t stamps [the child] with a badge of inferiority.
>
> The summation of the testimony is that the Negro children have road blocks put up in their minds as a result of this segregation, so that the amount of education that they take in is much less.[28]

As Henderson says, "the Other was in Court, and he was telling the Justices what it was *like* to be the Other."[29] The *Charter* gives the "other" a voice in Canada, and its narrative is legitimized as part of the courts' deliberations. Former Chief Justice Dickson declared that the courts are allies of Canadian democracy and will work to ensure that those who historically have not had a voice will be heard.[30]

The Canadian Supreme Court has stressed that in order to draw meaning from the *Charter,* it is necessary to identify its purpose. In *Hunter v. Southam,*[31] former Chief Justice Dickson stated that the purpose of the *Charter* "is to guarantee and to protect within the limits of reason, the enjoyment of the rights and freedoms it enshrines. It is intended to constrain governmental action inconsistent with those rights and freedoms."[32] In the subsequent decision of *R. v. Big M Drug Mart*, the former chief justice expanded further on a "purposive analysis":

> The meaning of a right or freedom guaranteed by the Charter was to be ascertained by an analysis of the purpose of such a guarantee; it was to be understood, in other words, in the light of the interests it was meant to protect.
>
> This analysis is to be understood, and the purpose of the right or freedom in question is to be sought by reference to the character and the larger objects of the Charter itself, to the language chosen to articulate the specific right and freedom, to the historical origin of the concepts enshrined, and where applicable, to the

---

26 Thurgood Marshall later became the first Afro-American to be appointed to the American Supreme Court.
27 *Supra* note 23 at 1596, quoting from Kasimar, *The School Desegregation Cases in Retrospect*, in Argument xvi.
28 *Ibid.* at 1597.
29 *Ibid.* at 1603.
30 *R. v. Holmes*, [1988] 1 S.C.R. 914 at 993.
31 *Hunter v. Southam,* [1984] 2 S.C.R. 145.
32 *Ibid.* at 156.

meaning and purpose of the other specific rights and freedoms with which it is associated within the text of the Charter.[33]

The purpose of a guaranteed right is to be found by reference to the objects of the *Charter*, to the language used, to the historical origins of the right, and to the meaning and purpose of other rights with which it may be associated. A purposive approach to defining the rights and freedoms is to be "a generous rather than a legalistic one, aimed at fulfilling the purpose . . . of the Charter,"[34] which is that "Canadian society is free and democratic."[35]

But, as former Justice Wilson has pointed out, even a purposive interpretation of a guaranteed right can lead to a rigid interpretation of the law. What is needed, she has urged, is a "contextual approach":

> Of the two possible approaches to the Charter's application one might be described as the abstract approach and the other the contextual approach. . . . Under each approach it is necessary to ascertain the underlying value which the right alleged to be violated was designed to protect. This is achieved through a purposive interpretation of Charter rights.[36]

To illustrate this point, Justice Wilson referred to the reasoning employed by her colleague Justice Cory in a case that challenged a court-imposed media blackout. The media were prohibited from publishing the names of a couple involved in a marital dispute, and the *Edmonton Journal* argued that its right to freedom of expression under section 2(b) of the *Charter* was contravened. Justice Wilson described Justice Cory's approach as abstract: "[T]he underlying value sought to be protected by section 2(b) of the *Charter* [was] determined at large."[37] Abstract decision-making, in this case, focussed solely on the fundamental importance of freedom of expression. But, as Justice Wilson said, "[t]he problem is that the values in conflict in the context of this particular case are the right of litigants to the protection of their privacy in matrimonial disputes and the right of the public to an open court process."[38] Although the ideal of upholding universal principles such as freedom of expression appears laudable, it often succeeds at the expense of the people in the middle. In this case, it was the couple who were seeking privacy in their turmoil. Justice Wilson concluded by saying, "I believe

---

33 *R. v. Big M Drug Mart Ltd.*, [1985] 1 S.C.R. 295 at 344.

34 *Ibid.*

35 *Oakes*, *supra* note 2 at 136. The values of a free and democratic society include respect for the inherent dignity of the human person, commitment to social justice and equality, accommodation of a wide variety of beliefs, and respect for cultural and group identity.

36 *Edmonton Journal v. Alberta (Attorney General)*, [1989] 2 S.C.R. 1326 at 1352.

37 *Ibid.*

38 *Ibid.* at 1353.

that the importance of the right or freedom must be assessed in context rather than in the abstract and that its purpose must be ascertained in context."[39] Justice Wilson's comments in this regard have been quoted with approval by other members of the Supreme Court.[40]

Thus the purposive approach to interpreting the *Charter* and the procedure involved in limiting rights has built a contextual interpretation, an ethic of care, into the *Charter*. This ethic of care requires judges to listen to the plight of the "other" and to reflect on the other's particular circumstances and on the repercussions of judicial decisions.

Caring in Education

One of the directions for education outlined in article 29 of the *Convention on the Rights of the Child* is to prepare children for life in democratic society. Lawrence LeBlanc, in his discussion of the *Convention on the Rights of the Child*, included the right to an education in the category of empowering rights, which "include all those rights that relate to a person being heard on matters that affect his or her life."[41] Other rights that fall into this category include freedom of expression and thought, freedom of conscience and religion, and freedom of association and assembly. David Purpel, an American professor of education, has argued that the public school is "the only major institution specifically charged with the responsibility for nourishing and sustaining democracy."[42] Education is central to developing an intellectual capacity that enables students to "think seriously and critically about what it means to live a good life; to examine and appraise actions, institutions and ideas; and to choose a course of action on the basis of such appraisals."[43]

If education is to attain its purpose of preparing students for life in a democratic society, the educational environment must emulate a democracy and empower students. The democratic model asks teachers and all those involved in the education system to "adapt their programs, instruction, and the learning environment to accommodate the developmental levels and learning needs of all students in the classroom."[44] Schools in Canada, in contrast, are by and large

---

39 *Ibid.* at 1356.

40 *Rocket v. Royal College of Dental Surgeons of Ontario,* [1990] 2 S.C.R. 232 at 246–47; *R. v. Keegstra,* [1990] 3 S.C.R. 697 at 737.

41 Lawrence J. LeBlanc, *The Convention on the Rights of the Child: United Nations Lawmaking on Human Rights* (Lincoln: University of Nebraska Press, 1995) c. 6 at 157.

42 David Purpel, *The Moral and Spiritual Crisis in Education: A Curriculum for Justice and Compassion in Education* (Massachusetts: Bergin and Garvey, 1989) at 49.

43 Jack Donnelly & Rhoda Howard, "Assessing National Human Rights Performance: A Theoretical Framework" (1988) 10 Human Rights Quarterly 214 at 235.

44 *The Adaptive Dimension in Core Curriculum* (Saskatchewan: Saskatchewan Education, 1992) at 6.

governed by a traditional authoritarian model that expects children to adapt or fit within the school environment.

Purpel has suggested that the need to control student behaviour reflects an obsession within the traditional authoritarian model of education. The need to control has placed a higher priority on productivity, efficiency, and uniformity than on flexibility, diversity, rights, and freedoms. Disciplinary rules are promulgated to reinforce control over students. School rules make it implicit or, if necessary, explicit that "it is the school that decides, the school that allows, lets, gives permission, waives, makes exceptions. It is the students who petition, request, and plead."[45]

Purpel contrasted the traditional model with the democratic model, which stresses "self determination and a process for both sustaining autonomy and adjusting conflict."[46] Purpel defined a democratic school setting as a student-centred environment with small classes, student input in decision-making, and attention to individual needs. In this atmosphere students and teachers get to know each other well. The school becomes a community of students, teachers, and administrators, who are all working together to nurture "fundamental humane and creative educational thinking, enabling them to bestow upon their pupils the happiness of school life and the joy of exchanging ideas with the teachers."[47] A democratic, nurturing, positive, and supportive environment promotes social networking, co-operative behaviour, and creative and self-enhancing independence.[48]

Educators have been criticized by Purpel and others for their obsession with technical matters, order, control, and consistency at the expense of caring. Where rules and regulations must be followed (rare exceptions allowed), educators have permission to overlook the unique circumstances of individual students. John Dewey, an American educational philosopher, advised teachers to abandon the technical stance and the comfort of a rut. He stated that "[t]he path of least resistance and least trouble is a mental rut already made."[49] He advocated for more sympathy, humanity, and reflection in dealing with students and educational matters. Sympathy, he said, "functions properly when used as a principle of reflection and insight. . . . Intelligent sympathy widens and deepens concern for consequences."[50]

---

45 *Supra* note 42 at 49.

46 *Ibid.*

47 Shalva Amonashvili, "Non-directive Teaching and the Humanization of the Educational Process" (1989) 19 Prospects 581 at 585.

48 Edward W. Schultz *et al.,* "School Climate: Psychological Health and Well Being in School" (1987) 57 Journal of School Health 432 at 432.

49 John Dewey, *How We Think: A Restatement of the Relation of Reflective Thinking to the Education Process* (New York: D.C. Heath, 1933) at 30.

50 John Dewey, *Theory of the Moral Life* (New York: Irvington, 1980) at 107.

Over ten years ago, Thomas Greenfield, a Canadian professor of educational administration, decried the loss of human passion from education. He believed that when educational administrators embraced the scientific study of organizations, they lost their humanity.[51] Greenfield was particularly contemptuous of Herbert Simon whose "adult" and "most fashionable" work brought the methods of science to administration.[52] Simon's vision was to build a theory of administration based on scientific knowledge. According to Greenfield, once Simon had convinced others in the field that science was on their side, his aim was to ensure that administrators made efficient and effective decisions. However, to do this, Greenfield says, they had to rid themselves of value, humanity, and passion.

Greenfield could be describing the justice perspective. The justice perspective relies on "an impartial logic . . . based on impersonal standards or universal principles."[53] Decision-makers who rely on universal principles to guide them in decision-making remove themselves from the complexities of another's situation. The result is that a decision, which may have untold consequences for another, is made in almost total disregard of that person's unique circumstances.

It is the caring perspective that is often missing from the structural rigidity of education.[54] And yet education is the very institution that requires more caring. After all, it is young, developing children who attend school. When courts interpret human rights legislation, especially in an educational context, it is not enough to ensure that rights, in a universal, abstract (ethic of justice) sense, are upheld. Education scholar Onara O'Neill argues that parents and educators need to expand their understanding of equality and fundamental freedoms to include "a fundamental obligation to be kind and considerate in dealing with children—to care for them—and to put ourselves out in ways that differ from those in which we must put ourselves out for adults."[55]

O'Neill cautioned against relying too heavily on the notion of student rights because of the rigidity of the obligation. She argued that those who meet only their obligation of living up to a student's rights will meet the "perfect obligation"

---

51 Thomas B. Greenfield, "The Decline and Fall of Science in Educational Administration"(1986) 17:2 Interchange 57 at 59–60. Greenfield is referring to the work of Herbert Simon whose book *Administrative Behavior* "offered . . . a method of value-free inquiry into decision making and administrative rationality" at 58.

52 Greenfield, *ibid.* Greenfield was reporting Simon's description of his own work.

53 Lyn Mikel Brown, ed., *A Guide to Reading Narratives of Conflict and Choice For Self and Moral Voice* (Harvard: Center for the Study of Gender, Education, and Human Development, 1988) at 111.

54 For a more expanded discussion, see Ailsa M. Watkinson, "Equality, Empathy and the Administration of Education" (1994) 5:3 Education and Law Journal 273.

55 Onara O'Neill, "Children's Rights and Children's Lives," in Philip Alston, Stephen Parker, & John Seymour, eds., *Children's Rights and the Law* (Oxford: Oxford University Press, 1992) at 24.

but not the "imperfect obligation." The distinction being that perfect obligations correspond to legal rights, "they specify completely or perfectly not merely who is bound by the obligation but to whom the obligation is owed."[56] They do not rely on specific social or political conditions. Perfect obligations correspond to the justice perspective; imperfect obligations are analogous to the ethic of care. The care perspective considers the particular other with sympathetic understanding, empathy, passion, and humanity. Imperfect obligations, O'Neill noted, are often trivialized as being "frightfully nice," as being matters of "decency," or as being "morally splendid."[57] They are considered supererogatory.[58] But "parents or teachers who meet only their perfect obligation would fail as parents or teachers."[59] A single focus on a rights-based approach, O'Neill warned, cannot take full account of the ways in which children's lives "are particularly vulnerable to unkindness, to lack of involvement, cheerfulness or good feeling. . . . Cold, distant or fanatical parents and teachers, even if they violate no rights . . . can wither children's lives."[60]

Educational administrators are informed how to lead, how to motivate staff, and how to develop morale, but their training contains scant discussion of issues such as

[r]adical and conservative critiques of school structure and curriculum, disputes over religion and language of instruction, the virtues of private versus public schools, class and cultural bias, unions, women, discipline, dress codes . . . and many other issues.[61]

Many of these issues are now being forced upon the consciousness of educational administrators, and they require empathic consideration.

There have been a number of *Charter* cases heard before the courts that involve educational institutions at various levels. The Supreme Court has ruled that section 23 of the *Charter* gives French-speaking parents the right to establish their own schools,[62] that the public's interest in public education is an overriding interest that cannot give way to a parent's wish for unapproved religious home schooling,[63]

---

56 *Ibid.* at 26.

57 *Ibid.* at 28.

58 *Ibid.*; Joy Kroeger-Mappes, "The Ethic of Care vis-a-vis the Ethic of Rights: A Problem for Contemporary Moral Theory" (1994) 9:3 Hypathia 108. Kroeger-Mappes wrote that "the supererogatory thesis asserts that the activity of caring, which is perceived as supererogatory for most men, is perceived as obligatory for most women" (at 113).

59 *Supra* note 55 at 27.

60 *Ibid.* at 28.

61 Greenfield, *supra* note 51 at 67.

62 *Mahe v. Alberta,* [1990] 1 S.C.R. 342.

63 *Jones v. The Queen,* [1986] 2 S.C.R. 284.

that the segregation of students with disabilities into special classrooms is a last resort,[64] that employees of school boards whose religion is different from the religion of the majority must be accommodated by adjusting the workplace so as to allow them to maintain their Sabbath,[65] and that a teacher's freedom of expression does not include the right to promote hatred against a protected class.[66] Other courts have ruled that reciting the Lord's Prayer and reading from the Bible in school are unconstitutional,[67] that harassment in schools violates the equality provisions of the *Charter*,[68] that students have a right to freedom of expression,[69] and that school authorities have an obligation to combat harassment by undertaking substantive educational measures to neutralize an environment that condones harassment.[70] Even so, Greenfield's 1986 comments are not out of date. In fact they are all the more poignant when one considers that the *Charter* has been used and is continuing to be used to challenge the decisions of educational administrators while there appears to be a continuing lack of any real consideration given to these issues in the educational setting.

The traditional authoritarian model of education has proven extremely resilient, with the result that democratic principles are being overridden and the democratic rights of students in the areas of fundamental freedoms and equality are being ignored. For example, how many schools have students represented on staff selection committees, provide procedures to ensure the students' right to fair and impartial hearings, develop policies expressly prohibiting harassment of students by other students and staff, develop policies supporting equality of representation in curriculum, allow students to control their own newspapers, or provide a mission statement that supports empowering pedagogical practices? Educators are much more comfortable talking about student responsibilities than about student rights. It is time to talk about student rights—their democratic right to equality and fundamental freedoms—and about the responsibility of educators to uphold those rights.

---

64 *Eaton v. Brant County Board of Education*, [1997] 1 S.C.R. 241.

65 *Central Okanagan School District No. 23 v. Renaud*, [1992] 2 S.C.R. 970.

66 *R. v. Keegstra*, [1990] 3 S.C.R. 697; *Ross v. School District No. 15*, [1996] 1 S.C.R. 825.

67 *Zylberberg et al. v. Sudbury Board of Education* (1989), 29 O.A.C. 23 (Ont. C.A.); *Russow v. British Columbia (A.G.)* (1989), 35 B.C.L.R. (2d) 29 (S.C.); *Canadian Civil Liberties Association v. Ontario (Minister of Education)* (1990), 71 O.R. (2d) 341 (Ont. C.A.); *Manitoba Association for Rights and Liberties Inc. v. Manitoba (Minister of Education)* (1992), 5 W.W.R. 749 (Man. Q.B.).

68 *Quebec Human Rights Commission v. Board of Education of Deux-Montagnes* (1994), 19 C.H.R.R. D/1.

69 *Lutes v. Board of Education of Prairie View School Division No. 74* (1992), 101 Sask. R. 232. A grade 9 student received a month of noon-hour detention for singing a rap tune, "Let's Talk About Sex." The student sang the song in the presence of the assistant director of the school division.

70 *Quebec Human Rights Commission, supra* note 68.

Educators need to consider why they govern schools the way they do, why teachers teach the way the do, what educators' premises are about students and student behaviour, and who is harmed by school rules and the "way things have always been." Thomas Sergiovanni, a professor of educational administration, has stated that "[t]he heart and soul of school culture is what people believe, the assumptions they make about how schools work, and what they consider to be true and real."[71] If the heart and soul of school culture remain ensconced in the traditional model, then increasing pressure from students and their parents on the subject of student rights will lead to conflict between those who attend schools and those who run them. If educators reject the traditional model and work instead to create a caring and democratic educational environment, then schools will be able to get on with the job of preparing children to take their places in a democratic society.

Conclusion

The new *Charter* obligations provide an exciting foundation on which to build a new school order, informed by the care orientation, that demonstrates through its educators respect for the dignity of all students, a commitment to social justice and the equality rights of all persons, acceptance of a wide variety of beliefs, and respect for diverse cultures and group identities.[72]

The courts' interpretations of the fundamental and equality rights contained in the *Charter* serve as evidence that the former expectations and practices of educational administrators are inappropriate, harmful, and possibly litigious. The care orientation is constitutionally demanded of educators, giving judicial clout to Professor Nel Noddings's contention that caring is a necessary credential to teach.[73] The ethic of care most certainly is essential in handling the current and sometimes volatile issues of racism, sexism, and the treatment of other minorities.[74] Only when educational institutions embrace this new order can we have faith in them. Only then can we honestly say that they "enhance the participation of individuals and groups"[75] in the educational setting and in so doing prepare students to take their places in the kind of democratic and caring society in which we purportedly wish to live.

---

71 Thomas J. Sergiovanni, *Leadership for the Schoolhouse: How Is It Different? Why Is It Important?* (San Francisco: Jossey-Bass, 1996) at 3.

72 *Oakes, supra* note 2.

73 Nel Noddings, *Caring: A Feminine Approach to Ethics and Moral Education* (Berkeley: University of California Press, 1984) at 197–200. See also Nel Noddings, "The Gender Issue" (1992) 49 Educational Leadership 65, in which she argues for an inclusion of women's culture in educational planning.

74 See Ailsa M. Watkinson, "Valuing Women Educators," in Samuel M. Natale & Brian M. Rothschild, eds., *Values, Work, Education: The Meanings of Work* (Atlanta: Rodopi, 1995).

75 *Oakes, supra* note 2 at 136.

Chapter 3 ■
Limiting Rights and Freedoms

School authorities are empowered, by their education acts, to set school rules, regulations, and policies. School rules, regulations, and policies that limit the rights and freedoms of students may be justified if they meet the requirements of section 1 of the *Charter.* Section 1 of the *Charter* reads:

> The Canadian Charter of Rights and Freedoms guarantees the rights and freedoms set out in it subject only to such reasonable limits prescribed by law as can be demonstrably justified in a free and democratic society.[1]

Although section 1 may be used by school authorities to justify limiting the rights and freedoms of students, the section clearly states that school authorities must justify any limits they impose. The onus placed on educational decision-makers to defend their reasoning provides students and their advocates with a powerful tool with which to question decisions and practices that restrict student rights. Section 1 may also become a useful evaluative tool for those who set school policies and school rules because it requires school officials to clearly articulate the justification for rules and policies that limit student rights.

Process

As noted earlier, whenever a court considers a *Charter* challenge, it employs a two-stage process. During the first stage, the court determines whether the law or practice that is being challenged limits a guaranteed right. The onus of proof at this stage is placed upon the individual who is challenging the law or government action:

> It is for the claimant to show that he or she had been denied a benefit or suffers a disadvantage compared with another person. It is also for the claimant to show the basis for imposing the burden or withholding the benefit. These matters are within the knowledge of the claimant.[2]

If the court finds that the challenged law limits a guaranteed right, this does

---

1 *Canadian Charter of Rights and Freedoms,* Part 1 of the *Constitution Act, 1982,* being Schedule B to the *Canada Act 1982* (U.K.), 1982, c. 11, s. 1.
2 *Miron v. Trudel,* [1995] 2 S.C.R. 418 at 485.

not mean that the law is unconstitutional. The court then moves to the second stage of deciding if the limit is a reasonable one and if it can be "demonstrably justified in a free and democratic society." The second stage puts the onus of proving that a limit is justified on the government or its agent. It is considered sound "to leave to the state the burden of justifying the restrictions it has chosen."[3] After all, it is the state that is in the position to defend its actions. To require the claimant to prove that the limit is based on irrelevant or irrational considerations "would be to require the claimant to lead evidence on state goals . . . beyond the reach of the ordinary person."[4]

The division between these two steps is crucial. As already discussed, each section of the *Charter* is to be interpreted in a broad and generous manner, leaving the justification for narrowing the right or freedom for conflicting social and legislative purposes to section 1.[5]

Interpretation

Four years after the *Charter* came into effect, the Supreme Court came head to head with the question: what constitutes a reasonable and justifiable limit to a right or freedom in a free and democratic society?[6] In a decision that is referred to as the Oakes test, the court outlined two criteria that must be satisfied before a limit can be considered reasonable and demonstrably justified in a free and democratic society. Limiting a right or freedom is acceptable if the court finds that the objective (the end) to be gained by the limit is sufficiently important and the method chosen (the means) to limit the right or freedom is reasonable and demonstrably justified.[7]

The standard to be used in measuring the worth of the objective must be high to ensure that "objectives which are trivial or discordant with the principles integral to a free and democratic society do not gain s. 1 protection."[8] The focus, at this point, is not the objective of the overall legislation or policy, but rather the particular limitation that infringes a *Charter* right. The focus of the inquiry is on the limitation that infringes the equality right, and the "pressing and substantial test is the objective not of the statute or section but of the infringing limitation in that statute of section."[9] At this stage, the court identifies the underlying functional

---

3   *B. (R.) v. Children's Aid Society of Metropolitan Toronto*, [1995] 1 S.C.R. 315 at 383.
4   *Miron, supra* note 2.
5   *Ibid.* at 486.
6   *R. v. Oakes,* [1986] 1 S.C.R. 103.
7   *Ibid.* at 138.
8   *Ibid.*
9   *Rosenberg v. Canada (Attorney General)*, (1998) 38 O.R. (3d) 577 at 584. The Ontario Court of Appeal ruled that the section of the *Income Tax Act* that permits the registration of a private pension plan with Revenue Canada only if the plan restricts survivor benefits to spouses of the opposite sex, thus excluding same-sex survivors,

values of the government's objectives so as to expose "legislation aimed at effecting a less than worthy goal [which] may be cloaked in the rhetoric of justice and reason."[10]

Once the objective to be gained by limiting a right has met the appropriate standard, the government or its agent invoking section 1 must show that the limit is reasonable and demonstrably justified. To do this, the government must address the three components of the Oakes test, which are designed to "balance the interests of society with those of individuals and groups."[11] First, the government or its agent must provide cogent and persuasive evidence that clearly shows that the method is designed to achieve the objective and is rationally connected to it. The court said, "Where a distinction or limit is irrelevant to the achievement of the objective the limit cannot be saved."[12] Second, the government or its agent must show that the method impairs as little as possible the right or freedom in question because there are no less restricting methods available that will achieve the same objective. Finally, the government or its agent must show that there is proportionality between the deleterious effects of the method and the objective to be met and its salutary effects.[13] This latter point was added in a 1994 decision when the court rephrased the third part of the Oakes test as follows:

> [T]here must be a proportionality between the deleterious effect of the measures which are responsible for limiting the rights and freedoms in question and the objective, and there must be a proportionality between the deleterious and the salutary effects of the measure.[14]

---

discriminates on the basis of sexual orientation and cannot be justified under s. 1. Justice Abella's discussion of s. 1 relied heavily on the earlier decision in *Vriend v. Alberta*, [1998] 1 S.C.R. 493. In *Vriend*, the Supreme Court found that the exclusion of sexual orientation from Alberta's *Individual's Rights Protection Act* infringed s. 15 of the *Charter* and could not be justified under s. 1.

10 *Miron, supra* note 2 at 503.

11 *Ibid.*

12 *Ibid.* at 559.

13 *Oakes, supra* note 6 at 139. Since the Oakes test was first articulated, it has suffered a great deal of criticism. The criticism was focussed not so much on the stringency of the test as on the court's diluting its impact. See Pamela Chapman, "The Politics of Judging: Section 1 and the *Charter of Rights and Freedoms*" (1986) 24 Osgoode Hall L.J. 867. The author argues that the Supreme Court has avoided using the Oakes test, using instead threshold tests (*R.W.D.S.U. v. Dolphin Delivery Ltd.*, [1986] 2 S.C.R. 573), bowing to legislative deference (*R. v. Edwards Books and Art Ltd.*, [1986] 2 S.C.R. 713), and ignoring it altogether (*Jones v. The Queen*, [1986] 2 S.C.R. 284). However, the more recent cases of *Vriend* and *Rosenberg, supra* note 9, show evidence of a return to the Oakes test as it was first understood.

14 *Dagenais v. Canadian Broadcasting Corp.*, [1994] 3 S.C.R. 835 at 888–89. In this case, the Supreme Court set aside a publication ban imposed on the CBC, prohibiting

At first glance, the Oakes test appears to be no more thorough than a technical analysis of policy-making. Although the standards to be met are high, there is little doubt that the process is more technical than philosophical. Attention is given only to ensuring that the means to the end are appropriate without questioning the values and mechanisms of the system within which the ends are set. But that is not the complete picture. It must be remembered that during the court's discussion of limits to rights, the former chief justice said that the purpose of the *Charter* is to ensure that "Canadian society is free and democratic,"[15] and that the values and principles of a free and democratic society include

> [r]espect for the inherent dignity of the human person, commitment to social justice and equality, accommodation of a wide variety of beliefs, respect for cultural and group identity, and faith in social and political institutions which enhance the participation of individuals and groups in society.[16]

Thus, "the same values undergird limits on rights as inform the rights themselves."[17] The limits on rights and freedoms are to be justified within the framework of respect for the inherent dignity of students, commitment to justice and equality, accommodation of a wide variety of beliefs, and respect for group and cultural differences.

Section 1 has been described as "distinctively Canadian because it fits well with parliamentary democracy by trying to reconcile individual and community rights."[18] Justice McLachlin compared the American and Canadian approaches to restricting rights and noted that one of the major differences was that the Canadian method of analysis permits

> a sensitive, case-oriented approach to the determination of their constitutionality. Placing the conflicting values in their factual and social context when performing the s. 1 analysis permits the courts to have regard to special features of the expression in question.[19]

Section 1 demands a contextual approach, as former Chief Justice Dickson said:

---

the broadcasting of the mini-series "The Boys of St. Vincent," a fictional account of sexual and physical abuse of children in a Catholic institution in Newfoundland.

15   *Oakes, supra* note 6 at 136.

16   *Ibid.*

17   Lorraine Eisenstat Weinrib, "The Supreme Court of Canada and Section One of the Charter" (1988) 10 Supreme Court L.R. 469 at 438.

18   Ruth Colker, "Section 1, Contextuality and the Anti Disadvantaged Principle" (1992) 42 U.T.L.J. 77 at 84.

19   *Rocket v. Royal College of Dental Surgeons of Ontario*, [1990] 2 S.C.R. 232 at 246–47. This quote was also quoted with approval in *R. v. Keegstra,* [1990] 3 S.C.R. 697.

It is important not to lose sight of factual circumstances in undertaking a s. 1 analysis, for these shape a court's view of both the right or freedom at stake and the limit proposed by the state; neither can be surveyed in the abstract.[20]

Chief Justice Dickson described the "synergetic" relationship between the values the *Charter* is intended to uphold and the circumstances of a particular case as central to judicial interpretation. He stated that "a rigid or formalistic interpretation to the application of s. 1 is to be avoided."[21] The determination of whether a limit meets the principles and values of a free and democratic society requires an examination of the context of an individual's or group's circumstances. The result of a contextual exploration often arouses feelings of empathy, filling the void of what former Justice Wilson described as the need for "a new humanity," one that requires judges "to enter the skin" of another before they judge.[22]

Application to Education

In a 1995 discussion on the role of section 1, Justice McLachlin of the Supreme Court discussed, by way of example, legislation that prohibits the issuing of a driver's licence to a person under the age of sixteen. On its face, this rule is discrimination on the basis of age. The reason for the rule is the government's concern for public safety. It is the government's duty, the court said, to show that most people under the age of sixteen are not competent and responsible drivers and thus that "the age of sixteen may be defended as a relevant marker of those who should be permitted to drive."[23] The court said that in such cases, a group or characteristic—in this case age—can be used to justify limiting a right or freedom if the group or characteristic "excludes most people who should be excluded given the goal of the legislation, and only a few who should not."[24] But using a marker such as age to restrict who may apply for a driver's licence would not be reasonable if the marker were not relevant in maintaining public safety, if there were another less restricting means available to protect public safety, or if the marker excluded more good drivers than bad.

In 1996 the Supreme Court considered the interpretation of section 1 in a case involving the right of a teacher to freely express his opinion and the right of students to a learning environment free of discrimination.[25] The court took heed

---

20 *Keegstra, ibid.*

21 *Ibid.* at 737.

22 Madame Justice Bertha Wilson, "Will Women Judges Really Make a Difference?" The Fourth Annual Barbara Betcherman Memorial Lecture, Osgoode Hall Law School, York University, 8 February 1990, at 22–23.

23 *Miron, supra* note 2 at 505.

24 *Ibid.* at 504.

25 *Ross v. School District No. 15*, [1996] 1 S.C.R. 825.

of the educational context in which this case appeared. It considered it highly relevant that a central function of a public school is "the inculcation of those fundamental values upon which a democratic polity rests."[26]

The case involved a teacher, Mr. Ross, who had made racist and discriminatory statements in writings and on public television. He had also published four books outlining his beliefs. The thrust of his argument was that "Christian civilisation was being undermined and destroyed by an international Jewish conspiracy."[27] A parent, Mr. Attis, filed a complaint with the New Brunswick Human Rights Commission alleging that the board of school trustees discriminated against him and his children, in breach of the New Brunswick *Human Rights Act,*[28] by failing to take appropriate action against Mr. Ross. A board of inquiry was established to investigate the complaint.

The board of inquiry concluded that the school board had discriminated against Mr. Attis and his children by failing to discipline Mr. Ross meaningfully. The board of inquiry considered the response of the school board to be one of indifference in that by continuing to employ Mr. Ross, the school board was endorsing his out-of-school activities and writings. The board of inquiry held that the inaction of the school board "resulted in an atmosphere where anti-Jewish sentiments flourished and where Jewish students were subject to a 'poisoned environment' with the school district which has greatly interfered with the educational services provided."[29]

The board of inquiry then issued an order that set forth four criteria directing that Mr. Ross be placed on a leave of absence, without pay, for a period of eighteen months; that he be appointed to a non-teaching job if a non-teaching job became available for which he was qualified; that his employment be terminated at the end of eighteen months if he had not been offered and accepted a non-teaching job; and that his employment with the school board be terminated immediately if, at any time, he continued to publish, write, or sell anti-Jewish material.[30]

The case was appealed, eventually being heard by the Supreme Court of Canada in 1996. The court was asked to consider two issues. The first issue was to determine whether the school board had violated section 5(1) of the New Brunswick *Human Rights Act,* thus discriminating against Mr. Attis and his children by continuing to employ Mr. Ross.[31] The second issue was whether the

---

26 *Ibid.* at 872.
27 *Ibid.* at 836–37.
28 *Human Rights Act*, R.S.N.B. 1973, c. H-11.
29 *Ross, supra* note 25 at 838 (quoting from the decision of the board of inquiry).
30 *Ibid.*
31 *Supra* note 28. S. 5(1) states: "5(1) No person, directly or indirectly, alone or with another, by himself or by the interposition of another shall . . . (b) Discriminate against any person or class of person with respect to any accommodation, services or facilities available to the public, because of race, colour, religion, national origin,

board of inquiry's order that Mr. Ross be removed from his teaching position infringed his fundamental freedoms under sections 2(a) (freedom of conscience and religion) and 2(b) (freedom of thought and expression) of the *Charter* and if it did, whether limiting his rights could be justified under section 1.

The Supreme Court, in a unanimous decision, found that the school board had failed to maintain a positive environment, and it quoted with approval the board of inquiry, which had said:

> In such situations it is not sufficient for a school board to take a passive role. A school board has a duty to maintain a positive school environment for all persons served by it and it must be ever vigilant of anything that might interfere with this duty.[32]

The Supreme Court then considered whether the board of inquiry's order violated Mr. Ross's right to freedom of religion and expression as found under sections 2(a) and 2(b) of the *Charter*. The court found that it did; however, it also found that limiting Mr. Ross's fundamental freedoms was justified because of the context of this case. In coming to this conclusion, the court considered the following points, as laid out in *Oakes*.[33]

1. The objective is of sufficient importance

The Supreme Court found that the board of inquiry's order to remove Mr. Ross from the classroom was necessary to combat the discrimination that had poisoned the educational environment.[34] The court acknowledged that the objective of eradicating discrimination was sufficiently important because it asserted Canada's commitment to the international community. Canada is a signatory to international conventions calling for the eradication of discrimination by prohibiting the dissemination of ideas based on racial or religious superiority. The Supreme Court referred to the decision of *Canada (Human Rights Commission) v. Taylor*,[35] in which the court found that "the objective of promoting equal opportunity unhindered by discriminatory practices based on race or religion was pressing and substantial."[36]

The sufficiently important objective to be gained by the board of inquiry's order, the court said, promoted the values of equality and multiculturalism enshrined in the *Charter* and acknowledged the pernicious effects of hate

---

ancestry, place of origin, age, physical disability, mental disability, marital status, sexual orientation or sex."

32 *Ross, supra* note 25 at 861.

33 *Supra* note 6.

34 *Ross, supra* note 25 at 879.

35 *Canada (Human Rights Commission) v. Taylor*, [1990] 3 S.C.R. 892.

36 *Ross, supra* note 25 at 879.

propaganda, which undermine the basic democratic values of the *Charter*. The court concluded that "[b]ased upon the jurisprudence, Canada's international obligations and the values constitutionally entrenched, the objective of the impugned order is clearly 'pressing and substantial.' "[37]

2. Method chosen is reasonable and demonstrably justified

The method chosen by the board of inquiry to remedy the poisoned educational environment was reasonable and demonstrably justified because

(a) The method chosen was designed to achieve the objective

The Supreme Court found that it was reasonable to anticipate "a causal relationship between [Mr. Ross's] conduct and the harm—the poisoned educational environment"[38] and that the poisoned educational environment was dependent upon Mr. Ross maintaining his teaching position. They reasoned that the causal relationship was anticipated because "of the significant influence teachers exert on their students and the stature associated with the role of teacher."[39] Thus it was necessary to remove Mr. Ross from his teaching position "to ensure that no influence of this kind is exerted by him upon his students and to ensure that the educational services are discrimination free."[40] However, the court noted that the fourth criterion in the order, that is that Mr. Ross's employment while on leave of absence or while employed outside the classroom be terminated immediately if he ever published, wrote, or sold anti-Jewish literature, was not rationally connected to the objective.

(b) The method impaired as little as possible the right or freedom

The Supreme Court agreed that the first three criteria in the board of inquiry's order were carefully tailored to meet the specific objective of ameliorating the poisoned educational environment and minimally impaired Mr. Ross's freedom of religion and freedom of expression. The court supported the board of inquiry's assertion that the harm caused by the teacher's beliefs could not be corrected through an apology and renunciation of Mr. Ross's views, nor could it be corrected through continual monitoring of his classroom because the influence of a teacher is "so much more complex."[41] The board had also rejected the idea of excluding Jewish children from his classes and the idea of offering monetary compensation for pain and suffering. However, the court concluded that the fourth criterion, which imposed a permanent ban on Mr. Ross's freedom of religion and expression, did not minimally impair the respondent's constitutional freedoms. Thus the fourth point in the board of inquiry's order could not be justified under section 1.

---

37 *Ibid*. at 880.
38 *Ibid*.
39 *Ibid*. at 881.
40 *Ibid*. at 881–82.
41 *Ibid*. at 883.

(c) There is a proportionality between the effects of the order and the objective

The Supreme Court found that the deleterious effects of the order upon Mr. Ross's freedom were limited to the extent necessary to attain the purpose. Mr. Ross, the court said, was still free to exercise his fundamental freedoms once he left his teaching position. The court reasoned that "the objectives of preventing and remedying the discrimination in the provision of educational services to the public outweigh any negative effects on the respondent produced by these clauses."[42]

Conclusion

Although the case discussed above considers limiting a teacher's rights, the same process is available to students who find their rights limited. The requirement of meeting a section 1 test is of value to those challenging the authority of school officials because it forces school officials to justify their decisions. In addition, section 1 is a useful tool, or filter, through which school officials can evaluate and reflect upon the decisions they make or contemplate making.

Some writers propose that policy analysts schooled in critical theory should be consulted whenever educational policies are drafted. These authors note that a critical policy analyst would be "openly political, adopting an advocacy stance rooted in a commitment to a 'vision of moral order in which justice, equality, and individual freedom are uncompromised by the avarice of a few.' "[43] The critical approach envisioned by the authors is one in which the analyst "would seek 'to expose the sources of domination, repression and exploitation that are entrenched in, and legitimated by, educational policy.' "[44] It is my position that the *Charter* does this for us. It gives us the right to advocate and to expose issues of domination, repression, exploitation, and inequality by placing the onus of justification on those with the power and authority to dominate and repress.

It is worth repeating that limits are to be screened against the backdrop of respect for the inherent dignity of the student, commitment to social justice and equality, and the accommodation of a wide variety of beliefs.[45] The educational context is important in any analysis of the actions of those in authority. Public education is designed to inculcate the fundamental values of a democratic society and, as was confirmed in the *Ross* decision,

---

42 *Ibid.* at 885.
43 Lyn Bosetti, Dale Landry, & Erwin Miklos, "Critical Perspectives on Educational Planning and Policy Analysis" (1989) 29:2 The Canadian Administrator 1 at 5, referring to J. Prunty, "Signposts for a Critical Educational Policy Analysis" (1985) 29:2 Australian Journal of Education 133.
44 *Ibid.*
45 *Oakes, supra* note 6.

every individual has a right to be educated in a school system that is free from bias, prejudice and intolerance; . . . any manifestation of discrimination on the basis of gender, race, ethnicity, culture or religion by any persons in the public school system is not acceptable; and . . . school programs and practices [are to] promote students' self-esteem and assist in developing a pride in one's own culture and heritage.[46]

When the rights of students are limited, school authorities must be able to show that the limit meets a sufficiently important objective, given the importance of education in awakening children "to the values a society hopes to foster and to nurture."[47] In addition, the limit must be reasonable and justifiable. It must be rationally connected to the objective, there must be no less restricting method available of achieving the same objective, and there must be a proportionality between the effect of the limit and the objective that is not excessively deleterious.

The educational landscape, influenced by the legal landscape, is changing. Students have rights—democratic rights—and any infringement upon them must be justifiable. Truncated justifications will not do. An analysis of policy within the framework of section 1 goes beyond a strict technical analysis to a careful consideration of whether school policy promotes or unduly impedes a democratic society.

---

46 *Supra* note 25 at 872. These are the guiding principles of the Government of New Brunswick's Ministerial Statement and they were considered "highly relevant" in this case—as they would be in any case dealing with public education.

47 *Ibid.*, paraphrasing with approval from the American case of *Brown v. Board of Education of Topeka*, 347 U.S. 483 (1954), in which the American Supreme Court stated: "Today education is perhaps the most important function of state and local governments. . . . It is the very foundation of good citizenship. Today it is a principal instrument in awakening the child to cultural values, in preparing him for later professional training, and in helping him to adjust normally to his environment" (at 493).

Chapter 4 ■
Freedom of Conscience and Religion

The fundamental freedoms enunciated under section 2 of the *Charter* are the foundations of a democratic society. Section 2 states:

> 2. Everyone has the following fundamental freedoms:
> (a) freedom of conscience and religion;
> (b) freedom of thought, belief, opinion and expression, including freedom of the press and other media communications;
> (c) freedom of peaceful assembly; and
> (d) freedom of association.[1]

These freedoms affect students' rights to freedom of religion and from religion, freedom of expression, including student publications, and the freedom of students to organize and demonstrate in the traditional democratic manner. Student fundamental freedoms are, without a doubt, among the most powerful forces behind the shift from the traditional authoritarian model to a more democratic model of school governance.

Fundamental freedoms have been one of the most litigated topics in the area of students' rights in American schools. The First Amendment of the American Constitution, which is similar to section 2 of the *Charter*, prohibits Congress from making laws that establish a religious belief or prohibit the free exercise of speech, press, or assembly. The importance of fundamental freedoms is underlined by an American Supreme Court decision that adopted the principle that "freedom of press, freedom of speech and freedom of religion are in a preferred position."[2] In referring to the position these rights hold in America, the Canadian Supreme Court concurred, saying: "It is this same centrality that . . . underlies their designation in the *Canadian Charter of Rights and Freedoms* as 'fundamental.' They are the *sine qua non* of the political tradition underlying the *Charter*."[3]

Canada's political tradition as a democracy is identified by "the ability of each citizen to make free and informed decisions [which] is the absolute

---

1   *Canadian Charter of Rights and Freedoms,* Part 1 of the *Constitution Act, 1982,* being Schedule B to the *Canada Act 1982* (U.K.), 1982, c. 11, s. 2.
2   *Murdock v. Pennsylvania,* 319 U.S. 105 at 115 (1943).
3   *R. v. Big M Drug Mart Ltd.,* [1985] 1 S.C.R. 295 at 346.

prerequisite for legitimacy, acceptability and efficacy of our system of self-government."[4] Freedom of assembly has been referred to as "speech in action." It is the physical act of meeting so as to communicate, share thoughts, and share emotions. This chapter looks at freedom of conscience and religion; the next chapter looks at freedom of expression and assembly.

Interpretation

The First Amendment of the American Constitution begins with the statement: "Congress shall make no laws respecting an establishment of religion."[5] It is referred to as the "establishment clause." The courts have interpreted this as erecting a "wall of separation between church and state."[6] Unlike the Constitution of the United States, the Constitution of Canada does not set up a wall between church and state; in fact, the *Charter* inextricably links the two. The preamble to the *Charter* states: "Whereas Canada is founded upon principles that recognize the supremacy of God and the rule of law." Even so, the Supreme Court has noted: "The Charter safeguards religious minorities from the threat of 'the tyranny of the majority.' "[7]

Freedom of religion under the *Charter* was first considered by the Canadian Supreme Court in the 1985 case of *R. v. Big M Drug Mart Ltd.* The case involved a challenge to an Alberta law forbidding stores to be open on a Sunday. The Canadian Supreme Court ruled that section 4 of the *Lord's Day Act,* which required businesses to close on Sundays, infringed the right to freedom of conscience and religion as guaranteed under section 2(a) of the *Charter*.

The court said:

> Freedom must surely be founded in respect for the inherent dignity and the inviolable rights of the human person. The essence of the concept of freedom of religion is the right to entertain such religious beliefs as a person chooses, the right to declare religious beliefs openly and without fear of hindrance or reprisal and the right to manifest religious beliefs by worship and practice or by teaching and dissemination.
> . . .

---

4   *Ibid.*

5   This provision specifically prohibits Congress from making such laws, but in 1940 the United States Supreme Court established that this also applies to the states in *Cantwell v. Connecticut*, 310 U.S. 296 (1940).

6   *Everson v. Board of Education of Ewing*, 330 U.S. 1 (1947). The establishment clause states that "Congress shall make no law respecting an establishment of religion, or prohibiting the free exercise thereof." See Francis Graham, *Wall of Controversy: Church-State Conflict in America* (Malabar: Florida: Robert E. Kreiger, 1986); Jesse H. Cooper, *Securing Religious Liberty* (Chicago: The University of Chicago Press, 1995).

7   *Big M Drug Mart Ltd., supra* note 3 at 337.

> Freedom in a broad sense embraces both the absence of coercion and constraint, and the right to manifest belief and practices. Freedom must mean that, subject to such limitations as are necessary to protect public safety, order, health, or morals or the fundamental rights and freedoms of others, no one is to be forced to act in a way contrary to his belief or his conscience.[8]

In other words, religious freedom is the right to openly declare one's religious beliefs without fear, coercion, or constraint. It is not, however, an absolute freedom.

> [It] is restricted by the right of others to hold and to manifest beliefs and opinions of their own, and to be free from injury from the exercise of the freedom of religion of others. Freedom of religion is subject to such limitations as are necessary to protect public safety, order, health or morals and the fundamental rights and freedoms of others.[9]

The fundamental right of religious freedom can be limited to protect public safety, order, health, morals, or the fundamental rights of others.

All legislation contested under the *Charter* has to undergo a "purpose test" to determine its constitutional validity. If it fails the purpose test, "there is no need to consider further its effects, since it has already been demonstrated to be invalid."[10] If, however, it passes the purpose test, but the law "interferes by its impact, with rights and freedoms,"[11] it may still be ruled invalid. The Alberta government had argued that even though the original purpose of the *Lord's Day Act*[12] had been to force businesses to observe the Christian Sabbath, its purpose had evolved into a secular one—a common day of rest. Therefore, the government argued, it was not in violation of the *Charter*. The Supreme Court disagreed, saying, "[E]ither an unconstitutional purpose or an unconstitutional effect can invalidate legislation."[13] Therefore the Supreme Court invalidated the legislation because its original purpose, the observance of the Christian Sabbath, violated the *Charter*.

In 1986 the Supreme Court considered a similar issue regarding the Sunday closing of retail businesses in Ontario. The court again reviewed the purpose of the legislation and found it to have been enacted for the secular purpose of providing uniform holidays for retail workers.[14] The court found that by enforcing

---

8   *Ibid.*
9   *Ross v. New Brunswick School District No. 15*, [1996] 1 S.C.R. 825 at 868.
10 *Big M Drug Mart Ltd., supra* note 3 at 334.
11 *Ibid.*
12 *Lord's Day Act*, R.S.C. 1970, c. L-13.
13 *Big M Drug Mart Ltd., supra* note 3 at 331.
14 *R. v. Edwards Books and Art Ltd.*, [1986] 2 S.C.R. 713 at 715.

Sunday closing, the act infringed the freedom of Saturday observers to manifest or practise their beliefs. However, the court ruled that although the *Retail Business Holiday Act* infringed section 2(a) of the *Charter*, it was saved by section 1. The court stated:

> All coercive burdens on religious practices, be they direct or indirect, intentional or unintentional foreseeable or unforeseeable, are potentially within the ambit of s. 2(a).
>
> This does not mean that every burden on religious practices is offensive to the constitutional guarantee of freedom of religion. Legislation or administrative action which increases the cost of practising or otherwise manifesting religious beliefs is not prohibited if the burden is trivial or insubstantial.[15]

A group of retired Royal Canadian Mounted Police officers challenged an amendment to the Royal Canadian Mounted Police Regulations[16] that allowed officers who were members of the Khalsa Sikh religion to wear turbans and other religious symbols.[17] The retired officers argued that the provision was inconsistent with section 2(a) of the *Charter* and infringed their religious freedom. The case was dismissed. The court said the program did not restrict anyone's religious freedom, rather "it was aimed at enlarging it."[18] The expressed purpose of the change was "to facilitate recruitment, to enable the Sikh community to exercise its religious freedom and reflect the new multicultural nature of Canada."[19]

Application to Education

Many provinces have faced challenges to religious practices in public schools. The challenge is made using section 2 of the *Charter* by arguing that religious practices in schools are a violation of freedom of religion.[20] The following discussion on education and religion is in reference to the publicly funded public education system and does not include denominational or separate schools. Denominational schooling in Canada is well established as a result of section 93 in the *Constitution Act, 1867*. Section 93 allows for the establishment of public and separate schools so as to protect religious Christian minorities. Its object was to

---

15 *Ibid.* at 715–16. The *Retail Business Holiday Act* was ruled constitutional using s. 1 because it was designed to meet a sufficiently important objective—promoting a regular day off work—and it allowed for some exemptions for religious minorities.

16 RCMP Regulations, 1988, SOR/88-361, s. 64.

17 *Grant et al. v. Attorney General of Canada et al.* (1995), 125 D.L.R. (4th) 556.

18 *Ibid.* at 558.

19 *Ibid.* at 559.

20 Not surprisingly, the arguments so far have applied only to public schools.

secure to the religious minority of one Province the same rights, privileges and protection which the religious minority of another Province may enjoy. The Roman Catholic minority of Upper Canada, the Protestant minority of Lower Canada and the Roman Catholic minority of the Maritime Provinces, will thus stand on a footing of entire equality.[21]

The establishment of public and denominational schooling under Canada's confederation is viewed today as an anomaly. Quebec has done away with denominational schools and, most recently, the province of Newfoundland received a constitutional amendment to allow it to abolish denominational schools and to function with one public education system.[22]

Historically, Canadian public educational institutions have incorporated religious study, school prayer, and patriotic exercises into the school program. Generally, students who did not wish to participate in these exercises were excused from the classroom. However, many of these religious practices in schools have now been challenged. Students and their parents have used the *Charter* to argue that Christian practices impede freedom of religion or freedom to be free from any type of religion.

The definition of freedom of conscience and religion in *Big M Drug Mart* included the right of a person not to be "forced to act in a way contrary to his belief or his conscience."[23] Coercion was defined to include "indirect forms of control which determine or limit alternative courses of conduct available to others."[24] This means that using the public school system to manifest Christianity has a coercive effect because, even though participation is voluntary, the fact that the majority of students participate impedes the freedom of other students to hold different beliefs.[25]

---

21 *Reference Re an Act to Amend the Education Act* (Ontario) (1987), 40 D.L.R. (4th) 18 at 42. Justice Wilson was citing from debates of U.K., H.L., Parliamentary Debates, 3rd. ser., vol. 185, col. 557 at 565 (19 February 1867). The case examined the constitutionality of the Ontario government's ability to make an amendment to Ontario's *Education Act* and to provide full funding to Roman Catholic separate high schools. The court ruled that the Government of Ontario could amend the act. It was a valid exercise of provincial power conferred on the government under s. 93 of the *B.N.A., 1867*. The court said this constitutional document is not subject to *Charter* review.

22 *Newfoundland Schools Act,* SN 1997, c. S-12.2. See also Frank Peters, "The Changing Face of Denominational Education in Canada" (1995–96) 7 Education & Law Journal 229.

23 *Supra* note 3 at 337.

24 *Ibid.* at 336–37.

25 *Zylberberg et al. v. Sudbury Board of Education* (1989), 29 O.A.C. 23.

School Prayer and Religious Practices

The major American cases that ruled religious practices and school prayer unconstitutional were decided in 1948 and 1962.[26] The Canadian cases dealing with the same issues were first considered in 1989.[27]

Perhaps one of the most highly charged educational issues to go before the American Supreme Court has been the question of school prayer. In 1962 the court considered the case of *Engel v. Vitale,*[28] which challenged the constitutional validity of repeating the following prayer in school: "Almighty God, we acknowledge our dependence upon Thee and we beg Thy blessings upon us, our parents, our teachers and our country." In a six to one decision, the court held that reciting the prayer in school violated the First Amendment because the recitation of the prayer was a state-sponsored religious activity. Even the reciting of the Lord's Prayer with an excusal privilege for those who do not wish to participate was ruled unconstitutional.[29] The court said:

> When the power, prestige and financial support of government is placed behind a particular religious belief, the indirect coercive pressure upon religious minorities to conform to the prevailing officially approved religion is plain.[30]

The case caused an uproar that can still be heard today.[31]

In reaching their conclusions in *Engel v. Vitale* and *R. v. Big M Drug Mart*

---

26 In 1948, the American Supreme Court ruled that religious practices conducted during school hours and in school buildings were unconstitutional (*McCollum v. Board of Education of School District No. 71,* 333 U.S. 203 (1948)). The religious classes in question were being taught in a school building in Champagne, Illinois, during school hours. Students who did not attend religious classes were required to leave the classroom to carry on with their studies. The American Supreme Court invalidated the program, pointing out that a tax-supported building was being used and the state's compulsory education provision was providing the pupils for the religious classes: "[N]ot only are the State's tax-supported public school buildings used for the dissemination of religious doctrines. The state also affords sectarian groups an invaluable aid in that it helps to provide pupils for their religious classes through use of the state's compulsory public school machinery. This is not separation of Church and State" (at 212). In 1962 the American Supreme Court considered a challenge to school prayer, *Engel, infra* note 28 and accompanying text.

27 *Zylberberg, supra* note 25; *Russow v. British Columbia (A.G.)* (1989), 35 B.C.L.R. (2d) 29; *Canadian Civil Liberties Association v. Ontario (Minister of Education)* (1990), 71 O.R. (2d) 341 (Ont. C.A.).

28 *Engel v. Vitale,* 370 U.S. 421 (1962).

29 *School District of Abington v. Schempp,* 374 U.S. 203 (1963).

30 *Engel, supra* note 28 at 431.

31 Presidential and congressional campaigns still focus on this issue.

Ltd., the American and Canadian Supreme Courts considered the historical context of freedom of religion. In *Engel v. Vitale,* the American Supreme Court said:

> The First Amendment was added to the Constitution to stand as a guarantee that neither the power nor the prestige of the Federal Government would be used to control, support, or influence the kinds of prayer the American people can say.[32]

In discussing the historical context in *R. v. Big M Drug Mart Ltd.,* Justice Dickson (as he was then) noted the *Charter*'s common goal with the American First Amendment by saying:

> What unites enunciated freedoms in the American First Amendment, s. 2(a) of the *Charter* and in the provisions of other human rights documents in which they are associated, is the notion of the centrality of individual conscience and the inappropriateness of governmental intervention to compel or to constrain its manifestations.[33]

In the case of *Zylberberg et al. v. Sudbury Board of Education,*[34] the Ontario Court of Appeal considered the religious rights of minorities. The facts of the *Zylberberg* case are as follows. The *Ontario Education Act,*[35] under section 28(1) of its regulations, required that public schools be opened or closed each school day with a reading of the Scripture or other suitable readings and the reciting of the Lord's Prayer or other suitable prayer. The regulation also permitted students to be excused from religious exercises if that was their desire. Some parents challenged section 28(1), saying that it violated section 2(a) of the *Charter,* which states that everyone has the fundamental freedom of conscience and religion, and further that it violated section 15 of the *Charter,* the section that deals with equality. The parents stated that they sent their children to a public school rather than a separate school in order to give them a secular education. The parents did not request that their children be excused from religious exercises because they did not want their children singled out from their peers because of their religious beliefs.

The Ontario Court of Appeal ruled that section 28(1) of the regulations violated the *Charter* because it imposed Christian religious exercises in the school. It is "antithetical to the *Charter* objective of promoting freedom of conscience and religion."[36] In reaching its decision, the court took into account the expert testimony of three psychologists. One psychologist, a witness for the parents,

---

32 *Supra* note 28 at 429.
33 *Supra* note 3 at 346.
34 *Supra* note 25.
35 *Education Act,* R.S.O. 1980, c. 129.
36 *Zylberberg, supra* note 25 at 34.

expressed the view that children who had to excuse themselves from class while the Lord's Prayer was being recited would be placed under pressure to conform, and that if they resisted this pressure they would be alienated from their peers. Another psychologist, brought in by the school board, asserted that children from minority religions were not harmed by the policy, and that religious exercises resulted in minority children "confronting the fact of their differences from the majority."[37] The court responded to this assertion by saying, "[T]his insensitive approach . . . not only depreciates the position of religious minorities but also fails to take into account the feelings of young children."[38] The Court of Appeal's empathic response to the comments of the psychologist was in sharp contrast to the lower court's decision that any infringement was so trivial and unsubstantive that it was not worthy of *Charter* protection.[39]

The parents had objected to the excusal clause that allowed students to be excused from religious practices because they viewed it as coercive. The Divisional Court found their objection "offensive to logic and common sense."[40] The Court of Appeal found otherwise, stating:

> From the majoritarian standpoint, the respondents' argument is understandable but, in our opinion, it does not reflect the reality of the situation faced by religious minorities. Whether or not there is pressure or compulsion must be assessed from their standpoint and in particular, from the standpoint of pupils in the sensitive setting of a public school.[41]

The Appeal Court judges invited decision-makers to assess the situation from the students' point of view. The court referred to the powerful influence of peer pressure, quoting from the dissenting opinion in the lower court:

> [I]f most of the pupils willingly conform, might not a few whose family faith is Moslem, or Hebraic or Buddhist, feel awkward about seeking exemption? Peer pressures, and the desire to conform, are notoriously effective with children.[42]

The excusal clause, the Court of Appeal reasoned, may be seen by the majority as conferring freedom of choice, but in reality it imposes on members of religious minorities "a compulsion to conform to the religious practices of the majority."[43]

---

37 *Ibid.* at 29, quoting from an affidavit filed by the school board.

38 *Ibid.* at 34.

39 *Ibid.* at 36, referring to the judgement of Justice O'Leary of the Ontario Divisional Court.

40 *Ibid.* at 35.

41 *Ibid.* at 34.

42 *Ibid.*

43 *Ibid.* at 35. The Court of Appeal quoted the comments of Justice Brennan regarding the use of excusal clauses in *Schempp, supra* note 29: "[E]ven devout children may

The defenders of school prayer argued that the practice served both educational and moral objectives and they justified the practice under section 1. The argument was rejected. The religious purpose of the legislation was clear, and it could not be saved by an appeal to section 1. To back its position, the court made reference to the words of Dr. Egerton Ryerson, the founder of Ontario's public school system, who wrote in a report on elementary education: "As Christianity is the basis of our whole system of elementary education, that principle should pervade throughout."[44]

The school board also tried to argue that the preamble to the *Charter*— "Whereas Canada is founded upon principles that recognize the supremacy of God"—was proof that their regulations on religious practices were consistent with the *Charter*. The Court of Appeal rejected this argument as well, saying that preambles are rarely referred to and if they are it is only for clarification of ambiguous operative provisions. The court stated: "There is no ambiguity in the meaning of s. 2(a) of the Charter."[45]

The school board then pointed to American religious cases, saying that they had been ruled unconstitutional not because they violated the free-exercise clause, but because they violated the establishment clause, which prohibits the American Congress from establishing a religion.[46] The court was not swayed. The judges said:

> The applicability of the *Charter* guarantee of freedom of conscience and religion does not depend on the presence or absence of an "anti-establishment principle" in the Canadian Constitution . . . a principle which can only further obfuscate an already difficult law.[47]

---

well avoid claiming their right and simply continue to participate in exercises distasteful to them because of an understandable reluctance to be stigmatized as atheists or nonconformists simply on the basis of their request. . . . Such reluctance to seek exemption seems all the more likely in view of the fact that children are disinclined at this age to step out of line or to flout 'peer group norms.' "

44 *Ibid.* at 39, quoting from Egerton Ryerson, "Report on a System of Public Elementary Instruction for Upper Canada" (Montreal, 1847) para. 57.

45 *Ibid.* at 36.

46 *Engel, supra* note 28; *Schempp, supra* note 29. It is interesting to note that *in obiter* in *Engel* and *Schempp,* the judges differed on whether the legislation also offended the free exercise clause. The Canadian Supreme Court agreed with Justice Brennan who wrote, in *Schempp,* that religious practices violated the free-exercise clause and that the excusal clause had a chilling effect of discouraging freedom of conscience and religion (at 38).

47 In *Big M Drug Mart Ltd., supra* note 3, Chief Justice Dickson warned that American decisions on freedom of religion must be applied with care in Canadian cases.

The Court of Appeal judges came to a different conclusion from that reached by the lower court, due in part to their ability to empathize with students in school. The Court of Appeal took "action brought about by experiencing the distress of another"[48] and in so doing ruled that policies that promoted and indoctrinated Christianity were contrary to the intent and purpose of the *Charter.*

Issues of school prayer and religious studies invariably pit parents against the school system. It is unusual for students to object. After all, as the courts have recognized, objecting would set them apart from their peers and peer pressure is a powerful force. For example, one student, who objected to the reciting of the Lord's Prayer suffered terrible personal consequences.[49]

Chris Tait objected to the reciting of the Lord's Prayer as part of the opening exercises at his school in Manitoba. His one-person protest, with the support of his family, led to his ostracism, harassment, and assault. Chris was to have been the valedictorian at his grade 12 graduation, but he was prevented from receiving the honour after he objected publicly to the religious practice. In the twenty-four hours before the graduation ceremony, Chris received seventy-five harassing and threatening calls. When he attended the graduation party, he saw himself burned in effigy. His ordeal ended when he was locked in a granary all night. He would not reveal everything that happened to him, but he said it was the scariest night of his life. It was not just Chris who was affected, his family members were shunned and their property was vandalized.[50]

Tait's case shows that the distress caused religious minorities by promoting religious (Christian) practices in school can cause physical, psychological, and emotional and spiritual distress. Chris Tait's case is not an isolated one. In another Ontario case, a young member of the Baha'i faith was taught that she would "go to hell" if she was not Christian. During the time she was receiving Christian religious instruction, she had recurring nightmares in which she was pursued by the Devil and felt that she was burning in hell.[51]

This case was similar to *Zylberberg,* in that a group of parents challenged the constitutional validity of providing religious instruction and also the provision that allowed students to be exempt from the instruction. The parents argued that the provision was of little consequence since they feared that if they used it their children would be further ostracized. The court agreed with the expert evidence of a psychology professor who said that children feel pressure to conform to Christian beliefs that are sponsored and supported by the school. He said that the students experience stress and discomfort when they are confronted with the

---

48 Lynn Henderson, "Legality and Empathy" (1987) 85 Michigan Law Review 1574 at 1579.

49 "Prayer Issue Settled, But Manitoba Family is Still Shaken" *The [Toronto] Globe and Mail* (25 March 1989) A1–A2.

50 *Ibid.*

51 *Canadian Civil Liberties Assn., supra* note 27.

pressure to conform to a religious belief that they know is different from their own.[52]

The crucial issue in this case was whether the purpose and effect of the regulation and the curriculum was indoctrination of Ontario school children in the Christian faith, contrary to section 2(a) and section 15 of the *Charter*. The Ontario Court of Appeal ruled that the practice of providing two-and-a-half hours per week of Christian religious education was indoctrination. At one time, the religious curriculum had been taught by members of the County Bible Club.

The Ontario Court of Appeal acknowledged that it is difficult to distinguish between indoctrination and education, but it provided the following eight-point test to assist those trying to determine the difference. The school may sponsor the study of religion, but it may not sponsor the practice of religion; the school may expose students to all religious views, but it may not expose students to any particular view; the school's approach to religion should be one of instruction not indoctrination; the school should educate students about all religions, not convert them to any one religion; the school's approach should be academic not devotional; the school should study what all people believe, but should not teach students what to believe; the school should strive for student awareness of all religions, but should not press for student acceptance of any one religion; the school should seek to inform students of various beliefs, but should not seek to conform them to any one belief.[53]

Although courts across Canada have consistently ruled school prayer and religious exercises to be contrary to the *Charter*, an anomaly exists in Saskatchewan and Alberta. In 1905, when Alberta and Saskatchewan entered confederation, Parliament ensured that although education was to be secular, religious instruction in schools would continue but would be limited to a defined period in the day. Relevant provisions of the 1901 North-West Territories' *School Ordinance*[54] were incorporated into the constitutional documents establishing Alberta and Saskatchewan as provinces.[55] The provisions of the North-West Territories' *School Ordinance* included the following:

---

52 *Ibid.* at 365.

53 *Ibid.* at 367. For a further discussion of prayer in schools, see Ailsa M. Watkinson, "Systemic Violence in Schools and Administrative Complicity," in Juanita Ross Epp & Ailsa M. Watkinson, *Systemic Violence in Schools: Promise Broken* (New York: State University of New York Press, 1997).

54 *The School Ordinance*, N.W.T.O. 1901, c. 29. For a discussion of the history and implications, see Richard W. Bauman & David Schneiderman, "The Constitutional Context of Religious Practices in Saskatchewan Public School: God Was in the Details" (1996) 60:2 Sask. L. Rev. 265.

55 *The Saskatchewan Act* 1905, 4-5 Edw. VII, c. 42; *The Alberta Act*, 1905, 4-5 Edw. VII, c. 3.

137(1) No religious instruction except as hereinafter provided shall be permitted in the school of any district from the opening of such school until one half hour previous to its closing in the afternoon after which time any such instruction permitted or desired by the board may be given.

(2) It shall however be permissible for the board of any district to direct that the school be opened by the recitation of the Lord's prayer.[56]

In 1993 a group of Saskatoon parents filed a complaint against the Saskatoon Public School Board with the Saskatchewan Human Rights Commission. They asserted that reciting the Lord's Prayer and reading from the Bible in public school violated sections 4 and 13 of *The Saskatchewan Human Rights Code*. The case was heard in the summer of 1999. The board of inquiry, chaired by retired judge Kenneth Halverson, ruled that even though there was overwhelming evidence of discrimination articulated cogently by a number of students, the 1901 constitutional document protected some religious practices in schools. However, the Saskatoon Public School Board's current discriminatory practices were not protected because the board of education did not "direct" the reciting of the Lord's Prayer but instead used "weasel words" in a policy statement encouraging and supporting the practice of Bible readings and the recitation of the Lord's Prayer.[57] The school board was ordered to cease sanctioning recitation of the Lord's Prayer to open public school days, to cease recitation of the Lord's Prayer at assemblies, and to cease the practice of Bible readings.[58]

Christian religious practice in schools does little to foster tolerance or respect for individual beliefs. In fact, it appears to do the opposite. Many wars have been fought because of religious intolerance, and many individuals have been persecuted because of their beliefs.[59] The historical context of freedom of conscience and religion is a common one of struggle, oppression, and

---

56 *Supra* note 54.
57 Saskatchewan Board of Inquiry Decision, July 23, 1999, (Halverson, J.) [unreported] at 24. It is important to remember that this case was heard under *The Saskatchewan Human Rights Code* and not under the *Charter*.
58 *Ibid.* at 25–28.
59 See A. Rebell, "Schools, Values and the Courts" (1987) 7 Yale Law and Policy Review, in which he recounts how in a 1946 case in the United States, a young student objected to patriotic exercises on the basis of his religion. The Supreme Court of the United States ruled against him. When the Supreme Court handed down its decision, the young boy was beaten and his father's store was boycotted (*Minersville School District v. Gobitis*, 310 U.S. 586 (1946)). The deeply religious Scottish philosopher David Hume condemned this Christian piety as serving no manner of purpose: "[W]e observe, on the contrary, that they cross all these desirable ends; stupefying the understanding and harden the heart, obscure the fancy and sour the temper," in David Hume, *Inquiries: Concerning the Human Understanding and Concerning the Principles of Morals*, 2nd ed. (Oxford: Clarendon Press, 1962) at 219.

persecution.[60] Its long and tortuous history makes it hardly surprising that it continues to be an emotional subject. But it is an issue that tests our understanding of a free and democratic society. Former Chief Justice Dickson said:

> A truly free society is one which can accommodate a wide variety of beliefs, diversity of tastes and pursuits, customs and codes of conduct. A free society is one which aims at equality with respect to the enjoyment of fundamental freedoms. . . . Freedom must surely be founded in respect for the inherent dignity and the inviolable rights of the human person.[61]

Indeed, that is the test for those schooled in the "common sense"[62] assumption that a little religion never hurt anyone and that religious exercises may be "good" for students. As the cases discussed above show, religious exercises may have deleterious effects on students. Christians do not have a corner on morality and to assume so is arrogant and certainly not founded in respect for the inherent dignity of students from a wide diversity of backgrounds.[63] It is not a violation of the majority's religious freedom to allow religious observances and practices in an "enlarging" way. Accommodating the religious practices of all groups without government coercion equalizes all religious practices.[64]

Compulsory Education and Religion

Laws that make education compulsory often bring parents into conflict with the law. Some parents withdraw their children from the publicly funded school system and enroll them in religious schools. If the schools are not recognized by the provincial department of education, the parents are penalized for breaking compulsory education laws.

Prior to the *Charter* coming into force, the conflict between public education

---

60   *Big M Drug Mart Ltd., supra* note 3 at 345.
61   *Ibid.* at 336.
62   "Common sense" is the taken-for-granted characteristic of the dominant group. Antonio Gramsci's "common sense" draws attention to normal and ordinary actions and practices whose banality renders them invisible; see Roxana Ng, "Racism, Sexism, and Nation Building," in Cameron McCarthy & Warren Crichlow, eds., *Race, Identity, and Representation in Education* (New York: Routledge, 1993) at 52.
63   In 1994, Rushworth Kidder interviewed two dozen women and men of conscience from around the world, representing different cultures, religions, and life experiences, and asked them: "If you could create a global code of ethics what would be on it?" The interviews revealed eight common values: love, truthfulness, fairness, freedom, unity, tolerance, responsibility, and respect for life (Rushworth Kidder, "Universal Human Values: Finding an Ethical Common Ground" (1994 July/August) The Futurist 8).
64   *Zylberberg, supra* note 25.

and religious beliefs had been challenged in the courts in a variety of ways.[65] In the majority of these cases, the courts ruled against the wishes of the parents. In 1919 the Manitoba Court of Appeal heard the case of *R. v. Hildebrand*,[66] in which a parent was accused of unlawfully neglecting to send his child to public school. The parent, a Mennonite, claimed that the *School Attendance Act* did not apply to Mennonites by virtue of a Dominion order-in-council passed in 1873, which assured Mennonites emigrating from Russia that they would have control over their children's education. The court ruled that the order-in-council was ineffective because jurisdiction for educational matters is a provincial responsibility and therefore the *School Attendance Act* applied.

In 1923 a parent challenged the *School Attendance Act* of Alberta, which required every child between certain ages to attend his or her district school.[67] In this case, the parent had sent his child to a German Lutheran Protestant school that was supported and maintained by the church. The parent was charged with neglecting to send his child to school. The case was heard in the Supreme Court of Alberta and the court ruled that the *School Attendance Act* was binding. In 1978, a similar challenge[68] to the *School Act* of Alberta, which regulated school attendance, was successful because by that time Alberta had passed the *Alberta Bill of Rights*,[69] which was used to uphold freedom of religion. The important thing to note in this case is that the challenge to compulsory school law was successful only because a relatively new provincial human rights statute protected freedom of religion.

In 1972, the American Supreme Court considered the issue of compulsory education and religion in the case of *Wisconsin v. Yoder*.[70] The case involved members of an Amish community who challenged Wisconsin's compulsory school attendance law, which required children to attend private or public school until they were sixteen. The Amish declined to send their children to school after they had completed grade 8. The parents were convicted by a lower court of violating the compulsory attendance laws and fined $5. The Supreme Court reversed the lower court decision, noting that the Amish belief concerning school attendance is basic to their religion.

The Amish are devoted to life in harmony with nature. Their belief requires community members to make their living by farming or other closely related

---

65 *Donald v. Board of Education of Hamilton* (1945), O.R. 518 (C.A.); *Ruman v. Board of Trustees of Lethbridge School* (1943), 3 W.W.R. 340 (Alta. S.C.); *Perepolkin v. Superintendent of Child Welfare* (1957), 120 C.C.C. 67 (B.C.C.A.); *R. v. Wiebe*, [1978] 3 W.W.R. 36 (Alta. Prov. Ct.); *R. v. Hildebrand*, [1919] 3 W.W.R. 286 (Man. C.A.); *R. v. Ulmer*, [1923] 1 W.W.R. 1 (Alta. S.C.).

66 *Hildebrand, ibid.*

67 *Ulmer, supra* note 65.

68 *Wiebe, supra* note 65.

69 *The Alberta Bill of Rights*, 1972 (Alta.), c. 1., ss.1, 2.

70 *Wisconsin v. Yoder*, 406 U.S. 205 (1972).

activities. The court was particularly impressed by the long history of the Amish way of life. This was not a group claiming some new and fashionable way of rearing children:

> The independence and successful social functioning of the Amish community for a period approaching almost three centuries and more than two hundred years in this country is strong evidence that there is at best a speculative gain in terms of meeting the duties of citizenship, from an additional one or two years of compulsory formal education. Against this background it would require a more particularized showing from the state on this point to justify the severe interference with religious freedom such additional compulsory attendance would entail.[71]

This was a most unusual case and the Supreme Court warned other courts to move with great care when determining whether a state's legitimate social concern for the education of children must give way to the claims of religious beliefs.[72]

A number of challenges to compulsory education laws in Canada have failed under the *Charter*. Generally, provincial laws allow students to be excused if the alternative program into which they will be enrolled meets the approval of the provincial department of education. This requirement was challenged in *R. v. Powell*.[73] Mr. Powell objected to the public school system, opting instead to teach his children at home. He submitted his home study program to the school board for approval. Board officials rejected the program because it did not meet either school board or provincial curricular requirements. Mr. Powell then argued that the compulsory education provisions of the *School Act* violated section 2(a) of the *Charter*. The court disagreed, saying that the purpose of the *School Act*, which reflects society's concern for the upbringing and education of children, is secular and the fact that it affected a person's religious convictions was not sufficient to say that it violated the *Charter*. The court referred to the Supreme Court decision in *R. v. Big M Drug Mart Ltd.* in which Justice Dickson (as he was then) quoted with approval the following:

> If the purpose or effect of a law is to impede the observance of one or all religions or is to discriminate invidiously between religions, that law is constitutionally invalid. . . . But if the state regulates conduct by enacting a general law within its power, the purpose and effect of which is to advance the State's secular goals, the statute is valid despite its indirect burden on religious observance unless the State may accomplish its purpose by means which do not impose such a burden.[74]

---

71   *Ibid.* at 226.
72   The dissenting judge questioned the right of the child as being separate from that of the parent. The court responded to these comments by saying that the issue was not dealt with because it had not been raised by either side.
73   *R. v. Powell* (1985), 39 Alta. L.R. (2d) 122 (Prov. Ct.).
74   *Braunfeld v. Brown,* 366 U.S. 599 at 607 (1960).

There have been a number of similar but unsuccessful challenges made before the courts.[75] One of them, *R. v. Jones*, was considered by the Supreme Court in 1986.[76] Pastor Jones was the pastor of a fundamentalist church. He refused to send his children to public school. Instead he taught them and other children in the basement of the church. He also refused to ask for an exemption from the *School Act,*[77] which would have excused the children from attending school if the at-home instruction was approved by the department of education or a superintendent of schools. Pastor Jones was charged with three counts of truancy and ordered to pay a fine or go to jail. He argued that the compulsory attendance provision of the *School Act* and the requirement that he apply for an exemption contravened section 2(a) and section 7 of the *Charter.* He reasoned that it was God, rather than the government, who had final authority over his children's education.

The Supreme Court ruled against Pastor Jones, saying that "the province has a compelling interest in education"[78] and that this interest requires the assurance that every child is receiving efficient instruction approved by secular authorities in all educational establishments. The court stated its belief that "the School Act does not offend religious freedom; it accommodates it. It envisions the education of pupils at public schools, private schools, at home or elsewhere."[79] The *School Act,* the court said, was a flexible piece of legislation that sought to ensure that all children received an adequate education whether they were educated in a public school, a private school, or a religious school. The court added:

> It would be very strange indeed if, just because a school had a religious approach to education, it was free from inspection by those whose responsibility it was to ensure that the standards of secular education set by the province were being met.[80]

The reasoning in *Jones* was applied by a lower court that was asked to determine if a parent was negligent in sending her child to a Christian school that was not recognized by the department of education.[81] The school had a staff of eighteen, only three of whom had teaching certificates, the curriculum was not approved by the department of education, and students who attended the

---

75 *R. v. Bienart* (1985), unreported decision (Alta. Prov. Ct.); *R. v. Corcoran* (1985), 52 Nfld. & P.E.I. R. 308 (Nfld. D.C.); *R. v. Jones,* [1986] 2 S.C.R. 284.

76 *Jones, ibid.*

77 *School Act,* R.S.A. 1980, c. S-3.

78 *Jones, supra* note 75 at 315.

79 *Ibid.* at 312.

80 *Ibid.*

81 *R. v. Kotelmach* (1990), 76 Sask. R. 116 (Q.B.). The mother and stepfather were convicted of two counts of neglecting to ensure the regular attendance of a school-aged pupil. The proceeding was brought by the child's father.

school were refused admittance to university.[82] The court reiterated the conviction that society's interest in the education of its citizens made it reasonable for the state to legislate and enforce a minimum standard of education, including compulsory school attendance.

A 1984 *Charter* case decided by the Newfoundland District Court ruled in favour of a teacher who wished to teach his ten-year-old daughter at home.[83] Unlike the cases discussed above, this case did not revolve around freedom of religion, but rather the parent's right under section 7. The teacher argued that section 7 gives parents the right to make certain decisions about their children and the right cannot be taken away without at least affording "the principle of fundamental justice" envisaged in section 7 of the *Charter*. The court ruled that the superintendent's refusal to approve the parent's program of instruction, which was based on a program obtained from the Manitoba Department of Education, violated the principles of fundamental justice because the parent had no right of hearing, appeal, or review.

In the more recent case of *Bal v. Ontario*,[84] parents representing Sikhs, Hindus, Muslims, Mennonites, and Christian Reformers argued that an amendment to the *Education Act*[85] that prevented the board from providing publicly funded alternative religious schools violated their religious freedom. The court relied upon an earlier case that had raised a similar argument and ruled against the parents.

In *Adler v. Ontario*,[86] parents argued that the absence of government funding for independent religious schools breached section 2(a) of the *Charter*. Chief Justice Dubin provided the following meaning of section 2(a) rights:

> The right involves the freedom to pursue one's religion or beliefs without government interference, and the entitlement to live one's life free of state imposed religions or beliefs. It does not provide, in my view, an entitlement to state support for the exercise of one's religion. Thus in order to found a breach, there must be some state coercion that denies or limits the exercise of one's religion.[87]

Clearly then, freedom of religion means freedom from government coercion and interference. It does not include government omission or neutrality. And although in some circumstances this may be troublesome, in the area of ensuring religious freedom and freedom from religion in schools, it accomplishes the

---

82   The school, The Christian Centre Academy in Saskatoon, has since had its curriculum approved by the department and it employs certified teachers.

83   *R. v. Kind* (1984), 50 Nfld. & P.E.I. R. 332 (Nfld. D.C.).

84   *Bal v. Ontario* (1994), 21 O.R. (3d) 681 (Ont. Ct. Gen. Div.).

85   *Education Act*, R.S.O. 1990, c. E.2, ss. 21, 51.

86   *Adler v. Ontario* (1994), 19 O.R. (3d) 1.

87   *Ibid.* at 10.

objective that public schooling is to be secular and neutral.[88]

Patriotic Exercises

Singing the national anthem and saluting the flag are patriotic exercises that many regard as necessary to demonstrate national loyalty or, at the very least, as harmless symbolic acts. But to members of some religious faiths they are objectionable. As early as 1945 Canadian courts concluded that these exercises do have devotional and religious significance.[89]

There have been a number of challenges to the practice of saluting the flag or singing the national anthem. In the case of *Ruman v. Board of Trustees of Lethbridge School,*[90] heard in 1943, the Alberta Supreme Court was asked to consider whether a school board could suspend students who refused to salute the flag. The students, of the Jehovah's Witness faith, objected to this type of patriotic exercise on the grounds of their religious beliefs. In 1943 there were no provincial, federal, or constitutional laws that protected freedom of religion.[91] The only consideration the court entertained was whether it was within the power of the school board to prescribe that patriotic exercises be conducted in the school and whether the school board had the power to suspend those students who refused to obey. The court concluded that the board had such powers and the matter ended there.

This finding is in sharp contrast to an American Supreme Court case heard the same year. In *West Virginia State Board of Education v. Barnette,*[92] the American Supreme Court struck down the flag salute requirement, saying that it transcended the constitutional limitations of government powers and invaded the sphere of intellect and spirit. The West Virginia State Board of Education had adopted a resolution ordering that the salute to the flag was to be a regular part of school programming. Failure to conform to this rule was seen as

---

88 See Greg M. Dickinson & W. Rod Dolmage, "Education, Religion, and the Courts in Ontario" (1996) 21 Canadian Journal of Education 363. The authors conclude their review of cases dealing with religion in schools with the comment "[w]hen individuals' religious freedom was perceived to be threatened by educational policy (e.g. Zylberberg and Elgin County [Civil Liberties]), the courts found for the applicants; when group rights were claimed (e.g. Adler and Bal) these rights were not extended." I am puzzled by their conclusion. The different conclusions, as I see it, are consistent with a rejection of government-sponsored religion in schools. I do not view it as an example of individual versus collective rights. In fact, if it were, it could be argued that "groups" carried every case.

89 *Donald, supra* note 65.

90 *Ruman v. Board of Trustees of Lethbridge School* (1943), 3 W.W.R. 340 (Alta. S.C.).

91 Except for s. 93 of the *British North America Act,* which dealt only with denominational schools.

92 *West Virginia State Board of Education v. Barnette,* 319 U.S. 624 (1943).

insubordination and those who did not conform were expelled. Students could not be readmitted until they complied. In finding the requirement to salute the flag a violation of the First Amendment, the court said:

> If there is any fixed star in our constitutional constellation, it is that no official, high or petty, can prescribe what shall be orthodox in politics, nationalism, religion, or other matters of opinion or force citizens to confess by word or act their faith therein.[93]

Two years later, a Canadian case confirmed the right of pupils to refrain from saluting the flag or singing the national anthem on religious grounds. This case ruled in favour of the student only because the relevant statutes and regulations recognized a right to refrain from taking part in religious exercises.[94] When considering whether saluting the flag and singing the national anthem should be considered as having devotional or religious significance, the court referred to *West Virginia State Board of Education v. Barnette*. The court quoted the following:

> Symbolism is a primitive but effective way of communicating ideas. The use of an emblem or flag to symbolize some system, idea, institution, or personality, is a short cut from mind to mind. Causes and nations, political parties, lodges and ecclesiastical groups seek to knit the loyalty of their followers to a flag or banner, a colour or design. The state announces rank, function and authority through crowns and races, uniforms and black robes; the church speaks through the cross, the crucifix, the altar and shrine, and clerical raiment. Symbols of state often convey political ideas just as religious symbols come to convey theological ones. Associated with many of these symbols are appropriate gestures of acceptance or respect; a salute, a bowed or bared head, a bended knee. A person gets from a symbol the meaning he puts into it, and what is one man's comfort and inspiration is another's jest and scorn.[95]

In *R. v. Big M Drug Mart Ltd.,* the Supreme Court said:

> [T]he guarantee of freedom of conscience and religion prevents the government from compelling individuals to perform or abstain from performing otherwise harmless acts because of the religious significance of those acts to others.[96]

This position may assist those who wish to challenge the use of patriotic exercises

---

93   *Ibid.* at 642.
94   *Donald, supra* note 65.
95   *Supra* note 92 at 632.
96   *Supra* note 3 at 350.

in schools. Those who wish to defend their use will, as always, need to show that they serve a legitimate objective and that they are reasonable and demonstrably justified.

Conclusion

The fundamental freedom of conscience and religion under the *Charter* has been defined to mean that school prayer and reading from the Bible in public schools are violations of a person's right to be free from state-imposed religious practices. The exceptions, as discussed above, are the education systems of Saskatchewan and Alberta. However, a 1999 Saskatchewan board of inquiry decision, based on an interpretation of *The Saskatchewan Human Rights Code* and the 1905 constitutional agreement bringing Saskatchewan and Alberta into confederation, was unequivocal in labelling the imposition of Christian practices in public schools, discrimination.[97] Nevertheless, school boards in these provinces can continue the practices if they do so according to the constitutional agreement. But, as the board of inquiry made clear, other jurisdictions (including Calgary) took "a multicultural approach to religion in public school nearly 30 years ago. . . . To its credit, Calgary elected to not utilize the 1901 Ordinance to compel use of the Lord's prayer."[98] Instead the city adopted a policy restricting Christian religious practices in its public schools. As Halverson noted in Saskatoon, "A willing Board of Education could craft similar policies."[99]

The Supreme Court has rejected the idea that compulsory education violates a parent's right to provide an education, arguing that the education of children is of such compelling interest to the public that educational standards are appropriate.

As of this date, the use of patriotic exercises in schools has not received much attention, but, as has been the case in the United States, patriotic exercises in school are open to constitutional challenge. Religious practices, which are distinct from religious studies, do not belong in public schools. The phrase "public school" denotes a gathering of students from various beliefs and backgrounds. Discontinuing Christian practices in public schools is a respectful acknowledgement that in today's society Canadian students represent a wide array of beliefs.

---

97   *Supra* note 57.

98   *Ibid.* at 29.

99   *Ibid.* at 30. There are indications that the Saskatoon Board of Education may eliminate some of the Christian practices, see Leslie Perreaux, "Trustees Support Ban on Prayer" *The [Saskatoon] StarPhoenix* (17 July 1999) A1. Following the board of inquiry hearing, trustees for the Saskatoon Public School Board were polled. Three of the five suggested religious practices be exchanged for education on religion. One trustee said he was considering proposing a motion to suspend the practice of prayer in schools. See also Leslie Perreaux, " 'Drop the Prayer': Yakel to Put End to Lord's Prayer in Public Classrooms" *The [Saskatoon] StarPhoenix* (29 July 1999) A1.

Chapter 5 ■
Freedom of Expression and Assembly

Freedom of expression is considered one of the most significant freedoms in a democratic society. John Stuart Mill, in his famous work *On Liberty*,[1] asserted that it is essential in a democratic society that the right to expose opposing views be protected. He believed that individual liberty must be protected from the tyranny of the majority. His theory is often referred to as "the marketplace theory," in which opinions are expressed freely as a means of seeking the truth.

In 1981, Walter Tarnopolsky, a professor of law, speaking before the Royal Commission on Newspapers, said: "Where freedom of expression exists, the beginning of a free society and a means for every extension of liberty are already present. Free expression is therefore unique among liberties: it promotes and protects all the rest."[2] The Canadian Supreme Court has affirmed that it would "be difficult to imagine a guaranteed right more important to a democratic society than freedom of expression."[3] It is a freedom that is critical to human dignity and autonomy, an essential element for the functioning of democratic institutions.[4]

Freedom of expression, as contained in section 2(b) of the *Charter,* includes "all forms of expression, whether they be oral, written, pictorial, sculptural, music, dance or film."[5] It includes such base expressions as the freedom to advertise[6]

---

1 John Stuart Mill, *On Liberty* (New York: Gateway, 1955).

2 Walter Tarnopolsky *et al.,* eds., *Newspapers and the Law,* vol. 3 (Ottawa: Research Publications of the Royal Commission on Newspapers, 1981) at 7.

3 *Edmonton Journal v. Alberta (A.G.),* [1989] 2 S.C.R. 1326 at 1336; aff'd in *R. v. Keegstra,* [1990] 3 S.C.R. 697.

4 *K Mart Canada Ltd. v. U.F.C.W., Local 1518* (1994), 24 C.L.R.B.R. (2d) 1. Union members were prohibited from distributing leaflets outside K Mart. The court ruled the prohibition violates s. 2(b) and the prohibition could not be justified under s. 1.

5 *Re Ontario Film and Video Appreciation Society and Ontario Board of Censors* (1983), 147 D.L.R. (3d) 58 (Ont. D.C.), aff'd (1984), 45 O.R. (2d) 80 (Ont. C.A.) at 65. See also C. Beckton, "Freedom of Expression," in W.S. Tarnopolsky & R. Beaudoin, eds., *Canadian Charter of Rights and Freedoms: Commentaries* (Toronto: Carswell, 1982); and David Schneiderman, *Freedom of Expression and the Charter* (Toronto: Thomson Professional, 1991).

6 *R.J.R.-MacDonald Inc.,* [1995] 3 S.C.R. 199. The court, in a split decision, ruled that an act prohibiting all advertisements and promotions of tobacco products was inconsistent with s. 2(b) of the *Charter* and could not be justified under s. 1; *Irwin*

and the loftier "means by which the individual expresses his or her personal identity and sense of individuality."[7] Freedom of expression has limitations. For example, freedom of expression does not include violent acts,[8] nor does it include the setting up of a peace camp on Parliament Hill,[9] nor unlimited spending by third parties during elections.[10] Section 2(b) also protects freedom of thought, belief, and opinion, which, unlike freedom of expression, are considered absolute freedoms.

Freedom of assembly has been referred to as "speech in action." It is the physical act of meeting so as to communicate and share thoughts, emotions, and friendship. It serves many essential functions: a communicative function, a pressure function, and an openly coercive function.[11] Students often find assemblies or demonstrations to be the only way that they can bring their grievances to the attention of the public.[12]

Toy v. Quebec (A.G.O), [1989] 1 S.C.R. 927. The company challenged the government's restrictions on advertising aimed at children under thirteen. The Supreme Court found the restrictions violated s. 2(b) but the limits were justified under s. 1.

7   *Ford v. Quebec*, [1988] 2 S.C.R. 712 at 749. This case challenged the French-language laws concerning public signage in Quebec. The Supreme Court found that certain sections of the *Charter of French Language* violated s. 2(b) of the *Charter* and were not justified under s. 1.

8   *Irwin Toy, supra* note 6 at 970.

9   *Weisfeld v. Canada (Minister of Public Works)* (1995), 116 D.L.R. (4th) 232 (C.A.). Forcibly removing a protester's "peace camp" from Parliament Hill did not violate his freedom of expression rights. It was not conduct amounting to expression. The protesters could still distribute material and verbally express their views.

10 *Libman v. Quebec (Attorney General)*, [1997] 3 S.C.R. 569. The court found the legislative objective in limiting third-party spending during a referendum to be laudable in that it was designed to enhance the right to vote by prosecuting political equality; however, the method overstepped the minimal impairment test of s. 1 and could not be saved.

11 A.D. Grunis, *Freedom of Assembly in Canada* (Ph.D. thesis, Osgoode Hall, 1976) [unpublished] at 21. See also Amy Gutmann, ed., *Freedom of Association* (Princeton: Princeton University Press, 1998). Gutmann stated that freedom of association also includes the creation and maintenance of intimate relationships, which are valuable for their own sake and for the pleasure they offer (chap. 1).

12 In November 1997 students protested against the presence of Indonesian president Suharto at the Asia Pacific Economic Co-operation Summit held at the University of British Columbia. The Royal Canadian Mounted Police attempted to break up the demonstrations by arresting demonstrators, taking down signs, and spraying protesters with pepper spray. The actions of the RCMP are currently under investigation by the RCMP Public Complaints Commission. See Naomi Klein, "The Real APEC Scandal" *Saturday Night* (February 1999) 41.

Freedom of Expression

The Canadian Supreme Court has clearly stated that the scope of freedom of expression is very broad. It is not restricted to popular views or even to truthful views, "[r]ather, freedom of expression serves to protect the right of the minority to express its view, however unpopular such views may be."[13] The purpose of freedom of expression is

> to permit free expression to the end of promoting truth, political or social participation, and self-fulfillment. That purpose extends to the protection of minority beliefs which the majority regard as wrong or false. . . . Tests of free expression frequently involve a contest between the majoritarian view of what is true or right and an unpopular minority view.[14]

The court has adopted a two-step approach to determine whether a person's freedom of expression has been infringed:

> The first step involves determining whether the individual's activity falls within the freedom of expression protected by the Charter. The second step is to determine whether the purpose or effect of the impugned government action is to restrict that freedom.[15]

A number of the cases heard so far under section 2(b) of the *Charter* have been challenges to government legislation.[16] In such cases the courts have examined whether the activity is a form of expression protected by the *Charter* and whether the government's legislation or actions are intended to restrict that expression. A court may well find that a person's freedom of expression has been infringed but the infringement or limitation on that right is justified in a free and democratic society.

Statutory limitations have been placed on a person's freedom of expression in matters relating to libel, slander, obscenity, and sedition. Since the arrival of the *Charter*, many of these limitations have been challenged. Invariably these cases

---

13   *Ross v. School District No. 15,* [1996] 1 S.C.R. 825 at 864.

14   *R. v. Zundel,* [1992] 2 S.C.R. 731 at 752–53.

15   *Ross, supra* note 13 at 865. The test was first articulated in *Irwin Toy, supra* note 6, and more recently in *Keegstra, supra* note 3.

16   For example, *Ross, supra* note 13, challenged an order issued by the New Brunswick Human Rights Board of Inquiry; *Keegstra, supra* note 3, challenged a section of the *Criminal Code* that prohibited the distribution of hate literature; *Irwin Toy, supra* note 6, challenged a legislative limitation on advertising; *Zundel, supra* note 14, challenged the "false news" provisions of the *Criminal Code*, particularly s. 181; *R. v. Butler,* [1992] 1 S.C.R. 452, challenged the obscenity prohibition in the *Criminal Code*.

turn on whether the limits meet the criteria of section 1 of the *Charter*. If the form of expression falls within the core values that underlie the protection of freedom of expression, such as "the search for truth, participation in the political process, and individual fulfillment,"[17] it will be a more onerous task to justify governmental limitations.[18] Other forms of expression, such as commercial advertising, pornography, and hateful messages, face lower thresholds of justification.

The power of a censorship board that limited freedom of expression without providing specific criteria by which artists might govern themselves was ruled contrary to the *Charter* because the criteria for censorship were not "prescribed by law" and were considered vague:

> It is accepted that law cannot be vague, undefined and totally discretionary; it must be ascertainable and understandable. Any limits placed on freedom of expression cannot be left to the whim of an official; such limits must be articulated with some precision or they cannot be considered to be law.[19]

Limiting the distribution of obscene material under section 163(8) of the *Criminal Code* was upheld by the Supreme Court. The court ruled that limiting this type of material was a reasonable limit, in part because of a "growing concern that the exploitation of women and children, depicted in publications and films can, in certain circumstances, lead to 'abject and servile victimization.' "[20]

In the case of the *Canada (Human Rights Commission) v. Taylor*,[21] the Supreme Court ruled that an order by the Canadian Human Rights Commission to halt

---

17 *Butler, ibid.* at 499.

18 *Ibid.* at 501.

19 *Re Ontario Film and Video, supra* note 5 at 67.

20 *Butler, supra* note 16 at 497. A merchant was charged with selling, possessing, and distributing obscene material contrary to the *Criminal Code*. The Supreme Court ruled that pornographic material is protected under s. 2(b) of the *Charter*, but that, in this case, limiting the distribution of obscene material was justified under s. 1. The case was initially lauded by women's groups, but it has been roundly criticized by gay and lesbian groups. The decision has been applied to justify limiting the distribution of gay and lesbian material. A continuous legacy has been the detention of gay and lesbian literature by Canada Customs officials. See Paul Wollaston, "When Will They Ever Get It Right? A Gay Analysis of *R. v. Butler*" (1993) 2 Dalhousie Journal of Legal Studies 251. Wollaston points out that while the rationale for prohibiting the distribution of such material was concern that the availability of the material harms society and in particular women, "[i]ronically, on April 30, 1992, the first obscenity charges after the Butler decision were laid against Glad Day Bookshop in Toronto for selling a lesbian magazine made by women for women about women's sexuality" (at 251).

21 *Canada (Human Rights Commission) v. Taylor*, [1990] 3 S.C.R. 892.

telephone hate messages intended to incite racial hatred was reasonable. The right of a professional organization to enforce a code of ethics that set out an appropriate procedure for one teacher to register criticism of another was upheld.[22]

Hate Propaganda

In the well-publicized case of *R. v. Keegstra*,[23] the Supreme Court ruled that limiting the free speech of teachers can be justified because of the harm their speech causes students. The *Keegstra* case involved a high school teacher who taught for about twelve years in Eckville, Alberta. In 1984 Mr. Keegstra was charged with unlawfully promoting hatred against an identifiable group by communicating anti-Semitic statements to his students.[24] According to the facts of the case, Mr. Keegstra attributed various evil qualities to Jews, describing them as "treacherous," "sadistic," "money loving," "power hungry," and "child killers."

> He taught his classes that Jewish people seek to destroy Christianity and are responsible for depressions, anarchy, chaos, wars and revolution. According to Mr. Keegstra, Jews "created the Holocaust to gain sympathy" and, in contrast to the open and honest Christians, were said to be deceptive, secretive and inherently evil. Mr. Keegstra expected his students to reproduce his teachings in class and on exams. If they failed to do so, their marks suffered.[25]

As a result, Mr. Keegstra was charged with promoting hatred against Jews. He argued, among other things, that the section of the *Criminal Code* under which he had been charged violated his freedom of expression as guaranteed under section 2(b) of the *Charter*.[26]

The court discussed the meaning of freedom of expression, saying that it was "an essential value of Canadian parliamentary democracy."[27] Referring to an

---

22 *Cromer v. B.C. Teachers Federation* (1986), 29 D.L.R. (4th) 641 (B.C.C.A.). Ms. Cromer was charged with breaching the British Columbia Teachers' Federation code of ethics by personally criticizing another teacher. Ms. Cromer argued that the code of ethics was in violation of her freedom of expression. Her submission was denied. Although her freedom of expression was limited, the limit was justified. The judge said that Ms. Cromer's comments were personal rather than directed at the issue. If her comments had been issue focussed, the court might have ruled in her favour.

23 *Keegstra, supra* note 3.

24 Keegstra was charged under s. 319(2) (then s. 218(2)) of the *Criminal Code*.

25 *Keegstra, supra* note 3 at 714.

26 S. 2(b) states: "Everyone has the following fundamental freedoms: freedom of thought, belief, opinion and expression, including freedom of the press and other media of communication."

27 *Keegstra, supra* note 3 at 726. The court identified the convictions fueling freedom of expression as "(1) seeking and attaining truth is an inherently good activity; (2)

earlier test in *Irwin Toy*,[28] the court ruled that hate propaganda was included under section 2(b) of the *Charter*. In other words, hate propaganda was opinion and expression. Thus, section 319(2) of the *Criminal Code* infringed Mr. Keegstra's freedom of expression. Former Chief Justice Dickson said:

> It is in my opinion, inappropriate to attenuate the s. 2(b) freedom on the grounds that a particular context requires such; the large and liberal interpretation given the freedom of expression . . . indicates that the preferable course is to weigh the various contextual values and factors in s. 1.[29]

As stated earlier, section 1 is integral to contextual reasoning because it examines the factual circumstances of each case, avoiding unquestioning adherence to an abstract universal principle.[30] The court, agreeing with former Justice Wilson's call for a "contextual approach" to *Charter* interpretation, said:

> [A] particular right or freedom may have a different value depending on the context. It may be, for example, that freedom of expression has greater value in a political context than it does in the context of disclosure of the details of a matrimonial dispute. The contextual approach attempts to bring into sharp relief the aspect of the right or freedom which is truly at stake in the case as well as the relevant aspects of any values in competition with it. It seems to be more sensitive to the reality of the dilemma posed by the particular facts and therefore more conducive to finding a fair and just compromise between the two competing values under section 1.[31]

Within the context of section 1, the court looked at the harm done by hate propaganda and said there are two sorts of injury caused by its dissemination.

---

participation in social and political decision-making is to be fostered and encouraged; and (3) diversity in forms of individual self-fulfillment and human flourishing ought to be cultivated in a tolerant and welcoming environment" (at 728).

28 *Irwin Toy, supra* note 6.

29 *Keegstra, supra* note 3 at 734.

30 *Ibid.* All limits imposed on a right or freedom are subject to s. 1 scrutiny. In this case, the respondents relied on American jurisprudence to argue the status given to free expression and America's implied aversion to content-based regulation of free expression. The Canadian Supreme Court questioned the perception of unlimited free expression in American cases, saying, "[T]he precedents are somewhat mixed" (at 738–44).

31 *Ibid.* at 737, quoting with approval from *Edmonton Journal, supra* note 3 at 1355–56. The court also quoted from a decision written by Justice LaForest, who argued that a mechanistic approach must be avoided when balancing interests under s. 1. See *United States of America v. Cotroni; United States of America v. El Zein,* [1989] 1 S.C.R. 1469 at 1489–90.

First, "there is harm done to members of the target group. It is indisputable that the emotional damage caused by words may be of grave psychological and social consequence."[32] Second, the hatred promoted by the words and writings can manifest itself in physical harm to persons belonging to a racial or religious group, the consequence of which is

> a response of humiliation and degradation from an individual targeted by hate propaganda. . . . A person's sense of human dignity and belonging to the community at large is closely linked to the concern and respect accorded the groups to which he or she belongs.[33]

The validity of limiting hate propaganda was reinforced in the court's mind by Canada's compliance with international human rights instruments and other sections of the *Charter,* in particular, section 15(1), the equality section. Former Chief Justice Dickson said that to allow hate messages free rein runs "counter to the values central to a free and democratic society."[34] The court rejected Mr. Keegstra's argument that the limiting of his freedom of expression was unreasonable, saying:

> [T]here can be no real disagreement about the subject matter of the messages and teachings communicated by the respondent, Mr. Keegstra: it is deeply offensive, hurtful and damaging to target group members, misleading to his listeners, and antithetical to the furtherance of tolerance and understanding in society.[35]

Upon close examination of this case, it seems that the Canadian Supreme Court reached its decision to limit free expression by empathizing with the feelings of humiliation, degradation, and helplessness experienced by minorities—an ethic of care response. One year after the Canadian Supreme Court's decision in *Keegstra* and in stark contrast, the former president of the United States, George Bush, spoke publicly about limiting free expression, saying:

> Ironically on the 200th anniversary of our Bill of Rights, we find free speech under

---

32 *Keegstra, supra* note 3 at 746. As an example, the court referred to the use of words that, in the context of sexual harassment, constitute harassment.

33 *Ibid.* at 746. In *Butler, supra* note 16 at 497, the court made reference to its earlier decision in *Keegstra* and ruled that the distribution of sexually explicit obscene material brings with it harmful consequences, such as discrimination and violence against women and children.

34 *Supra* note 3 at 756.

35 *Ibid.* at 761. See also Sanjeer S. Anand, "Beyond *Keegstra:* The Constitutionality of the Wilful Promotion of Hatred Revisited" (1998) 9 N.J.C.L. 117. The author argues that the court's approach to considering the wilful promotion of hatred was appropriate.

assault throughout the United States. The notion of "political correctness" has ignited controversy across the land. What began as a cause for civility has soured into a cause of conflict and even censorship.[36]

Bush appealed unquestioningly to the universal principles of free expression thus subsuming the minorities' burden[37]—an ethic of justice response.

Material and Substantial Disruption

The most well-known case on the right of students to express themselves freely is *Tinker v. Des Moines,*[38] which was heard by the American Supreme Court in the midst of the tumultuous Vietnam War. The case resulted from a school regulation prohibiting the wearing of black armbands in school. School officials in Des Moines heard that some protesters planned to wear black armbands to symbolize their opposition to the Vietnam War. In anticipation of this event, the principal adopted a policy that stated that any student who wore an armband to school would be asked to remove it. If the student refused, the student would be suspended. John, Mary Beth, Paul, and Hope Tinker, along with Christopher Eckhardt, wore armbands to school. They were sent home. They did not return to school until after the planned period of protest had expired.

The students filed for an injunction restraining the board from disciplining them and also sought nominal damages. The lower court upheld the constitutionality of the school authorities' action on the grounds that it was reasonable in order to avoid a disturbance. The Supreme Court did not agree. In an often-quoted passage the court said: "It can hardly be argued that either students or teachers shed their constitutional rights to freedom of speech or expression at the school house gate."[39] In addition, the court repeated its repudiation of the principle that a state might conduct its schools so as to "foster a homogeneous people." It quoted with approval its earlier decision in *Keyishan v. Board of Regents:*[40]

---

36 D'Arcy Jenish, "A War of Words: Academics Clash Over 'Correctness' " *Maclean's* (27 May 1991) 44.

37 Robin West, "Love, Rage and Legal Theory" (1989) 1 Yale Journal of Law and Feminism 100. Empathic understanding is, West argues, essential to a moral response to another's situation: "When we care about the 'differences' of others . . . we do so because we are moved to lessen their burden, not just understand it" (at 106).

38 *Tinker v. Des Moines,* 393 U.S. 502 (1969).

39 *Ibid.* at 506. Of interest here is the Canadian Supreme Court's ruling that teachers do, in fact, shed their right to free speech at the schoolhouse gate.

40 *Keyishan v. Board of Regents,* 385 U.S. 589 (1967). This case involved a faculty member of the State University of New York who refused to sign a certificate that he was not a Communist and never had been a Communist. Failure to sign the certificate would mean his dismissal. The Supreme Court held for the teacher, saying that the certificate interfered with his constitutional rights.

The vigilant protection of constitutional freedom is nowhere more vital than in the community of American schools (*Shelton v. Tucker*). . . . The classroom is particularly the "marketplace of ideas." The nation's future depends on leaders trained through wide exposure to that robust exchange of ideas which discovers truth "out of a multitude of tongues," [rather] than through any kind of authoritative selection.[41]

The most important issue for the American Supreme Court was whether "the students' activities would materially and substantially disrupt the work and discipline of the school."[42] The basic premises in the case were that students do not forfeit their rights when they walk through the schoolhouse gate, and they retain their freedom of expression in the public school "as long as their exercise of that freedom does not unduly hinder the school's achievement of its educational mission."[43] The court noted, "There is no evidence whatever of petitioners' interference, actual or nascent, with the school's work or of collision with the rights of other students to be secure and to be left alone."[44]

Out of this case came the "material and substantial disruption" test, which places the burden on the school authorities to show that free speech is likely to interfere with the proper operation of the school and to collide with the rights of students to be left alone. A fear of disruption will not pass the test. The Supreme Court said an "undifferentiated fear or apprehension of disturbance is not enough to overcome the right to freedom of expression."[45]

Lewd and Indecent Speech

The "material and substantial disruption test" does not apply to student speech that is considered lewd and indecent. In 1986, the American Supreme Court considered the case of *Bethel School District No. 403 v. Fraser*.[46] A student, Fraser, used sexual innuendo in a nominating speech before a student assembly. An earlier ruling by a lower court had applied the "material and substantial disruption test" and had ruled in favour of Fraser. The Supreme Court, in overturning the previous decision, pointed out that there was a marked distinction between political messages, such as wearing an armband, and the sexual content of Fraser's speech.[47] The court said: "This Court's First Amendment jurisprudence

---

41 *Tinker, supra* note 38 at 507.
42 *Ibid.*
43 Mark Yudof, "Tinker Tailored: Good Faith, Civility, and Student Expression" (1995) 68 St. John's Law Review 365 at 366.
44 *Tinker, supra* note 38 at 508.
45 *Ibid.*
46 *Bethel School District No. 403 v. Fraser*, 106 S. Ct. 3159 (1986).
47 *Ibid.* at 3163. Yudof, *supra* note 43, considers Fraser's comments on political speech, after all he was nominating a colleague for political office: "If a nominating speech for political office is not political speech, then what constitutes political speech?" (at 373).

has acknowledged limitations on the otherwise absolute interest of the speaker in reaching an unlimited audience where the speech is sexually explicit and the audience may include children."[48]

In reference to the use of vulgar and offensive speech in schools, the court said that it is an appropriate function of school boards to determine "what manner of speech in the classroom or in school assembly is inappropriate."[49] The court noted that the role and purpose of the public school system is to prepare pupils for citizenship, and to this end the schools must inculcate the habits and manners of civility: "The undoubted freedom to advocate unpopular and controversial views in schools and classrooms must be balanced against the society's countervailing interest in teaching students the boundaries of socially appropriate behaviour."[50]

The *Tinker* decision was rights based, whereas the *Fraser* decision was restrictive and premised in society's belief in its obligation to inculcate in students what society deems to be appropriate behaviour. On its face this may sound reasonable, but it is conceivable that student protest in time of war, as was the case in *Tinker,* could be seen to exceed socially appropriate behaviour and could be judged to be an affront to true citizenship and thus not worthy of protection.

"Socially appropriate behaviour," like "community standards," is a troublesome criterion, vulnerable to prevailing community bigotry, homophobia, and intolerance. Part of the Supreme Court of Canada's test for determining obscenity is the "community standard" test, which is concerned "not with what Canadians would not tolerate being exposed to themselves, but what they would not tolerate *other* Canadians being exposed to."[51] And as Paul Wollaston, a student of law at Dalhousie University, commented, "The community as a whole, and therefore the community standard is not as tolerant of explicit gay sexual material as it is of explicit heterosexual material."[52]

Compare the American case of *Fraser* with the case of Chris Lutes, a grade 9 student in Saskatchewan.[53] Chris Lutes sang the song "Let's Talk About Sex" during noon hour on the main street of Milestone within earshot of a school division official, who reported the incident to the school administration. Chris was disciplined by the vice-principal because the song had been "banned" at school.[54]

---

48 *Fraser, supra* note 46 at 3165.
49 *Ibid.* at 3165.
50 *Ibid.* at 3164.
51 *Butler, supra* note 16 at 478.
52 Wollaston, *supra* note 20.
53 *Lutes v. Board of Education of Prairie View School Division No. 74* (1993), 101 Sask. R. 232.
54 The vice-principal later stated that in using the word "banned" he did not intend to convey the meaning that the song was prohibited from ever being played or sung. The song was not banned, he said, it was just not permitted in keyboard class. The judge was not persuaded by the clarification of the meaning of "banned."

Chris had his noon-hour privileges of going downtown revoked for a month. Chris and his mother argued that the punishment was wrongful because the song did not contain any offensive lyrics and had been used in schools to inform students of the perils of AIDS. They also argued that the punishment violated Chris's freedom of expression. The court ruled that Chris's freedom of expression had been violated and that the action of the administration could not be justified under section 1. The judge said:

> I am satisfied Chris has established a strong prima facie case that his freedom of expression as guaranteed under s. 2 of the Charter has been violated and that the actions of the school cannot be justified under s. 1. This song, which intended to educate young people about safe sex and AIDS, was unfortunately characterized by a School official . . . as an inappropriate song.
>
> In my view, this whole problem arose as a result of overreaction to an inoffensive song that carried a powerful message.[55]

The judge also said that Chris was entitled to proceed with his action for damages against the school for allegedly infringing his freedom of expression.[56]

The Canadian Supreme Court has said that the objective to be gained in limiting a right or freedom must be of sufficient importance and "necessary to protect public safety, order, health or morals, or the fundamental rights and freedoms of others."[57] Clearly the court found that Chris Lutes was not usurping public safety, order, health, morals, or the rights of others.

Student publications, dress codes, and the selection of reading material, all educational issues, fall within the ambit of freedom of expression and have been subject to restrictions. The restrictions may be justified. The test employed to establish whether a person's freedom of expression has been limited and whether the limitation is justified involves a number of steps. First, is the activity a form of expression? Second, is the governmental action, in the form of school regulations, limiting the expression?[58] The next step is for school officials to articulate clearly

---

55 *Supra* note 53 at 239.

56 There is no evidence that Chris Lutes continued in this vein with his challenge. The court did not provide an interim injunction preventing the school from proceeding with its punishment, saying that since the detention period was coming to an end at the time of the hearing, the request was academic.

57 *R. v. Big M Drug Mart Ltd.*, [1985] 1 S.C.R. 295 at 337. At the time of writing, an RCMP inquiry has been established to review the role of the RCMP and the federal government in limiting the freedom of expression of students at the University of British Columbia. Students protested with signs condemning the human rights records of international leaders attending the Asia Pacific Economic Co-operation meetings in Vancouver in November 1997. All signs were taken down by the police and students protesters were sprayed with pepper spray. See W. Wesley Pue, "The Rule of Law, APEC and Canada" (1998) 56 The Advocate 217.

58 *Ross, supra* note 13.

why the restriction is necessary. Is the restriction necessary to maintain a positive learning environment, public safety, or to protect the fundamental rights of others? Lastly, is the method chosen to limit the freedom of expression reasonable and demonstrably justified?

Student Publications

Student publications may raise topics some would rather not read about, but they are forms of expression. American courts have distinguished between student publications that are written and produced by students, and student publications that are written by students as part of class assignments. The latter have not been given constitutional protection because they are not considered free expression but rather class assignments, which are not constitutionally protected.[59]

It may be helpful at this point to consider a matter reported in a newspaper concerning the limiting of a student's free expression. The case was not challenged in court. According to newspaper reports, a high school student hired by the local newspaper to report on school activities was censored by her high school principal. The student was required to submit her report to the principal for his approval before sending it to the newspaper. Her report was a commentary on the cancellation, by school authorities, of a student talent night because the show contained sexist and racist material. The principal objected to the student's report and suggested she not submit it. She hesitated at first but gave in after, she said, it was made clear to her that there would be "grave consequences," including suspension or expulsion.[60]

Newspaper reporting is a closely guarded freedom. Section 2(b) specifically mentions freedom of the press as a fundamental freedom. The student was restricted by the principal from publishing her report, thus limiting freedom of the press. There may be some argument over whether or not it was a direct order. Even so, it could be argued that a "suggestion" coming from an authority figure is tantamount to a direct order.[61]

---

59 *Hazelwood School District v. Kuhlmeier*, 108 S. Ct. 562 (1988). In this case, the school principal deleted two articles from a school newspaper published by journalism students. The principal believed the articles, which were on the topic of teenage experiences with pregnancy and parental divorce, might reveal the identity of students and portray parents in a poor light. The students charged that the principal violated their constitutional freedom of expression under the First Amendment. The Supreme Court disagreed, saying that educators can exercise substantial control over school-sponsored activities such as student publications.

60 Paul Spasoff, "Student Claims Expulsion Threatened Over News Story" *The [Saskatoon] StarPhoenix* (15 April 1993) A1; see also Paul Spasoff, "Principal Admits Asking Student to Keep Story Out of Newspaper" *The [Saskatoon] StarPhoenix* (17 April 1993) A3.

61 See *R. v. H.* (1985), 43 Alta. R. 250 (P.C.).

For the sake of this discussion, let us assume that the student was limited in expressing herself freely. The onus is then placed on school officials to demonstrate clearly and cogently that there were pressing and substantial reasons for limiting her free expression. For example, publication of her article would have threatened the equality rights or fundamental freedoms of others; created an environment that was not conducive to learning; or threatened public safety, order, health, and morals. Once a sufficiently important objective has been articulated to justify limiting freedom of expression, clear evidence is required to show that the censoring of the report minimally interfered with the student's right to freedom of expression, no other means were available to limit this right and still meet the sufficiently important objective, and there were few deleterious effects.

The facts of this case differ significantly from the American case referred to above. In the American case, the high school newspaper was published by journalism students. It was not characterized as free expression because the newspaper was part of a class assignment and therefore school officials retained the right to impose reasonable restrictions on what was printed in the newspaper. The court noted that students published the paper and received grades and academic credits for their performance. This fact, the court said, removed the newspaper from the realm of constitutional protection.[62] In contrast, the student discussed above was hired by the local newspaper. She was not working on a school assignment and she was not working for the school. The difference between these cases is important. Given the facts as presented, it appears likely that the student in the latter case would have had a good chance in challenging the actions of the school officials.

Appearance

In the 1970s the issue of appearance for students centred on hairstyles, a means of expression. More than 150 American cases involved male head and face hairstyles in public schools.[63] Some of these cases may seem frivolous today, but they are important because they show how much things change. The distracting issues of today may be classified as silly irritants tomorrow. Perhaps we can learn something from a review.

---

62 *Hazelwood, supra* note 59. This case is a controversial one. Many expressed shock at the court's willingness to limit freedom of the press. Others see it as appropriate, see, for example, Bruce C. Hafen & Jonathan O. Hafen, "The Hazelwood Progeny: Autonomy and Student Expression in the 1990's" (1995) 69 St. John's Law Review 379. These authors see the decision as rescuing students from their own innocent autonomy. They critique those who lament the Supreme Court's decision.

63 E.E. Reutter, *The Law of Public Education* (New York: The Foundation Press, 1985) at 683.

Lower American courts used the *Tinker* test to make their decisions and held a number of hair rules unconstitutional because the schools were unable to support their need by showing incidents of disruption within the school. In the case of *Massie v. Henry,*[64] the student, Massie, had hair and sideburns that were not in accordance with the school regulations. The court ruled against the school regulation because the school authorities provided no evidence that anyone else was impaired by the length of hair and there was no proof of any "disruptive event" caused by the student's action. Hair rules have been upheld where school authorities have demonstrated that long hair actually caused a disruption in the school:

> Incidents of disruption that have been shown to result from long hair have been in the nature of harassment, use of obscene or derogatory language, fights, health and sanitation problems, physical dangers, obscene appearance, and distraction of these students.[65]

In *Ward v. Blaine Lake School Board,* a student in Saskatchewan who was suspended for violating a school board rule on the length of hair attempted to use the *Tinker* case to support his right to express himself through his hairstyle.[66] The court rejected any reference to the *Tinker* test because it had been decided as a constitutional matter. Canada's *Charter* was not entrenched in the Constitution until ten years after *Ward.* The court said: "[U]nder our system of democratic local self-government, our school system was established by the laws of our province. . . . [T]he duty and power to manage the educational affairs of each school . . . has been vested in the [school board]."[67] But this exclusivity is no more. The duty and power of school boards to manage is now subject to *Charter* scrutiny and *Charter* justification.

Restricting dress, another form of expression, may be justified under the *Charter* if it can be shown that the dress interferes with the learning environment or is necessary to create an effective learning environment, but dress codes that prohibit girls from wearing pants will probably violate section 15 of the *Charter* in that the school regulation discriminates on the basis of sex. In a 1970 American case, a court upheld a dress code prohibiting scantily clad students "because it is obvious that the lack of proper covering, particularly with female students, might tend to distract other students" and disrupt the educational process.[68] It is to be

---

64 *Massie v. Henry,* 455 F. 2d 779 (4 Circ. 1972).
65 *Sims v. Colfax Community School District,* 307 F. Supp. 485 at 487 (1970).
66 *Ward v. Blaine Lake School Board,* [1971] 4 W.W.R. 161 (Sask. Q.B.).
67 *Ibid.* at 167.
68 *Bannister v. Paradis,* 316 F. Supp. 185 (D.N.H. 1970), referred to in Louis Fischer, David Schimmel, & Cynthia Kelly, *Teachers and the Law* (New York: Longman, 1991).

hoped that judges and school officials will no longer attempt to justify limiting expression on the basis of gendered assumptions.

The issue for the 1990s in the United States is gang clothing identified by such seemingly innocuous signs as jewellery or the colour of shoelaces. Some school officials have attempted to restrict gang clothing with varying degrees of success, arguing that gang clothing intimidates other students and interferes with their learning.[69]

Reading Material

Censorship of curriculum materials, text books, and library books is a common occurrence. Even so, to date, there has not been a Supreme Court *Charter* decision on this issue.

In 1982 the American Supreme Court considered its first case of censorship in public schools.[70] Some members of the school board, who had just returned from a conservative parents' organization meeting, objected to ten books in the school library and removed them. Students led by Steven Pico challenged their decision. The majority on the Supreme Court, although recognizing a school board's right to determine library content, made it clear that this right does not supersede the constitutional rights of students. The court ruled that the removal of the books violated the First Amendment rights of students to freedom of speech and expression and affirmed that a library is a special place for the recognition of the First Amendment rights of students who, by using it, are enriched through self-education and reading.[71] The court listed several legitimate motivations for removing library books, including pervasive vulgarity, educational suitability, and inappropriateness to age and grade level.

In the spring of 1997, the Surrey School Board in British Columbia voted to ban gay and lesbian resource material from its schools. One of its first acts under the new policy was to ban three children's book featuring same-sex parents.[72]

---

69 See Paul D. Murphy, "Restricting Gang Clothing in Public Schools: Does a Dress Code Violate a Student's Right of Free Expression?" (1991) 64 South California Law Review 1321.

70 *Board of Education, Island Trees Union Free School District No. 26 v. Pico*, 457 U.S. 853 (1982).

71 See Richard S. Vacca & H.C. Hudgins, *The Legacy of the Berger Court and the Schools, 1969–1986* (Kansas: National Organization on Legal Problems of Education, 1991).

72 The banned books are *Asha's Mums, Belinda's Bouquet*, and *One Dad, Two Dads, Brown Dad, Blue Dad*. The continuing uproar over the school board's decision is reported in a number of articles, see, for example, K. Bolan, "Surrey School Chair Linked to Anti-Gay Group" *The Vancouver Sun* (6 May 1997) A1 & A8. The chair of the Surrey school board is reported to be "a director of the Citizen's Research Institute, a non-profit society circulating anti-homosexual material to parents and school

The policy, on its face, appears to contravene the fundamental freedom of expression as well as the equality rights of gays, lesbians, and bisexuals under section 15 of the *Charter*. The policy is currently being challenged.

Some schools in Canada have prohibited students from reading the popular children's series "Goosebumps." School officials ban reading materials at their peril unless, of course, they can establish a persuasive argument detailing the harm caused by reading such books and the harm to be remedied by prohibiting them.[73]

Freedom of Assembly

The purpose of an assembly is to attract attention in order to make an opinion known. Justice Berger, former justice of the Supreme Court of British Columbia, has noted that "[a]ssemblies, parades and gatherings are often the only means that those without access to the media may have to bring their grievance to the attention of the public."[74] American courts have used the *Tinker* test of substantial disruption as their touchstone in cases involving freedom of assembly.

In the case of *Grayned v. City of Rockford*,[75] demonstrators challenged a city ordinance that prohibited pickets or demonstrations within 150 feet of primary or secondary school buildings during school hours.[76] The demonstrators in this case were black students and their family members and friends. The demonstrators were marching around on a sidewalk about 150 feet from a school building. Many carried signs that read "Black Cheerleaders to Cheer Too," "Black History with Black Teachers," "Equal Rights, Negro Counsellors." Also, some made the "Power to the People" sign. A disturbance erupted, but the evidence as to who caused it, the police or the demonstrators, was contradictory. The demonstrators were warned by the police to disperse. When they did not, Mr. Grayned, along with other demonstrators, was arrested. Mr. Grayned was tried and convicted of violating the city ordinance. The court considered the question of how to accommodate First Amendment rights and the special characteristics of the school

---

districts, according to documents obtained by the Vancouver Sun" (at A1); Kent Spencer & Barbara McLintock, "Surrey Board Faces Firing" *The [Vancouver] Province* (6 May 1997) A4. The headline is a paraphrase of comments made by Education Minister Paul Ramsey.

73 I have read two of these books in response to a CBC inquiry about their suitability for children. One of my own children was an avid reader of the Goosebumps series. I found them, as the name implies, spooky but surprisingly well written. One of the concerns with the series is the belief that they validate the occult. I was not alarmed by them.

74 Thomas Berger, "The Supreme Court and Fundamental Freedoms: The Renunciation of the Legacy of Mr. Justice Rand" (1980) Supreme Court L. R. 460 at 466.

75 *Grayned v. City of Rockford*, 408 U.S. 104 (1972).

76 An exception was made for school labour disputes, as long as they were peaceful.

environment. It upheld the city ordinance because it punished only conduct that disrupted or was about to disrupt normal school activities, and it noted that the anti-noise ordinance went no further than the *Tinker* test says it was reasonable to go to prevent interference with its schools.

In 1969 a group of ex-students from a high school in Ontario gathered in the school halls to distribute printed material that was critical of the operation of the school.[77] The students were charged with trespassing. They argued that they had a right to freedom of assembly. This argument was not considered, as the court found them guilty of trespassing. If this case were heard today, school officials would have to justify their authority to regulate the time, manner, and place in which materials are to be distributed using the section 1 test.

If the right to peaceful assembly interferes with the rights of other students to receive an education, the courts may follow the reasoning in *La Fédération des Etudiants v. l'Université de Moncton*.[78] In this 1982 case, students from the University of Moncton occupied an administration building to protest an increase in tuition fees. The following year some of the students were refused readmittance to the university. They argued that their expulsion was a denial of their right to peaceful assembly. This argument failed. The judge stated that the collective right to an unimpeded education prevailed. *Tinker* was not referred to in this case. Wayne MacKay, a law professor at Dalhousie University and former director at the Nova Scotia Human Rights Commission, believed that the courts would most likely follow this type of reasoning when faced with a similar question in the public schools.[79] This does not preclude, however, peaceful occupations that do not interfere with the collective rights of others to an unimpeded education.

Canadian courts will have to decide whether limiting the right of peaceful assembly in or around a school is justified by balancing the constitutional right against a legitimate need for an environment in which learning can occur. A peaceful assembly in which demonstrations do not disrupt classes or intimidate students or staff should be allowed.

Conclusion

One of the true tests of the democratizing of public education is the willingness of educational decision-makers to accept and learn from students' rights to express their views. These rights are also supported by the *Convention on the Rights of the Child*.[80] Articles 12, 13, 14, and 15 of the convention parallel the rights

---

77 *R. v. Burko* (1969), 3 D.L.R. (3d) 330 (Ont. Mag. Ct.).

78 *La Fédération des Etudiants v. l'Université de Moncton* (1982), unreported decision (N.B.Q.B.).

79 A. Wayne MacKay, *Education Law in Canada* (Canada: Emond-Montgomery, 1984) at 306.

80 *Convention on the Rights of the Child*, U.N. Doc. A/RES/44/25 (1989).

discussed in this chapter. They provide that State Parties to the convention shall assure that children who are capable of forming their own views are given the right to express them; that children shall have the right to seek, receive, and impart information and ideas of all kinds; that children shall have the right to freedom of thought, conscience, and religion, and the right to freedom of association and peaceful assembly. As with section 1 of the *Charter*, these rights under the convention can be limited on the basis of national security, public safety, public order, health or morals, or the fundamental rights and freedoms of others.

The rights discussed in this chapter are especially empowering for students. They affirm their ability to think, form opinions, and take action. These rights confront the traditional authoritarian mode of school governance. They are both liberating and a challenge. Educators are encouraged to work with students so that when they exercise their rights, they do so effectively and respectfully.

Chapter 6 ∎
Race, Gender, Economic Status, and Sexual Orientation

The students in any classroom are not a homogeneous group. Their experiences vary depending on their heritage, culture, gender, class, sexual orientation, and ability. Today's students represent a diverse society, one far removed from the homogeneous student population that the Canadian education system was originally designed to serve. This diversity presents teachers with many challenges and obligations.

Diversity, as it is used here, refers to individuals and groups who have historically suffered discrimination and disadvantage due to their cultural heritages, racial and ethnic identities, gender and class experiences, and mental and physical abilities.[1] It is students from these diverse groups who, according to a 1994 report, "are, on average, performing somewhat worse [in schools] than students from other communities."[2] The reasons for the discrepancies are many, but there is little doubt that the historical and social patterns of discrimination and inequality experienced overtly and covertly by members of diverse groups adversely affects their educational chances. The inequality of educational outcomes among the diverse student population is a human rights issue, one that is governed by the *Charter* and other human rights legislation, as well as by societal values.

The *Convention on the Rights of the Child*,[3] provincial human rights legislation, and the *Charter* all guarantee the right of students to receive an education without discrimination. The impact of the equality rights section of the *Charter* on education may prove to be profound. Section 15(1) states:

---

1   The definition is adapted from Robert A. DeVillar, Christian J. Faltis, & James P. Cummins, *Cultural Diversity in Schools: From Rhetoric to Practice* (New York: State University of New York Press, 1994) at 76.

2   Minister of Education and Training, Monique Begin & Gerald Caplan, co-chairs, *For the Love of Learning: Report of the Royal Commission on Learning* (short version) (Ottawa: Queen's Printer, 1994) at 44.

3   *Convention on the Rights of the Child,* U.N. Doc. A/RES/44/25 (1989). See arts. 2, 28, & 29. Article 2(1) states: "State Parties shall respect and ensure the rights set forth in the present Convention to each child within their jurisdiction without discrimination of any kind, irrespective of the child's or his or her parent's or legal guardian's race, colour, sex, language, religion, political or other opinion, national, ethnic or social origin, property, disability, birth or other status."

15.(1) Every individual is equal before and under the law and has the right to the equal protection and equal benefit of the law without discrimination, and in particular, without discrimination based on race, national or ethnic origin, colour, religion, sex, age or mental or physical disability.[4]

Interpretation

Section 15 of the *Charter* protects the rights of all citizens to equal protection and equal benefit of the law. The purpose of the equality guarantee is

> to prevent the violation of human dignity and freedom by imposing limitations, disadvantages or burdens through the stereotypical application of presumed group characteristics rather than on the basis of individual merit, capacity, or circumstance.[5]

Section 15 is the "section of the *Charter*, more than any other, that recognizes and cherishes the innate human dignity of every individual."[6] It serves two purposes:

> First, it expresses a commitment—deeply ingrained in our social, political and legal culture—to the equal worth and human dignity of all persons. . . . [Section 15(1)] "entails the promotion of a society in which all are secure in the knowledge that they are recognized at law as human beings equally deserving of concern, respect and consideration." Secondly, it instantiates a desire to rectify and prevent discrimination against particular groups "suffering social, political and legal disadvantage in our society."[7]

In order to undertake a *Charter* challenge,

> [a] person claiming a violation of s. 15(1) must first establish that, because of a distinction drawn between the claimant and others, the claimant has been denied "equal protection" or "equal benefit" of the law. Secondly, the claimant must show that the denial constitutes discrimination on the basis of one of the enumerated grounds listed in s. 15(1) or one analogous thereto.[8]

---

4   *Canadian Charter of Rights and Freedoms,* Part 1 of the *Constitution Act, 1982,* being Schedule B to the *Canada Act 1982* (U.K.), 1982, c. 11, s. 15.
5   *Miron v. Trudel,* [1995] 2 S.C.R. 418 at 486–87.
6   *Egan v. Canada,* [1995] 2 S.C.R. 513 at 584, referred to in *Vriend v. Alberta* (1998), 1 S.C.R. 493 at 552.
7   *Eldridge v. British Columbia (Attorney General),* [1997] 3 S.C.R. 624 at 667.
8   *Ibid.* at 669.

The case of *Andrews v. Law Society of British Columbia*[9] was the first section 15 case heard by the Supreme Court. It involved the right of a British subject, permanently resident in Canada, to practise law in British Columbia. The province of British Columbia required that lawyers wishing to practise in the province be Canadian citizens.[10] The question before the court was whether the citizenship requirement infringed or denied the rights guaranteed by section 15(1).

Prior to *Andrews*, lower courts had given their interpretations to section 15(1) and the record had not been hopeful for those relying on section 15(1) to bring about changes for the disadvantaged.[11] In fact in many ways the decisions were more restrictive than the Supreme Court's earlier rulings on human rights cases under human rights legislation.[12] Researchers found that women were initiating fewer cases than men, and that men were using the *Charter* to strike down women's hard-won protection and benefits. For example, men have successfully challenged sections of the *Criminal Code* which

> made sexual intercourse with a girl under age 14 an offence . . . which made indecent assault of a female person an indictable offence and . . . which contained protection for vulnerable young women, such as protection for foster daughters against men in positions of authority such as foster fathers.[13]

Lower courts were interpreting section 15(1) in a manner consistent with the justice orientation, whereby they relied on a universal principle of equality— which means treating everyone the same regardless of their personal, historical, or social circumstances. This interpretation has been referred to as "equality with a vengeance."[14]

The Women's Legal Action Fund (LEAF), which intervened in *Andrews*, urged the Supreme Court to give section 15 a substantive interpretation that would

> benefit individuals and groups which historically have had unequal access to social and economic resources, either because of overt discrimination or because of the adverse effects of apparently "neutral" forms of social organizations premised on the subordination of certain groups and the dominance of others.[15]

---

9   *Andrews v. Law Society of British Columbia*, [1989] 1 S.C.R. 143.

10 *Barristers and Solicitors Act*, R.S.B.C. 1979, c. 26.

11 See Gwen Brodsky & Shelagh Day, *Canadian Charter Equality Rights for Women: One Step Forward or Two Steps Back?* (Ottawa: Canadian Advisory Council on the Status of Women, 1989), in which they review equality cases heard under s. 15 prior to *Andrews, supra* note 9.

12 *Ibid.*

13 *Ibid.* at 58–59.

14 *Schacter v. Canada et al.*, [1992] 2 S.C.R. 679.

15 *Andrews, supra* note 9 (LEAF Intervenor Factum at 10).

The Supreme Court issued its historic decision on February 2, 1989, giving section 15(1) substantive meaning in its interpretation of equality, discrimination, and analogous groups protected by section 15(1). The court rejected an exclusively legalistic and procedural interpretation to section 15(1), saying:

> It is not every distinction or differentiation in treatment at law which will transgress the equality guarantees of the Charter . . . for the accommodation of differences, which is the essence of true equality, it will frequently be necessary to make distinctions.[16]

Treating everyone equally in order to realize equality is consistent with the ethic of justice. It is reciprocal—"I'll treat you the same if you treat me the same"—but it is based on the naive assumption that all are equal in the first place.[17] Viewing equality in this manner rarely allows for a consideration of the effect of the inequalities that some groups have suffered throughout history. Clinging to the view that in order to be fair we must treat everyone the same obfuscates any consideration of the social, political, and legal conditions of disadvantaged individuals and groups. Equality is considered in the abstract rather than in its context. A procedural interpretation of equality focuses on equal treatment; a substantive interpretation is contextual, considering the circumstances of the particular other. Thus equal treatment or equal opportunity is not enough. In fact treating everyone the same can exacerbate inequality. An interpretation of equality that includes equality of results forces decision-makers to consider the particular individual and his or her circumstances.

Discrimination

Canadian courts have recognized two types of discrimination: direct discrimination and indirect discrimination.[18] The term "systemic discrimination" includes both types.[19]

Direct discrimination is based on stereotypical assumptions of the personal characteristics of a protected group and "has the effect on the claimant of imposing a burden, obligation or disadvantage not imposed upon others or of withholding or limiting access to benefits or advantages which are available to others."[20]

---

16 *Ibid.* at 168.

17 Catherine MacKinnon put it succinctly when she wrote that the only equality in this argument is that "men's differences from women are equal to women's differences from men. There is an *equality* there." Catherine A. MacKinnon, *Feminism Unmodified: Discourse on Life and Law* (Cambridge: Harvard University Press, 1987).

18 See, for example, *Eldridge, supra* note 7; *Huck, infra* note 37.

19 Colleen Sheppard & Sarah Westphal, "Equity and the University: Learning from Women's Experience" (1992) 5 C.J.W.L. 5.

20 *Miron, supra* note 5 at 485.

Direct discrimination occurs when a student is not allowed to attend her neighbourhood school because of her disability[21] or when girls and boys are streamed into home economics and industrial arts classes because of stereotypical gender assumptions.[22]

Indirect discrimination, sometimes referred to as "adverse impact discrimination," arises from practices that apply to everyone. The practices appear neutral but either impose more of a burden on a protected class or deny them equal benefits. Adverse impact discrimination is rarely motivated by ill-will, but regardless of whether there was an intent to discriminate or not, the courts have ruled that if an action, practice, or convention disadvantages or imposes a burden on a protected class of people, then it is discrimination.[23] An educational example of adverse impact discrimination is placing a child with a disability in an integrated classroom, then ignoring the differences and forcing the student "to sink or swim within the mainstream environment"[24] without the benefit of accommodation in the form of positive steps or special measures.[25] Another example is the use of assessment procedures that result in a higher percentage of minority students being labelled as less academic than the majority group.[26] The problem is not with the students but with the measuring tool.[27]

---

21   *Eaton v. (Brant County) Board of Education* (1995), 22 O.R. (3d) 1 (C.A.); *Elwood v. Halifax County-Bedford District School Board* (1987). For a complete discussion of the case, see A. Wayne MacKay, "The Elwood Case: Vindicating the Educational Rights of the Disabled," in M. Csapo & L. Goguen, eds., *Special Education Across Canada: Issues and Concerns for the 90's* (Vancouver: Centre for Human Development & Research, 1989) at 149.

22   *Tillie v. Moose Jaw School Div. No. 1* (1995), 23 C.H.R.R. D/87. Two female students successfully argued that they had been discriminated against on the basis of their sex under s. 13 of *The Saskatchewan Human Rights Code* when they were denied entry into an industrial arts class and instead placed in a home economics class.

23   *Ontario Human Rights Commission and Simpson-Sears Ltd.,* [1985] 2 S.C.R. 536. Other cases expanded on this meaning of equality, see *Bhinder v. C.N.R.*, [1985] 2 S.C.R. 561; *C.N.R. v. Canadian Human Rights Commission,* [1987] 1 S.C.R. 1114. See also *Vriend, supra* note 6 at 547.

24   *Eaton v. Brant County Board of Education,* [1997] 1 S.C.R. 241 at 273.

25   *Eldridge, supra* note 7 at 680.

26   See Jim Cummins, "From Multicultural to Anti-Racist Education," in Rore Skutmabb-Kangas & Jim Cummins, eds., *Minority Education: From Shame to Struggle* (Philadelphia: Multilingual Matters, 1988) at 127.

27   In 1995 an Aboriginal student enrolled in one of my classes wrote in her journal: "[T]he inequality of the educational system brings to mind when I wrote a Stanford-Binet I.Q. test on the reserve when I was in grade school. It had so many alien concepts such as objects I'd never seen or heard of—electrical appliances and Caucasian formats. It made me feel dumb and incompetent not realizing I couldn't possibly respond to ideas and concepts I have never heard of" [quoted with permission].

According to the courts, realizing equality means focusing on the outcome, the end, the result. If the end result of an education program is that a certain group of students does worse than other groups, the program requires closer scrutiny. It could mean the existence of systemic barriers within the program that bring about the discriminatory results. As noted earlier, the discrimination is likely unintentional, but it still impedes the potential of some students.

Justice LaForest, speaking for a unanimous Supreme Court, said:

> [D]iscrimination can arise both from the adverse effects of rules of general application as well as from express distinctions flowing from the distribution of benefits. . . . I can think of no principled reason why it should not be possible to establish a claim of discrimination based on the adverse effects of a facially neutral benefit scheme. Section 15(1) expressly states, after all, that every individual is "equal before and under the law and has the right to the equal protection and equal benefit of the law without discrimination . . . " The provision makes no distinction between laws that impose unequal burdens and those that deny equal benefits.[28]

The authors of a task force on education have argued that if the education system were working equitably there would be an equal distribution of achievement across demographic or community lines, but there is not.[29] Jim Cummins, an education professor at OISE, has noted that the students who tend to have the most difficulty in schools are those who have experienced a long history of discrimination, subjugation, and prejudice.[30] The evolving legal definitions of equality and discrimination, which consider the impact of systemic practices, policies, and school rules, invite educators to heed the impact of historically accepted school practices that are taken for granted on the educational opportunities of historically disadvantaged students.

Application to Education

Students and their advocates have used and will continue to use section 15 to argue that the education system discriminates against them and denies them equal benefit of the education system. Section 15 has been used to argue that a teacher's anti-Semitic views impede the rights of students to equal benefit of the education system[31] and that children with disabilities have a right to an integrated education.[32] There are most certainly other challenges ahead. It is conceivable that there may

---

28 *Eldridge, supra* note 7 at 680.
29 Begin & Caplan, *supra* note 2.
30 Jim Cummins, *Empowering Minority Students* (Sacramento: California Association of Bilingual Education, 1989) at 8.
31 *R. v. Keegstra,* [1990] 3 S.C.R. 697; *Ross v. New Brunswick School District No. 15,* [1996] 1 S.C.R. 825.
32 See, for example, *Eaton, supra* note 24.

be challenges to curricula that exclude the experiences and histories of marginalized groups such as Aboriginal people, persons with disabilities, gays, lesbians,
and bisexuals. There may be challenges to the inequities of spending on girl's
and boy's sports, as well as challenges by the Aboriginal community and other
marginalized groups on the basis that the education system as a whole is failing
their students.[33]

A claim of inequality in education may be directed at a number of systemic
practices and conventions, some of which appear innocuous and certainly not
intended to elicit inequality. There are times when treating everyone equally—
giving everyone the same opportunity—is appropriate. Few would argue with
the principle that every child should have the right to attend school regardless of
his or her ancestry, colour, or ethnic background; however, the idea that no two
students are the same and that to treat them in exactly the same way may
disadvantage one over the other is also an accepted principle.

Consider, for example, the case of Laura, who taught students with behavioural
problems. She discussed the need to treat students differently and to administer
different consequences depending on the student. Laura illustrated this point
with reference to one of her students, Tom, who reacted angrily whenever one
particular student looked at him. Tom swore and threatened him. If another student
had acted this way, Laura might have sent the student home until he or she had
calmed down. However, Laura knew that Tom had been severely sexually abused
and that the other student reminded him of the abuser. She also knew that sending
Tom home might make him vulnerable to more abuse. She said:

> It wasn't that I was still approving of Tom's swearing or anything, it was sort of a
> catharsis for him as opposed to someone else who would be deliberately swearing
> at me. . . . I tell [my students] that they're not going to be treated equally and that
> equal is not always fair.[34]

In Laura's estimation, treating Tom differently was fair considering Tom's
history and social circumstances. To have treated him the same as the other

---

33 See Jim Cummins, "Empowering Minority Students: Framework for Intervention,"
in Lois Weis & Michelle Fine, eds., *Beyond Silenced Voices: Class, Race, and Gender
in United States Schools* (Albany: State University of New York Press, 1993) c. 5.
Cummins notes that "when the patterns of minority student school failure are examined
from an international perspective, it becomes evident that power and status relations
between minority and majority groups exert a major influence on school performance"
(at 105). For example, Finnish students in Sweden, where they are considered a low-
status group, experience more academic failure than they do in Australia, where they
are considered a high-status group.

34 Ailsa M. Watkinson, *Honouring Diversity in the Classroom* (Saskatoon: Saskatchewan
Teacher's Federation, 1996). The example is based on a factual incident related to
me by the teacher.

students, a practice some might see as "fair," would have discounted his personal circumstances and even put him at further risk. Although this example is not a legal human rights case, it illustrates the well-established practice among educators of taking a student's personal circumstances into account.

True equality for students from diverse backgrounds cannot be achieved by treating everyone the same because equality in that case is void of context. Canadian courts—in particular, the Supreme Court—have repeatedly asserted that identical treatment, otherwise referred to as "formal equality," does not constitute true equality or "substantive equality."[35] Formal equality is an unreflective approach to dealing with inequality; it is a "thin and impoverished" notion of equality.[36]

The identical treatment of everyone does not necessarily mean that there has been no discrimination, nor does it mean that equality has been achieved.[37] To expose all students to the same educational opportunities will not guarantee that the legal obligation of equality has been realized. The test is in the outcomes— the results. To this end, educators are obliged to "take special measures to ensure that disadvantaged groups are able to benefit equally from government services."[38] There is no doubt that there is an inequality in educational outcomes in Canadian schools. The question is whether this inequality arises from discrimination within the service provided by the government, namely public education.

Racialized Students

It is estimated that by the year 2011 approximately one-third of the school population in Saskatchewan will be of Aboriginal ancestry, almost doubling the number of Aboriginal children in the school system.[39] Within the next few years,

---

35 See, for example, *Vriend, supra* note 6 at 543; *Eldridge, supra* note 7 at 671; and *Andrews, supra* note 9 at 164.

36 *Eldridge, supra* note 7 at 678.

37 *Michael Huck v. Odeon Theatres Limited* (1985), 6 Canadian Human Rights Reporter D/2682 (Court of Appeal) at D/2689. The court found that the failure of a theatre to provide a disabled person a choice of place from which to view a film comparable to that offered to the general public was discriminatory. See also Donna Greschner, "The Right to Belong: The Promise of *Vriend*" (1998) 9 N.J.C.L. 417. Greschner equates "substantive equality," as opposed to "formal equality," with "full membership." Full membership begins with a presumption of inclusion. "It proclaims that everyone is a member [of community] and cannot be treated as an outsider or subordinate. . . . The promotion of belonging for everyone means that diversity is recognized and accepted as part of the essence of human condition and as necessary for human flourishing" (at 429–30).

38 *Eldridge, supra* note 7 at 680.

39 Saskatchewan School Trustees Association, *Saskatchewan 2000* (Regina: Saskatchewan School Trustees Association, 1991).

one-half of all kindergarten students in Saskatchewan will be of Aboriginal ancestry.[40] In 1991, however, only 12 percent of Aboriginal students completed grade 12,[41] compared with an overall graduation rate in the province of 78.2 percent.[42] Another study, reporting the highest level of education attained by Aboriginal and non-Aboriginal people, showed 11 percent of Aboriginal students attained grade 12, compared with 18.9 percent of the non-Aboriginal population. At the other end of the scale, however, 24 percent of Aboriginal people had less than grade 9, compared with 13.8 percent of the non-Aboriginal population.[43]

Although it is difficult to get a clear picture of the success rate among Aboriginal students, educational researchers have recognized that they do not reap the same benefits as non-Aboriginal students. The situation forces educators to consider "why schooling has continued to be such an alienating experience for Aboriginal children and youth."[44] The 1995 *Saskatchewan Education Indicators Report* stated:

> With the increasing number of Aboriginal youngsters, it becomes more critical than ever that Aboriginal traditions and history be reflected in instructional materials and classroom practices, and that Aboriginal teachers provide positive role models.[45]

No one has yet argued, under human rights legislation or the *Charter*, that the lack of Aboriginal material and Aboriginal teachers in schools denies Aboriginal students equal benefit of a public service, but the argument is there to be made. The argument could conceivably be that the prevalence of curriculum material that is either explicitly racist[46] or by omission diminishes the contributions and

---

40 The Honourable Pat Atkinson, Minister of Education, Opening Remarks, Canadian Association of School Administrators Meeting, Radisson Hotel, Saskatoon, 28 September 1997.

41 *Saskatchewan Education Indicators Report, Update 1995* (Regina: Saskatchewan Education, 1995) at 11. These statistics were drawn from a survey conducted by Statistics Canada, in which nineteen to twenty-four year olds who identified themselves as Aboriginal were asked whether they had completed some or all of their secondary education.

42 *Ibid.* at 21. These statistics were drawn from a survey of seventeen and eighteen year olds who, after starting grade 10, completed grade 12 within three years. If it had included those who had returned to school after four or five years, the completion rate would have been higher. This survey did not include band-run or private schools.

43 Report of the Royal Commission on Aboriginal Peoples, *Gathering Strength,* vol. 3 (Canada: Minister of Supply and Services, 1996) at 440. The survey included persons still attending school who were fifteen years and over.

44 *Ibid.*

45 *Supra* note 41 at 7.

46 There are numerous examples of texts and books that portray Aboriginal people negatively, for example, see *Prejudice in Social Studies Textbooks* (Saskatoon: Saskatchewan Human Rights Commission, 1973–74). Some of these books are still

history of Aboriginal people; the lack of Aboriginal role models in teaching and administrative positions; and even the strict reliance on school rules that have a detrimental impact on Aboriginal students all act as systemic barriers to educational benefits.[47]

The historical, social, and political contexts of Aboriginal people are other powerful pieces in the argument that the education system has not served Aboriginal students well. Aboriginal children were forced to attend residential schools run by the federal government and various religious denominations. Forced expulsion from their family homes had a profound impact:

> Our Indigenous nations were once strong and self-sufficient. We maintained our cultures through adherence to a philosophy that was rich and vibrant. However, the last one hundred years of our history is full of black holes made by the theft of our language, our religious practices and traditions. Especially sad are the decades of torment our nations' children had to endure in the church-run, government sponsored residential schools.[48]

The effects of this dislocation are still felt. Parents of Aboriginal students have expressed the fear that their children are failing to develop a positive sense of their identities and that curricula rarely reflect their history and culture.[49] Parents believe that Aboriginal students either drop out or are being suspended and expelled out of all proportion to their numbers. They worry about racist attitudes towards their children and about the lack of adequate counselling and support services that might make a difference.[50] These parents could launch a challenge to the education system alleging under section 15 of the *Charter* that their children are not reaping the same benefits provided by law in the establishment of public education and that the unequal distribution of benefits is based on their children's ancestry and race. This same argument of systemic

---

on library bookshelves. As recently as 1995, a book by Jeanette Lee Thompson, *Old Mose of Fort Whoop-Up: A True Story* (Edmonton: Canadian Social Sciences Services, 1971), was found in the Education Library at the University of Saskatchewan. The book "is a story told through the eyes of a dog who lived at a trading post called Fort Whoop-Up, where fur trading Indians drink whiskey, get drunk and mean and go home to beat their wives and children. NorthWest Mounted Police are described as brave and noble." Betty Ann Adam, "Pull Racist Book: Educator" *The [Saskatoon] StarPhoenix* (23 October 1995) A3.

47 Report of the Royal Commission, *supra* note 43.
48 Linda Jaine, ed., *Residential Schools: The Stolen Years* (Saskatoon: University Extension Press, 1993). See also Report of the Royal Commission on Aboriginal Peoples, *Looking Forward Looking Back,* vol. 1 (Canada: Minister of Supply and Services, 1996) c. 10.
49 Begin & Caplan, *supra* note 2 at 41.
50 *Ibid.*

discrimination is open to others who believe that the education system does not provide historically disadvantaged students with the same chance to meet their potentials as it provides to students who have not been historically disadvantaged.

Immigrant students face additional problems, most notably with language. An Alberta study found that 74 percent of English as a Second Language (ESL) students dropped out of school. The reasons varied from their limited ability in English combined with limited first-language proficiency, the requirement that ESL students leave school by the age of nineteen, and their own sense of impending failure.[51] In order for these students to benefit from public education, the government must provide them with special services.[52]

Other members of racialized minorities face systemic hurdles within the education system as well. Black students do not achieve as well as others and it appears that the education system is failing them. The Report of the Royal Commission on Learning stated that "a disproportionate number of black students were not going to get a high school diploma and were going to face, like other dropouts, poor job prospects, and possible social marginalization."[53]

These facts are serious. The first step in improving the situation is to ask what it is within the practice and culture of education that impedes the learning opportunities of minority members, women, and persons with disabilities. The next step is to take positive action to eliminate the barriers and to structure the education process more equitably.

Gender

Girls and young women continue to face barriers in education even though the *Saskatchewan Education Indicators Report* showed that in 1994–95 female students outperformed their male counterparts in all grade 12 subject areas, including math and sciences.[54] Research has shown that traditional pedagogy

---

51 David L.E. Watt & Hetty Roessingh, "Some You Win, Most You Lose: Tracking E.S.L. Student Drop Out in High School" (1994) 26:3 English Quarterly 5–6.

52 *Eldridge, supra* note 7.

53 Begin & Caplan, *supra* note 2 at 44. See also Jennifer Kelly, *Under the Gaze: Learning to Be Black in White Society* (Halifax: Fernwood, 1998); Carol Schick, "By Virtue of Being White: Resistance in Anti-Racist Pedagogy" (forthcoming) Race, Ethnicity and Education.

54 *Saskatchewan Education Indicators Report: Kindergarten to Grade 12, Update 1996* (Regina: Saskatchewan Education, 1996) at 14. The only exception is rural Mathematics 30, where boys outperform girls. These are encouraging findings considering that other studies show that girls start school ahead of boys in reading and basic computation skills but by the time they graduate from high school, boys have higher scores in both areas. Doug White, "After the Divided Curriculum" *The Victorian Teacher* (March 1983) 7.

favours boys' learning patterns more than girls'.[55] It has also shown that teachers interact more with boys than with girls and that their interactions with boys are more meaningful.[56] The effect is that the learning environment stunts the intellectual growth of girls. Girls also encounter a learning environment poisoned by sexual harassment.[57]

Motherhood has negative consequences for young women in school, and yet there is a lack of consideration given to students with young children. It has been and continues to be a struggle to convince educational decision-makers to provide childcare so that mothers can learn. The struggle continues even though statistics show that 50 percent of single mothers and 75 percent of married mothers drop out of school.[58] The consequence is almost certain poverty for the mothers and their children.[59] Even though the mothers are not denied entry into school, they are forced out because childcare is not considered an educational or gender matter. Measures such as childcare and flexible attendance rules are needed to keep mothers in school and to improve their chances in life, as well as the chances of their children.

School sports and the financial support they receive have been questioned as discriminatory. The sport that takes the biggest part of an athletic budget is football; it is male dominated if not male exclusive. If it can be shown that the money spent on male-dominated sports exceeds that spent on women's sports, sports programs and their budgets may be challenged as discriminatory.

Despite the fact that the authors of one report stated: "[W]e've been dismayed by the evidence of how far we have yet to come in giving girls and young women the same respect as we give to boys,"[60] many directors of education do not consider gender inequality an issue. In Saskatchewan, directors of education were asked about activities to ensure gender equity in their school divisions. Thirty-six percent did not respond to the question about obstacles to gender

---

55 Myra Sadker & David Sadker, *Failing at Fairness: How America's Schools Cheat Girls* (Toronto: Macmillan, 1994); Patricia Ann Lather, *Getting Smart: Feminist Research and Pedagogy* (New York: Routledge, 1991).

56 *Ibid.* See also *How Schools Shortchange Girls* (American Association of University Women, 1992). Referred to in Cecelia Goodnow, "Boys' World: Girls' Education Short Changed by Sexism" *The [Saskatoon] StarPhoenix* (18 April 1994) B15.

57 This matter is discussed at length in chapter 8. See also Nan Stein, Nancy L. Marshall, & Linda R. Tropp, *Secrets in Public: Sexual Harassment in Our Schools* (Massachusetts: Center of Research on Women, Wellesley College, and NOW Legal Defence and Education Fund, 1993).

58 Michelle Fine, *Framing Dropouts: Notes on the Politics of an Urban Public High School* (New York: State University of New York Press, 1991) at 22.

59 *Ibid.* at 23. Although slightly fewer women than men drop out of school, a woman's chances of finding paid work after she has dropped out of school are less than her male counterpart's (at 259).

60 Begin & Caplan, *supra* note 2 at 43.

equity, and another 16 percent said "that there was no need for gender equity measures in their school division or that it is not a targeted concern."[61]

Sexual Orientation

Gays and lesbians are a protected class under the *Charter*.[62] In addition all provincial and human rights legislation protects gays and lesbians from discrimination.[63] Gay, lesbian, and bisexual students face a myriad of hurdles within education and in their public lives. They are left out of the curriculum altogether and are often subjected to overt harassment.[64]

One Canadian school board has attempted to ensure that gay and lesbian material continues to be left out of the curriculum. In April 1997, the Surrey School Board in British Columbia passed a motion instructing the administration, teaching, and counselling staff that resources from gay and lesbian groups such as GALE BC (Gay and Lesbian Education BC) were not to be used or distributed in their division. Two weeks later the school board banned three children's books featuring same-sex parents.[65] The board's actions were described in the media as creating a climate of intolerance.[66] The board's actions were challenged in

---

61 *Saskatchewan Education Indicators Report, supra* note 54.

62 *Egan, supra* note 6; *Vriend, supra* note 6; *Rosenberg v. Canada (Attorney General)* (1998), 38 O.R. 577 (Ont. C.A.).

63 Alberta was the only province that had human rights legislation that did not include sexual orientation. The omission was challenged by Delwin Vriend as a violation of s. 15 of the *Charter*. The case was eventually heard by the Supreme Court, which ruled in favour of the complainant. The Supreme Court ruled that the omission of sexual orientation from the *Alberta Individual's Rights Protection Act* (R.S.A. 1980, c. 1-2), as amended *Human Rights, Citizenship and Multiculturalism Act* (R.S.A. 1996, c. H-11.7), violated s. 15 of the *Charter* and could not be saved by s. 1. The court ruled that sexual orientation was to be "read in" to the provincial legislation. *Vriend, ibid.* at 576.

64 See, for example, Bruce MacDougall, "Silence in the Classroom: Limits on Homosexual Expression and Visibility in Education and the Privileging of Homophobic Religious Ideology" (1998) 16 S.L.R. 41.

65 The banned books are *Asha's Mums, Belinda's Bouquet,* and *One Dad, Two Dads, Brown Dad, Blue Dad.* K. Bolan, "Surrey School Chair Linked to Anti-Gay Group" *The Vancouver Sun* (6 May 1997) A1 & A8.

66 Kent Spencer & Barbara McLintock, "Surrey Board Faces Firing" *The [Vancouver] Province* (6 May 1997) A4. The statement is a paraphrase of comments made by Education Minister Paul Ramsey. See also "Meet Rick: He's Gay and Living in Fear" *The [Vancouver] Province* (20 April 1997) A14. "Rick" lives in constant fear that his secret will get out. He refused to be photographed for the interview and used a different name. The article reported that "life at school is marked by intolerance and physical violence against gays." See also Paula Brooks, "War on Words" *Chatelaine* (December 1998) 46.

the B.C. Supreme Court. In December 1998, Supreme Court Justice Mary Saunders ruled that the ban could not be justified. "She found that the School Board is required to adhere to 'a high moral line' which is consistent with the Canadian Charter of Rights and Freedoms."[67] In January 1999 the Surrey School Board announced it was appealing the decision to the British Columbia Court of Appeal.

An American national gay and lesbian task force studied two thousand gay, lesbian, and bisexual adults. Ninety percent said they were subjected to verbal or physical harassment, and one in five lesbians and one in two gay men said they were victims of hate crimes in school.[68] A large percentage of gays, lesbians, and bisexuals drop out of schools.[69] The effects of homophobia are distressing. The United States Department of Health and Human Services estimated that 30 percent of all youth suicides are committed by gay, lesbian, and bisexual youth.[70] Lisa Loutzenheiser, a graduate student in educational policy, reported that "they are three to five times more likely to attempt suicide than their heterosexual peers and are more likely to succeed when they do."[71]

Their lack of strong role models in schools and elsewhere, their absence from school curricula, or alternatively their negative portrayal in school curricula, sustain the myth that they are abnormal. One writer noted that "gay people are the only minorities that do not have a parent as a role model."[72] And their chances of having a gay, lesbian, or bisexual teacher as a role model are minute since, despite human rights protection, a teacher who declares such a sexual orientation will likely lose his or her job. The exclusion of any discussion of the sexual orientation of some of the famous people who have given us many examples of heroism, courage, and works of art contributes to the perception of abnormality.[73]

---

67   "Court Strikes Down Surrey Board's Book Banning" http://www.lesbigay.com/bigots/press%20release.htm (16 December 1998).

68   Lisa W. Loutzenheiser, "How Schools Play 'Smear the Queer' " (1996) 10:2 Feminist Teacher 59 at 60.

69   Fine, *supra* note 58 at 19 & 22.

70   Reported in Loutzenheiser, *supra* note 68 at 59.

71   *Ibid*. at 59. See also Pierre J. Tremblay, "The Homosexuality Factor in the Youth Suicide Problem" (Paper presented at the Sixth Annual Conference of the Canadian Association for Suicide Prevention, Banff, Alberta, 11–14 October 1995) [unpublished].

72   G.J. Krysial, "A Very Silent and Gay Minority," (1987) 34 (4) The School Counsellor 304, referred to in Richard A. Friend, "Choices, Not Closets: Heterosexism and Homophobia in Schools," in Lois Weis & Michelle Fine, eds., *Beyond Silenced Voices: Class, Race, and Gender in United States Schools* (Albany: State University of New York Press, 1993) c. 10 at 213.

73   One professor asked his students to compile a list of twenty gay and lesbian luminaries. The final list was an extraordinary compilation of household names who had contributed to arts, politics, science, and other social endeavours. I was familiar with the homosexual orientation of only a few.

Poverty

It is estimated that poverty affects 20.9 percent of children in Canada.[74] Two recent studies found that children from poor families have a much higher illiteracy and failure rate than their middle-class peers.[75] One study found that in nineteen countries studied by the Organization for Economic Cooperation and Development, including Canada, "a disproportional number of students who failed came from economically disadvantaged families."[76] The other study found that "young adults from poorer backgrounds in the Prairie provinces and Quebec scored as though they had two fewer years of schooling than those from middle-class homes. In Ontario, British Columbia and the Atlantic provinces, the gap was between four and five years."[77]

The Supreme Court of Canada has yet to rule on just where poverty fits as an element of a litigant's claim to be a member of an historically disadvantaged group; however, the Nova Scotia Supreme Court took poverty into account in a *Charter* decision regarding the rights of a public housing tenant.[78] The tenant, a single, black mother of two children, had lived in public housing for over ten years. Ms. Sparks had been given one month's notice to move out of her residence. According to the *Residential Tenancies Act*, tenants in private housing who have lived in their residences for five years cannot be evicted from their homes unless a judge is satisfied that the tenants are in default of obligations under their leases.[79] The law protecting private housing tenants, however, is not extended to public housing tenants. The court ruled in favour of the tenant, noting that "[p]overty is, in addition, a condition more frequently experienced by members of the three groups identified."[80] The law adversely affected protected groups under the *Charter*, namely single parents, females, and blacks.

Recent statistics bear out the close association of female lone-parent families with poverty. Children in female lone-parent families are five times as likely to be in low-income situations as those in two-parent families. The report conducted

74　Douglas Durst, "Phoenix or Fizzle? Background to Canada's New National Child Benefit," in Douglas Durst, ed., *Canada's National Child Benefit: Phoenix or Fizzle* (Halifax: Fernwood, 1999) 11 at 23.

75　Victor Dwyer, "The Roots of Failure" *Maclean's* (22 September 1997) 70. The author is reporting on two studies, one conducted by Statistics Canada, the other by the Organization for Economic Cooperation and Development (OECD).

76　*Ibid.*, referring to the OECD study.

77　*Ibid.*, referring to the Statistics Canada study.

78　*Re Dartmouth/Halifax County Regional Housing Authority v. Sparks* (1993), 101 D.L.R. (4th) 224 (N.S.C.A.).

79　The *Residential Tenancies Act*, R.S.N.S. 1989, c. 401, gives residential tenants protection of residency. However, ss. 10(8)(d) and 25(2) of the act exempt public-housing tenants from the same benefit.

80　*Sparks, supra* note 78 at 233.

by the Organization for Economic Cooperation and Development noted that 60.8 percent of female lone-parent families had low incomes, compared with 11.8 percent for two-parent families.[81] The connection between female lone-parent families and poverty, the lower educational attainment of poor children, and the recent ruling in *Sparks*, which also took into account ancestry and colour, raise the possibility of a successful *Charter* challenge.

Human rights legislation in some provinces provides protection to persons who are on social assistance. The *Convention on the Rights of the Child*,[82] under article 27, states that every child has the right to a standard of living adequate for the child's physical, mental, spiritual, moral, and social development. Article 28 recognizes the child's right to education on the basis of equal opportunity. The impact of poverty on students is devastating and regardless of whether it falls under the *Charter* or human rights legislation it is a human rights issue. Governments have a moral obligation to take positive action to ameliorate the disadvantages experienced by children living in poverty.

Conclusion

Equality issues in education are some of the most important issues facing public education today.[83] The Supreme Court of Canada has quoted with approval from the well-known case of *Brown v. Board of Education of Topeka,* in which the American Supreme Court said:

> Today, education is perhaps the most important function of state and local governments. . . . It is the very foundation of good citizenship. . . . It is a principal instrument in awakening the child to cultural values, in preparing him for later professional training and in helping him to adjust normally to his environment. In these days it is doubtful that any child can reasonably be expected to succeed in life if he is denied the opportunity of an education. Such an opportunity where the State has undertaken to provide it, is a right which must be made available to all on equal terms.[84]

Educational decision-makers have a legal and moral obligation to take positive steps, to adjust the way things have always been done, and to create new and

---

81 *Supra* note 75; see also the collection of articles in Durst, *supra* note 74.

82 *Convention on the Rights of the Child,* U.N. Doc. A/RES/44/25 (1989).

83 Saskatchewan Minister of Education, the Honourable Pat Atkinson, Opening Session (League of Educational Administrators, Directors and Superintendents Annual Policy Conference, Ramada Hotel, Saskatoon, Saskatchewan, 1 March 1998) [unpublished].

84 *Brown v. Board of Education of Topeka,* 347 U.S. 483 at 493(1954). This case was referred to with approval in *R. v. Jones,* [1986] 2 S.C.R. 295, and *Ross v. School District No. 15,* [1996] 1 S.C.R. 825.

perhaps trail-blazing means to provide an education for all students on equal terms.[85]

The final report of the Royal Commission on Aboriginal Peoples provides some guidance through recommendations that may assist educational decision-makers in their quest to expunge the inequities from education. Many of the commission's recommendations apply to other disadvantaged groups as well. The report calls for legislation guaranteeing Aboriginal representation on school boards where population numbers warrant.[86] Depending on the population served by a school board, similar provisions could be made to guarantee representation from other disadvantaged groups. This would provide some assurance that the needs of the disadvantaged were being considered and would overcome one of the most insidious outcomes of democratic elections: the election of only majority group members.

In 1985 the Saskatchewan Human Rights Commission issued *Education Equity: A Report on Indian/Native Education in Saskatchewan.*[87] The report found special favour with the Royal Commission and was the foundation of their recommendations calling upon provincial and territorial governments to require school boards to implement education strategies along with Aboriginal parents, elders, and educators. Again the recommendations may be applied where appropriate to assist other disadvantaged groups. The recommendations called for the hiring of more Aboriginal teachers and administrators; the hiring of Aboriginal support workers such as counsellors, community liaison workers, psychologists, and speech therapists; the inclusion in all curricula of the perspectives, traditions, beliefs, and world views of Aboriginal Peoples; the involvement of Aboriginal elders in teaching; the inclusion of language classes; the development of family and community involvement mechanisms; as well as the development of educational programs to combat stereotypes, racism, prejudices, and biases. The recommendations concluded with a call for accountability indicators tied to board or district funding and for public reports of results.[88]

Many school jurisdictions have implemented some or all of these recommendations. But, as Cummins has noted, discrepancies still prevail despite many good efforts. Cummins has identified four areas that are often overlooked.

---

85 *Eldridge, supra* note 7.

86 *Supra* note 43 at 471: Recommendation 3.5.7.

87 *Education Equity: A Report on Indian/Native Education in Saskatchewan* (Saskatoon: Saskatchewan Human Rights Commission, 1985). The eventual report was a culmination of work undertaken by the commission, beginning in 1982, following an unreleased report on the high drop-out rate of Aboriginal students from urban schools in Saskatchewan. See Ailsa M. Watkinson, "Affirmative Action: A New Direction for Schools" (1984) 13(3) S.H.R.C. Newsletter. The article was the discussion paper leading to the education equity initiative.

88 *Supra* note 43 at 474: Recommendation 3.5.9.

The first two are included in the recommendations listed above but are worthy of repetition. Cummins noted that incorporating the language and culture of dominated minorities into school programs constitutes a significant predictor of their academic success;[89] community participation, meaning real community empowerment, is another factor he identified in the success of students from dominated communities.[90] Cummins also identified pedagogy, the process of teaching, as a variable that contributes to the success or failure of disadvantaged students in school. Students who are engaged in the process of learning and teaching are engaged in a higher level of cognitive skills than just factual recall. Their language use and experiences intertwine to develop "a sense of efficacy and inner direction in the classroom" and confirm that what they have to say is important.[91] The final variable that Cummins identified is assessment. He stated that "historically, assessment has played the role of legitimizing the disabling of minority students."[92] The designation of students as "learning disabled" or "language impaired," for example, depends on who is doing the testing—a psychologist or a speech pathologist. He concluded that "with respect to students' actual behaviour, the label was essentially arbitrary."[93]

These recommendations provide a framework for the development of strategies designed to ferret out inequities within the education system and to construct positive steps to overcome their impacts. The end result of such endeavours is, of course, the design of a vitally important public service: public education in a non-discriminatory manner.[94]

---

89 *Supra* note 33 at 107–08.
90 *Ibid.* at 109.
91 *Ibid.* at 112.
92 *Ibid.*
93 *Ibid.* at 113.
94 *Eldridge, supra* note 7.

Chapter 7 ■
Students with Disabilities

Students with disabilities present schools with a broad range of differences. A student with a learning disability such as dyslexia may require educational adjustments that differ markedly from the requirements of a student with a physical disability. The differences force educators to think about how best to provide an education for each student. At one time, placing disabled students in segregated schools was a popular option. Today, with the inclusion of persons with disabilities in human rights legislation, more parents are advocating for the right of their children to be educated in an integrated educational setting.[1] In many cases, the parents have turned to the courts for help.

Promoting the rights of children with disabilities in education has been and continues to be hindered by the courts' willingness to defer to educators. The judicial tendency of deference to educational decision-makers is resilient and perplexing. Although educators may be experts in public education, they are not necessarily experts in the rights of students with disabilities.[2] It is for this reason that parents often appeal to the courts in the hope that the courts will consider these educational matters within a human rights context. It is not unusual, however, for the courts to turn back to educational decision-makers for their opinions, which may be clouded by previous "best practices," by cost implications, or by a lack of understanding of the changes brought about by human rights legislation and in particular by the *Charter*.[3] There is also the confounding trend of appeal courts overturning successful challenges to administrative decisions to place children in segregated settings.

---

1   Persons with physical disabilities were included in human rights legislation in the 1970s. Quebec's legislation provided protection for physically and mentally handicapped persons, but it was not until the 1980s that persons with mental disabilities were included in human rights legislation in other provinces. The *Charter* provides protection for persons with both physical and mental disabilities.

2   Frank Peters & Craig Montgomerie, "Educators' Knowledge of Rights" (1998) 23 Canadian Journal of Education 29.

3   *Ibid*. See also, Frank Peters & Craig Montgomerie, "Educators' Attitudes Towards Rights." Paper presented at The Canadian Association for the Practical Study of Law in Education (CAPSLE), Saskatoon, May 1994.

Application to Education

There have been a number of cases brought forward under provincial human rights legislation. The results have been, to say the least, varied, and in many cases disheartening, especially on appeal. One example is a case taken under the Ontario human rights legislation. The case of *Hickling v. Lanark, Leeds and Grenville Roman Catholic Separate School Board* was heard by a human rights board of inquiry.[4] It involved the right of three sisters with mental disabilities to attend their neighbourhood school in a full-time, integrated setting. The board found in favour of the parents and agreed that the children were being discriminated against because of their disabilities. The case was appealed and the Ontario High Court of Justice overturned the board's decision.[5]

Such was also the case for Danny Rouettes.[6] Again, a human rights tribunal had ruled in favour of Danny's parents, who had requested that he be placed in his "neighbourhood comprehensive school, secondary 1 level, general education with support measures and adapted program."[7] The Quebec Court of Appeal overturned the tribunal's decision and ruled that the request could not go forward because school officials believed a segregated setting was more appropriate for Danny.[8]

In the case of Nathalie Robichaud, an injunction had been granted requiring the school board to place Nathalie in a regular class. On appeal the New Brunswick Court of Appeal overturned the injunction and ruled that decisions concerning the appropriate placement of children were matters for school officials to decide. In this case the school officials decided that Nathalie was to be kept in a segregated setting.[9] The tables were temporarily turned in the case of Emily Eaton, but not for long.

The Emily Eaton Case

In 1995 the Ontario Court of Appeal overturned a lower court decision that had ruled against the wishes of Emily Eaton's parents, who wanted their child

4 *Hickling v. Lanark, Leeds and Grenville Roman Catholic Separate School Board* (1986), 7 C.H.R.R. D/3546 (Ont. Bd. of Inquiry).

5 *Re Lanark Roman Catholic Separate Board and Ontario Human Rights Commission et al.* (1987), 60 O.R. (2d) 441, aff'd (1989), 67 O.R. (2d) 479 (C.A.).

6 *Quebec (Commission des droits de la personne) v. Chauveau (Commission scolaire)* (1994), 64 Q.A.C. 31, referred to in A. Wayne MacKay & Vincent C Kazmierski, "And on the Eighth Day, God Gave Us . . . Equality in Education: *Eaton v. Brant (County) Board of Education* and Inclusive Education" (1996) 7 N.J.C.L. 1 at 25.

7 MacKay & Kazmierski, *ibid.*

8 *Ibid.* at 27.

9 *Robichaud v. Nouveau-Brunswick (Commission Scolaire No. 39)* (1989), 99 N.B.R. (2d) 341 (C.A.).

integrated into a regular classroom. The parents of Emily, a ten-year-old girl with cerebral palsy, asserted that she was entitled to an education in a regular classroom, in her local school. Emily did not speak and had no established alternative communication system. She had some visual impairment. Emily could walk short distances with the aid of a walker but she usually used a wheelchair.[10]

When Emily began kindergarten she attended her local public school with a full-time assistant. At the end of grade 1, the Identification, Placement, and Review Committee granted the school board's request to have Emily placed in a special class. Emily's parents objected and unsuccessfully appealed the decision through the education ministry to the Ontario Special Education Tribunal and then to the Divisional Court. Their case was subsequently heard by the Ontario Court of Appeal. The Appeal Court ruled in their favour, but the decision was overturned by the Supreme Court of Canada.[11]

Emily's parents submitted that there ought to be a presumption in favour of including disabled children into regular classes, and that those who proposed a segregated classroom had the burden of proving its worth. They based their argument on section 15 of the *Charter*, which prohibits discrimination on the basis of disability. Emily's parents, on her behalf, challenged the school authorities' contention that Emily's interests were best served by placing her in a special education class. The parents argued that placing Emily in a segregated class against their wishes constituted discrimination under section 15(1) of the *Charter*.[12]

Justice Louise Arbour, speaking for the Court of Appeal, agreed and in so doing overturned a lower court decision that had ruled in favour of the school board by upholding the ruling of the Ontario Special Education Tribunal.[13] The Court of Appeal ruled that Emily's right to equality meant that she had the right to stay in a regular classroom with the necessary support required "so that her education experience can be as close as possible to that of her peers."[14] The norm, the Court of Appeal said, is integration. It is important to note, however, that the court did not rule out segregated settings altogether. It recognized that

---

10 *Eaton v. (Brant County) Board of Education* (1995), 22 O.R. (3d) 1 (C.A.).

11 *Eaton v. Brant County Board of Education*, [1997] 1 S.C.R. 241. The Supreme Court issued an oral judgement on the day of the hearing, saying that the case would be overturned. The swiftness of the decision caught many off-guard. The initial concern was that some of the grounds for overturning the decision were technical because the Attorney General had not been provided with notice that the government's legislation was being challenged. Nevertheless, in its written decision, the Supreme Court disagreed with the Court of Appeal's analysis on the merits of the case.

12 *Supra* note 10.

13 *Ibid.* The Ontario Special Education Tribunal had been asked by Emily Eaton's parents to set aside the placement decision of the Identification, Placement and Review Committee placing Emily Eaton in a special education class.

14 *Ibid.* at 13.

segregated settings might be the choice of some parents. The court said:

> [U]nless the parents of a child who has been identified as exceptional by reason of a physical or mental disability consent to the placement of that child in a segregated environment, the school board must provide a placement that is the least exclusionary from the mainstream and still reasonably capable of meeting the child's special needs.[15]

The Court of Appeal commented on the pedagogical debate about whether integration or segregation works best for students. The theories cannot be considered as two conflicting theories, the court said, when one theory, segregation, produces discrimination and the other does not.[16] The discrimination occurs when one group is burdened or disadvantaged by a decision. In Emily's case, the court ruled that to place Emily in a segregated setting would burden her by depriving her of the "opportunities to learn how other children work and how they live. And they will not learn that she can live with them, and they with her."[17] The court concluded that "[t]he decision to educate Emily Eaton in a special classroom for disabled students is a burden or disadvantage for her and therefore discriminatory within the meaning of s. 15 of the Charter."[18]

The Court of Appeal also took issue with the fact that the tribunal had not examined other less restricting alternatives for Emily such as

> providing Emily with a modified integrated setting, such as assigning her to a regular class but with a different teacher, more experienced in integrating disabled students, or withdrawing her periodically from the classroom for individual instruction.[19]

The Court of Appeal's decision was significant in that it used as its framework an equality rights perspective, and it followed closely the analysis established in *Andrews*.[20] The historical pattern of discrimination against persons with disabilities and their struggle for inclusion in society were indications that segregation was a burden or disadvantage and therefore discriminatory.[21]

The case was appealed and the Court of Appeal's decision was subsequently

---

15 *Ibid.* at 21.

16 *Ibid.* at 12.

17 *Ibid.* at 15. Justice Arbour was discussing "belonging," the interest protected by s. 15. For a discussion of belonging or the "full membership approach" to s. 15, see Donna Greschner, "The Right to Belong: The Promise of *Vriend*" (1998) 9 N.J.C.L. 417.

18 *Ibid.* at 15–16.

19 *Ibid.* at 22.

20 *Andrews v. Law Society of British Columbia,* [1989] 1 S.C.R. 143.

21 *Eaton, supra* note 10 at 16.

overturned by a unanimous Supreme Court.[22] The Supreme Court's decision in *Eaton* is puzzling in light of previous section 15 decisions[23] and in light of its succeeding decision in *Eldridge v. British Columbia (Attorney General).*[24] In *Eldridge*, the court, using an equality rights framework similar to that of Justice Arbour, unanimously affirmed the rights of hearing-impaired persons to "equal benefit" of the law. For this reason, the impact of the Supreme Court's decision in *Eaton* may be short-lived. Before proceeding with an examination of the implications for persons with disabilities arising from *Eaton* and *Eldridge,* the facts of *Eldridge* and the reasoning behind the decision need to be looked at.

Eldridge and *Eaton* Compared

The *Eldridge* case considered the right of Deaf people to sign-language interpreters.[25] The appellants contended that the absence of interpreters impaired their ability to communicate effectively with their doctors and other health-care providers, and that the failure to provide sign-language interpreters as an insured benefit under the medical services plan infringed their equality rights under section 15(1) of the *Charter*. The question for the court was whether the appellants had been afforded "equal benefit of the law without discrimination" in the provision of public health services.

The issue was one of adverse impact discrimination. The Medicare system did not single out Deaf persons and make an explicit distinction based on disability for different treatment.[26] However, the court noted that "[e]ffective communication is quite obviously an integral part of the provision of medical services."[27] And because sign-language interpreters were not made available, the court asked:

> [H]ow can it be said that they receive the same level of medical care as hearing persons? Those who hear do not receive communication as a distinct service. For

---

22 *Supra* note 11.

23 Most notably *Andrews, supra* note 20; *R. v. Turpin,* [1989] 1 S.C.R. 1296; *Miron v. Trudel,* [1995] 2 S.C.R. 624; *Egan v. Canada,* [1995] 2 S.C.R. 513.

24 *Eldridge v. British Columbia (Attorney General),* [1997] 3. S.C.R. 624.

25 The case was brought forward by three complainants who were born deaf. Robin Eldridge was required to visit a general physician and a specialist a number of times a year and found visiting her doctor, without an interpreter, to be very stressful and confusing. John and Linda Warren also saw their doctor frequently. They had planned to hire an interpreter for the birth of their twins, but the girls were born prematurely and an interpreter was not available on short notice. "During the birth, the nurse communicated to her through gestures that the heart rate of one of the babies had gone down. After the babies were born, they were immediately taken from her. Other than writing a note stating that they were fine, no one explained their condition to the mother" (*ibid.* at 638).

26 *Ibid.* at 670.

27 *Ibid.* at 676.

them an effective means of communication is routinely available, free of charge, as part of every health care service. In order to receive the same quality of care, deaf persons must bear the burden of paying for the means to communicate with their health care providers, despite the fact that the system is intended to make ability to pay irrelevant.[28]

Sign language is essential in ensuring that the Deaf receive the same quality of care as the hearing population, and the absence of sign language is a systemic barrier to a state benefit. The court said:

[O]nce the state does provide a benefit, it is obliged to do so in a non-discriminatory manner. . . . In many circumstances, this will require governments to take positive action, for example by extending the scope of a benefit to a previously excluded class or person.[29]

The court referred to human rights cases that had developed the principle that discrimination can arise from a failure to take positive steps to ensure that disadvantaged groups are provided equal benefit from services offered to the public.[30] The justices repeated the position that governments are "required to take special measures to ensure that disadvantaged groups are able to benefit from government services."[31] The court ruled that

the failure of the Medical Services Commission and hospitals to provide sign language interpretation where it is necessary for effective communication constitutes a prima facie violation of the s. 15(1) rights of deaf persons. This failure denies them the equal benefit of the law and discriminates against them in comparison with hearing persons.[32]

If there are reasons that cause a government to limit its responsibility to ameliorate disadvantages in the provision of benefits and services, those reasons are to be considered under section 1 of the *Charter*.[33] The court noted that it is well established that the duty to take positive steps to ensure that disadvantaged

---

28 *Ibid.* at 677.

29 *Ibid.* at 678.

30 *Michael Huck v. Odeon Theatre Limited,* [1985] 6 C.H.R.R. D/2682 (C.A.). The court found that even though the theatre was accessible to persons who used wheelchairs, in many respects it did not provide a disabled person a choice of place from which to view the movie. This restriction was deemed discriminatory; *Howard v. University of British Columbia* (1993), 18 C.H.R.R. D/353. The university was obliged to provide a Deaf student with a sign-language interpreter for his classes.

31 *Eldridge, supra* note 24 at 680–81.

32 *Ibid.* at 682.

33 *Ibid.* at 680–81.

groups benefit equally from services offered to the public is subject to the principle of reasonable accommodation. In the context of the *Charter*, this is the same as "reasonable limits" under section 1. The court stated clearly that reasonable accommodation was not to be considered under section 15, saying: "It should not be employed to restrict the ambit of s. 15(1)."[34]

It is important to consider *Eldridge* within any discussion of *Eaton* because the Supreme Court dealt with *Eaton* in a substantially different way from other equality rights cases.[35] Any concerns that the Supreme Court was having second thoughts regarding its treatment of equality rights cases as a result of *Eaton* were put to rest after *Eldridge*.

The Rights of Persons with Disabilities

It is no small matter when the Supreme Court of Canada unanimously decides a case. Normally it would be seen as a final, irrevocable decision. But less than a year after issuing its directive concerning the right of Emily Eaton to attend school in an integrated setting, the court considered the *Eldridge* case. As noted earlier, the *Eldridge* decision is compatible with the *Andrews* decision and with other equality rights cases heard by the Supreme Court. As a result, it raises serious questions about the import of *Eaton*.

A number of major issues were clarified in *Eldridge*. First, the Supreme Court affirmed that the *Charter* applies to provincial legislation and covers the actions of delegated decision-makers.[36] Second, the court affirmed that if the effect of legislation is that it denies someone equal protection or equal benefit of the law, even if it was never intended to be thus, the legislation is discriminatory.[37] Third, the court affirmed that section 15 does not distinguish between laws that impose unequal benefits or unequal burdens on disadvantaged groups compared with the mainstream population.[38] Fourth, the court affirmed that discrimination can

---

34 *Ibid.* at 682.

35 See *supra* note 23.

36 *Supra* note 24 at 666.

37 *Ibid.* at 670. The Supreme Court affirmed its earlier ruling in *Andrews* on this issue, as well as its decision in *Rodriguez v. British Columbia (Attorney General)*, [1993] 3 S.C.R. 519 (the court found that the criminalizing of assisted suicide discriminated against disabled persons under s. 15 of the *Charter* but was saved by s. 1); *Central Okanagan School District No. 23 v. Renaud*, [1992] 2 S.C.R. 970 (the court ruled that work schedules are to be adjusted to accommodate religious observances up to the point of undue hardship for the employer and union). In addition, the court made note of human rights cases in which it had also confirmed this principle, see *Ontario Human Rights Commission v. Simpson-Sears Ltd.*, [1985] 2 S.C.R. 536 (the court ruled that a requirement that employees be available for work on Friday evenings and Saturdays discriminated against those observing a Saturday Sabbath).

38 *Eldridge, supra* note 24 at 680. The court referred again to an earlier human rights case in which the same principle had been affirmed. In *Brooks v. Canada Safeway*

accrue from the failure of governments to take positive steps to ensure that disadvantaged groups benefit equally from services offered to the general public.[39] And finally, the Supreme Court confirmed that limiting rights through "reasonable accommodation" or "reasonable limits" is to be considered under a section 1 analysis and not under section 15.[40] With these principles in mind, a closer look at the Supreme Court's decision in *Eaton* may be helpful.

In the *Eaton* case, the Supreme Court and the Court of Appeal diverged significantly in some areas and appeared to agree on others. One significant difference is the analysis undertaken by each court. The Court of Appeal considered Emily's case as a case of equality rights. It considered the decision to place Emily in a segregated classroom in its historical, social, and political context, a context replete with the struggles of persons with disabilities and their attempts to gain acceptance and belonging in the mainstream. Within the equality rights framework, integration was the norm and segregation was suspect. The segregation of children with disabilities into special classes could only be justified under a section 1 analysis.

The Supreme Court rejected the equality framework, employing instead the criterion of the "best interests of the child." This framework is a troubling one because it can so readily be adapted to suit the needs of administrators, educators, and even parents. In taking this approach, the Supreme Court restored judicial deference towards educational decision-makers. Those who believe that educators know what is in the "best interests of the child" run the risk of sacrificing the child's equality rights.[41]

The Supreme Court set out some basic principles that it determined should be used to test the validity of the decision to place Emily in a segregated setting. The principles are, first, that not every distinction on a prohibited ground constitutes discrimination;[42] second, that reasonable accommodation is required to overcome "headwinds" so that persons with disabilities are not banished;[43]

Ltd., [1989] 1 S.C.R. 1219, the court had found that the employer's accident and sickness insurance plan discriminated on the basis of pregnancy and sex because it did not entitle pregnant women to receive benefits for any reason during a certain period.

39 *Eldridge, supra* note 24 at 681. In support of the need to take positive steps to ensure that disadvantaged groups benefit equally from services offered to the public, the court made reference to the case of *Huck, supra* note 30.

40 *Eldridge, supra* note 24 at 682.

41 *Eaton, supra* note 11. Justice Sopinka, speaking for the court, did not abandon an equality rights analysis altogether, in fact he affirmed many important principles. The problem with the decision was that it lacked any consistency with other equality rights cases because the analysis focused on the "best interest of the child" outside an equality rights and subsequent s. 1 analysis.

42 *Ibid.* at 272.

43 *Ibid.* Justice Sopinka refers to the "headwinds" as characteristics "of this group" rather than the effect of a socially constructed environment based on the attainments of the majority and thus the more powerful.

third, that the "difference dilemma" can mean segregation is either a burden or a benefit;[44] and finally, that the presumption that integration is the norm can work to the disadvantage of students who require special education in order to achieve.[45] These principles are problematic, particularly the latter three. As noted in *Eldridge*, it is well established that "reasonable accommodation" is to be considered under section 1 as part of the test used to justify limiting equality rights. Yet in *Eaton*, the Supreme Court considered "reasonable accommodation" under section 15. This made it easier to restrict the equality right and to justify segregation as a benefit because other less restrictive alternatives had not been considered.[46]

If the court had begun the process by affirming clearly that integration was the norm, the usual process would have unfolded: integration is the norm, positive steps are to be taken to ensure that Emily Eaton is provided with educational opportunities commensurate with her potential and her rights, and then, if integration is not appropriate, the court will consider what reasonable accommodation or alternate measures can be made to meet her needs. By removing the discussion on alternate measures from its rightful place under section 1, the court was drawn into a dichotomous ruling. Without a doubt the evidence presented regarding Emily's isolation in her classroom and her increased crying was compelling,[47] but if the evidence had been considered under section 1, the school authorities would have been obliged to show that alternative means had been tried. Accommodation, in the *Eaton* case, meant segregation, a restricting of the promise of equality under section 15. In *Eldridge*, accommodation meant ensuring that positive steps were taken to ameliorate the disadvantages and thus enhance the inclusion of historically disadvantaged groups into the wider society.

Ensuring that members of disadvantaged groups benefit equally from services offered to the general public requires meaningful intervention and positive measures to bring their equality right of access up to the same standard others enjoy. Any backing away from this affirmation of substantive equality is to be discussed within the principle of reasonable accommodation. This principle, the court said,

> is best addressed as a component of the s. 1 analysis. Reasonable accommodation, in this context, is generally equivalent to the concept of "reasonable limits." It should not be employed to restrict the ambit of s. 15(1).[48]

---

44 *Ibid.* at 274.

45 *Ibid.*

46 Justice Arbour, in her decision, raised the lack of alternative measures sought by the school board as problematic, *supra* note 10.

47 *Eaton, supra* note 11 at 256. The court agreed with the tribunal that it was not possible to meet Emily's intellectual and academic needs in the integrated setting without "isolating her in a disserving and potentially insidious way" (at 275). The court referred to this phrase three times in its decision. See also 254 & 276.

48 *Eldridge, supra* note 24 at 682.

The principle of reasonable accommodation was used in *Eaton* to limit the ambit of section 15(1). In contrast, *Eldridge* is concomitant with *Andrews* and other cases that have laid the groundwork for the interpretation of section 15. It is my submission that in the *Eaton* case accommodation—which is more akin to "positive steps" or "measures" as identified in *Eldridge*—was confused with "reasonable accommodation" or "reasonable limits." The error in *Eaton*, I submit, was in the restricting or limiting of a section 15 right in the interpretation of section 15. That should have been conducted, as affirmed in *Eldridge*, under section 1.

The confusion between positive steps and reasonable accommodation may have arisen from the fact that sometimes it is appropriate to acknowledge differences. This is especially true in cases of disability. The "difference dilemma" need not be a difficult one, however, if, as the court itself has said, the proposed solution can be viewed as either a burden or a benefit when placed in the context of the group's social, political, and legal status. As the Supreme Court noted in *Andrews*, "s. 15 is designed to protect those groups who suffer social, political and legal disadvantage in our society."[49]

In *Eaton*, the Supreme Court was reluctant to confirm a presumption in favour of integration as the Court of Appeal had done. But it is clear from a full reading of their decision that it did not reject integration as the norm. It said:

> While integration should be recognized as the norm of general application because of the benefits it generally provides, a presumption in favour of integrated schooling would work to the disadvantage of pupils who require special education in order to achieve equality.
>
> . . .
>
> Integration can be either a benefit or a burden depending on whether the individual can profit from the advantages that integration provides.[50]

The Supreme Court's comments were nothing new. In fact, they differed little from Justice Arbour's Court of Appeal decision. She, too, acknowledged that there are circumstances when integration will not work. However, the Supreme Court was concerned with the Court of Appeal's assertion that, having found integration to be a constitutional imperative, a child's parents could automatically displace the decision.[51]

---

49 *Andrews, supra* note 20 at 154; *Egan, supra* note 23; *Vriend v. Alberta*, [1998] 1 S.C.R. 493.

50 *Supra* note 10 at 274. The Supreme Court also made note of a 1971 provincial report that stated that integration was the preferred accommodation.

51 *Ibid.* at 279. The Supreme Court in *B. (R.) v. Children's Aid Society of Metropolitan Toronto*, [1995] 1 S.C.R. 315 at 368, ruled that parental rights under s. 7 of the *Charter* do not include the right to determine the type of medical treatment a child receives when it may cause the child harm.

The Supreme Court again appeared to affirm the norm of integration when Justice Sopinka outlined the steps decision-making bodies must take to determine that the appropriate accommodation for an exceptional child is in the child's best interests. First, the decision-making body must determine "whether the integrated setting can be adapted to meet the special needs of an exceptional child."[52] If this cannot be done, "that is where aspects of the integrated setting which cannot reasonably be changed interfere with meeting the child's special needs, the principle of accommodation will require a special education placement outside of this setting."[53] For children who can communicate their wishes and needs, "their own views will play an important role in the determination of best interests."[54] But for children who are limited in communicating their wishes the decision-makers must make a decision based on the evidence before them.[55] These comments seem to confirm the principle that integration is the norm, despite the justice's earlier protestations to the contrary.[56] In this respect, the Supreme Court's decision came to the same conclusion as the Court of Appeal—integration of children with disabilities is the norm.[57]

Conclusion

The principles to be drawn from the *Eldridge* decision have some exciting and promising spin-offs for other disadvantaged students. It is to be hoped that the recent discussion in *Eldridge* will bring a halt to the ambivalence surrounding the need to protect the rights of students with disabilities. The Supreme Court's decision in *Eldridge* affirmed that integration is the norm and that with integration comes an obligation to provide positive measures so that equality can be realized. Positive measures may include such things as teacher aides, specialized equipment, supplementary curricula, or adjustments to teaching methods. The point is that alternatives must be tried. If, however, educators believe that integration cannot be achieved, the onus is on them to explain why it cannot be accomplished. At this stage, it is appropriate to consider "reasonable accommodation" or limiting absolute integration in accordance with the criteria established by the courts under section 1. The requirement placed on educators is to consider the equality rights of each student and to evaluate each student's situation within the framework of respecting the student's potential and quest for equality and dignity.

---

52   *Eaton, ibid.* at 278.

53   *Ibid.*

54   *Ibid.*

55   *Ibid.*

56   *Ibid.* at 276 & 278.

57   Saskatchewan has continued to maintain that integration is the norm, despite the Supreme Court's ruling in *Eaton*. See *Saskatchewan Education Indicators: Kindergarten to Grade 12, Update 1996* (Regina: Saskatchewan Education, 1996) at 12.

Chapter 8 ■
Sexual Harassment[1]

According to a United Nations declaration, violence against women means

> any act of gender-based violence that results in, or is likely to result in, physical, sexual or psychological harm or suffering to women, including threats of such acts, coercion or arbitrary deprivation of liberty whether occurring in public or private life.[2]

Seventeen, a popular magazine for girls, featured an article on sexual harassment in schools in the September 1992 edition. Sexual harassment was described as behaviour that makes girls "feel ugly, exposed, humiliated and really bad."[3] It includes

> rude comments about your period, your thighs, your underarms, your intelligence, the way you walk, the way you smell. . . . It can be when a group of people rate guys or girls when they walk by or rate their features in study hall. Or pushing or shoving or cornering you or pinching you.[4]

The article concluded with thirteen questions that asked readers to describe what was going on in their schools.[5] The response was overwhelming. More than four thousand girls responded to the survey, including over three hundred from Canada.[6] In 1990, the Canadian Teacher's Federation asked girls and young women about their concerns, realities, and perceptions.[7] And another Canadian

---

1   This chapter is based on an article that appeared in The Canadian Administrator (May 1995) 34:8.
2   United Nations, *Declaration on the Elimination of Violence Against Women,* U.N. Doc. A/48/49 (1993).
3   "Harassment in the Halls" *Seventeen* (September 1992) 163 at 164. The article described sexual harassment and then contained a questionnaire for reader responses.
4   *Ibid.*
5   *Ibid.* The findings were compiled and analyzed by Nan Stein *et al., infra* note 11.
6   Nan Stein, personal communication, 20 November 1993. The Canadian responses were not included in the findings reported in her study.
7   *A Cappella: A Report on the Realities, Concerns, Expectations and Barriers Experienced by Adolescent Women in Canada* (Ottawa: Canadian Teacher's Federation, 1990).

study investigated adolescent perceptions of self, including self-esteem, self-image, health, and sexual abuse.[8]

These studies illustrate that the lives of girls in school and elsewhere are overshadowed by fear and resentment engendered by the sexual violence perpetrated against females by males. And who can blame them? And who dares to convince them that it isn't that bad? Consider the following statistics. One-half of all Canadian women have experienced at least one incidence of violence (considered an offence under the Canadian *Criminal Code*) since the age of sixteen,[9] and 54 percent of women have experienced some form of unwanted or intrusive sexual experience before reaching the age of sixteen.[10] Similar sex-based violence is prevalent in schools and so is the fear. One thirteen-year-old said: "I was always scared to go to school, or at least the one class it happened in, but it still happened in the halls. I got scarder and scarder everyday."[11]

Legislation

All provincial, territorial, and federal governments have human rights legislation that prohibits sex discrimination in employment and in places customarily open to the public. Some human rights legislation, including *The Saskatchewan Human Rights Code,* speaks specifically to the educational opportunities of children, declaring that students are entitled to enjoy an education without interference from sex discrimination.[12] Other jurisdictions have ruled that educational institutions are places customarily open to the public and thus students in school

---

8   Janelle Holmes & Elaine Leslau Silverman, *We're Here, Listen to Us! A Survey of Young Women in Canada* (Ottawa: Canadian Advisory Council on the Status of Women, 1992).

9   The Daily Statistics Canada: The Violence Against Women Survey (18 November 1993).

10 The Canadian Panel on Violence Against Women, Pat Freeman Marshall & Marthe Asselin Vaillancourt, co-chairs, *Changing the Landscape: Ending Violence—Achieving Equality, Final Report* (Ottawa: Minister of Supply and Services, 1993).

11 Nan Stein, Nancy L. Marshall, & Linda R. Tropp, *Secrets in Public: Sexual Harassment in Our Schools* (Boston, Massachusetts: Center for Research on Women, Wellesley College and NOW Legal Defense and Education Fund, 1993) at 3–4.

12 *The Saskatchewan Human Rights Code,* S.S. 1979, c. S-24, prohibits discrimination in education on the basis of sex. S. 13 states, "(1) Every person and every class of persons shall enjoy the right to education in any school, college, university or other institution or place of learning, vocational training or apprenticeship without discrimination because of his or their race, creed, religion, colour, sex, marital status, disability, nationality, ancestry or place of origin. (2) Nothing in subsection (1) prevents a school, college, university or other institution or place of learning from following a restrictive policy with respect to enrolment on the basis of sex, creed, religion or disability, where it enrols persons of a particular sex, creed or religion exclusively, or is conducted by a religious order or society, or where it enrols persons who are disabled."

are protected from sex discrimination and sexual harassment.[13] It appears clear that sexual harassment in schools contravenes human rights legislation, including the *Charter* and the international *Convention on the Rights of the Child.*

Section 15 of the *Charter* is of particular importance in dealing with the issue of sexual harassment in schools. Education is offered to the public through various statutes. In Saskatchewan, for example, *The Saskatchewan Education Act* compels all children between the ages of six and fifteen to attend school[14] and states that all students between the ages of six and twenty-one have a right to attend school.[15] Thus no student can be denied equal benefit of a law, which in this case provides a public education, because of his or her sex. In other words, a female student's legal right to educational benefits cannot continue to be burdened by her sex, which historically has made her vulnerable to sexual harassment.[16]

The eradication of inequality in education is one of the goals of the recently adopted international *Convention on the Rights of the Child.* Article 29(d) states that the education of the child shall be directed to:

[t]he preparation of the child for responsible life in a free society, in the spirit of understanding, peace, tolerance, equality of sexes, and friendship among all peoples, ethnic, national and religious groups and persons of indigenous origin.[17]

A learning environment poisoned by sexual harassment ill prepares a child for a responsible life imbued with an understanding of equality of the sexes and of friendship among all people.

Human rights legislation, the *Charter,* and the *Convention on the Rights of the Child* provide adequate standards of legal protection from sexual harassment in schools. The duty and obligation of emulating the law's vision and ensuring the protection of students lies with educational decision-makers.

Interpretation

Much of our understanding of sexual harassment has come from employment situations. However, the principles learned in the workplace can be applied to

---

13   See, for example, *Attis v. New Brunswick School Division No. 15* (1992), 15 C.H.R.R.D/339 at D/350-D/351 (para. 65). The board of inquiry made reference to an earlier New Brunswick Court of Appeal decision. This decision had concluded that public education falls within the purview of the provincial *Human Rights Act.* The court had said that to rule otherwise would "frustrate the legislative intent of the *Human Rights Act,*" which is to be given a "fair, large and liberal interpretation."

14   *The Saskatchewan Education Act,* R.S.S. 1978, c. S-175, s. 155.

15   *Ibid.,* s. 144.

16   See M.A. Hickling, "Employer's Liability for Sexual Harassment" (1988) 17 Man. L. J. 124 at 127.

17   *Convention on the Rights of the Child,* U.N. Doc. A/RES/44/25 (1989), art. 29(d).

education. After all, there is a strong parallel between employment opportunities and educational opportunities.

In a 1992 decision issued pursuant to a complaint by one student of sexual harassment by another,[18] the chair of the hearing, Marvin A. Zucker, relied heavily upon employment cases. Zucker quoted, with approval, the Supreme Court's directive that human rights laws must be given a broad interpretation. Zucker made reference to former Chief Justice Dickson, who had said that the interpretation of human rights legislation must be given full meaning, recognition, and effect, and who had warned that "[w]e should not search for ways and means to minimize these rights and to enfeeble their proper impact."[19] Thus, in order to maximize the rights of students, it is appropriate to draw upon case law as it pertains to employment.

Educational institutions have, according to Zucker, "long been confronted with the problem of sexual harassment."[20] Zucker said:

> The academic environment existing at an educational institution is extremely important in determining the benefit that a student receives from attending that institution. A sexually abusive environment inhibits, if not prevents, a harassed student from developing her full intellectual potential and receiving the most from the academic program.[21]

As noted earlier, Zucker referred to a number of important employment cases and for that reason it seems prudent to review some of the courts' comments in these cases.

Scope of Behaviour Considered Sexual Harassment

One of the first Canadian cases to rule that sexual harassment was sex discrimination provided the following definition:

> The forms of prohibited conduct that, in my view, are discriminatory run the gamut from overt gender based activity, such as coerced intercourse to unsolicited physical contact to persistent propositions to more subtle conduct such as gender based insults and taunting, which may reasonably be perceived to create a negative psychological and emotional work environment.[22]

---

18 *A. v. E.* (1992) Education and Law Journal 310.
19 *Action Travail des Femmes v. Canadian National Railways,* [1987] 1 S.C.R. 1114 at 1134.
20 *A. v. E., supra* note 18 at 326. In a break with tradition, the editors of the journal decided to print the entire decision of *A. v. E.* "given both the currency and prominence of sexual harassment issues at universities and other educational institutions."
21 *Ibid.*
22 *Bell v. Ladas* (1980), 1 C.H.R.R. D/155 (Ontario Board of Inquiry), quoted with approval in *A. v. E.*

This 1980 definition included a wide range of situations and behaviours, ranging from a negative work environment to sexual assault. Even so, some lower Canadian courts and American courts have made a distinction between what is commonly termed *quid pro quo* harassment and sexual harassment that results in a hostile environment. *Quid pro quo* harassment is harassment that carries with it tangible consequences such as lost employment opportunities. The hostile environment is harassment that requires employees to endure sexual posturing at work. However, the Canadian Supreme Court has ruled that this distinction is not necessary:

> The main point in allegations of sexual harassment is that unwelcome sexual conduct has invaded the workplace, irrespective of whether the consequences of the harassment included a denial of concrete employment rewards for refusing to participate in sexual activity.[23]

Therefore, it does not matter if, in spite of the harassing environment, girls and young women show no signs of educational impediment. The fact that they must endure an intimidating and hostile learning environment is sufficient to constitute sexual harassment.

Sexual Harassment: An Abuse of Power

In 1993, the Supreme Court of Canada noted that sexual harassment is

> an expression of power or desire or both. Whether it is from supervisors, co-workers, or customers, sexual harassment is an attempt to assert power over another person.
> . . .
>   [It] is any sexually-oriented practice that endangers an individual's continued employment, negatively affects his/her work performance, or undermines his/her sense of personal dignity. Harassment behavior may manifest itself blatantly in forms such as leering, grabbing, and even sexual assault. More subtle forms of sexual harassment may include sexual innuendoes, and propositions for dates or sexual favours.[24]

The Supreme Court of Canada has described sexual harassment as "the concept of using a position of power to import sexual requirements into the workplace thereby negatively altering the working conditions of employees who are forced

---

23 *Janzen v. Platy Enterprises Ltd.* (1989), 10 C.H.R.R. D/6205 (S.C.C.) at D/6227. The court stated that the distinction might have been necessary at a time when sexual harassment was not viewed as actionable.

24 *Ibid.* at D/6225, quoting from Arjun P. Aggarwal, *Sexual Harassment in the Workplace*. See also Kathleen Gallivan, "Sexual Harassment After *Janzen v. Platy*: The Transformative Possibilities" (1993) 48 U.T. Fac. L. Rev. 27.

to contend with sexual demands."[25] It has stated further that sexual harassment

> has been widely accepted by other adjudicators and academic commentators, [as] an abuse of power. When sexual harassment occurs in the workplace, it is an abuse of both economic and sexual power. Sexual harassment is a demeaning practice, one that constitutes a profound affront to the dignity of the employees forced to endure it.[26]

Fellow students are the educational equivalent of co-workers and although they may not have economic power to assert over their classmates, they do have sexual power.[27] Often those who are forced to endure this sexual power are those who have no power of their own:

> Perpetrators of sexual harassment and victims of the conduct may be either male or female. However, in the present sex-stratified labour market, those with the power to harass sexually will predominantly be male and those facing the greatest risk of harassment will tend to be female.[28]

The sex-stratified labour market is a reflection of our sex-stratified society which is mirrored again in a sex-stratified school environment.[29]

The Reasonable Woman

Perhaps one of the most interesting adjustments to legal reasoning has been the development of the "reasonable woman" standard. This standard has been used to determine when the work or study environment is poisoned by sexual harassment. In the 1991 American case of *Ellison v. Brady,* the defendant argued that a woman who had charged him with sexual harassment was "idiosyncratic"

---

25 *Janzen, ibid.* at D/6225.
26 *Ibid.* at D/6227.
27 See Rix Rogers, chair, *Reaching for Solutions: The Summary Report of the Special Advisor to the Minister of National Health and Welfare on Child Sexual Abuse in Canada* (Ottawa: Minister of Supply and Services, June 1990).
28 *Janzen, supra* note 23 at D/6227.
29 Research has repeatedly shown that school is more user friendly for boys than for girls, see chapter 6. Schools are organized hierarchically, an organizational design found to be more comfortable for men. In addition, educational decision-makers, the ones with the power to ensure schools maintain an environment in which learning can take place, are men. See Kathy E. Ferguson, *The Feminist Case Against Bureaucracy* (Philadelphia: Temple Press, 1984); Ailsa M. Watkinson, "A Feminist Paradigm: Leaders in Opposition or 'Darling You're Imagining Things,'" in Katherine Therrin & Nick Kach, eds., *Educus Wrecks: Proceedings of the 1991 Tri-University Educational Foundations Conference* (Edmonton: University of Alberta, 1992) at 83.

or "hyper-sensitive" in her objection to his behaviour.[30] The court disagreed, saying:

> [W]e believe that in evaluating the severity and pervasiveness of sexual harassment, we should focus on the perspective of the victim. . . . A complete understanding of the victim's view requires, among other things, an analysis of the different perspectives of men and women. Conduct that many men consider unobjectionable may offend many women.[31]

The court dismissed both the reasonable man's perspective as well as that of the reasonable person. Instead, it adopted "the perspective of a reasonable woman primarily because we believe that a sex-blind reasonable person standard tends to be male-biased and tends to systematically ignore the experiences of women."[32] The standard was elaborated upon further in a later decision in which the court pointed out that in order to determine the severity and pervasiveness of a given behaviour, one cannot "carve the work environment into a series of discrete incidents and measure the harm."[33] The court reasoned :

> [A] holistic perspective is necessary, keeping in mind that each successive episode has its predecessors, that the impact of the separate incidents may accumulate, and that the work environment created thereby may exceed the sum of the individual episodes.[34]

Zucker has also made reference to the "reasonable woman" standard. He stated that "[a] reasonableness standard does not mean perpetuation of the status quo by validating group norms at the expense of individual rights."[35]

The challenge for educational administrators, the vast majority of whom are men, is to acknowledge that they may not be able to perceive sexual harassment in the same way as women and thus they may be unable to empathize with the victims of sexual harassment. Incidents that may seem trivial to them must be placed within the entire educational and social milieu.

Application to Education

First of all, let me say that being sexually harassed since 5th grade has gone beyond the damage of affecting the way I feel. . . . Now, at age 15 and a sophomore in high

---

30 *Ellison v. Brady,* 924 F. 2d 872 (9th Cir. 1991).
31 *Ibid.* at 878.
32 *Ibid.* at 879.
33 *Robinson v. Jacksonville Shipyards, Inc.,* 760 F. Supp. 1486 (M.D. Fla. 1991) at 1524.
34 *Ibid.*
35 *A. v. E,. supra* note 18 at 327.

school, I have no pride, no self-confidence and still no way out of the hell I am put through in my school. . . . I have been depressingly desperate for something to make me feel like I actually am not a slutty bitchy whore. (14 year old)[36]

The results of the *Seventeen* survey are reported in a document entitled *Secrets in Public.*[37] Ninety-two percent of the girls between the ages of twelve and sixteen who responded to the survey had been sexually harassed in school.[38] Ninety-six percent had been harassed by other students and 4 percent had been harassed by teachers, administrators, or other school staff.[39] The harassers in student-to-student cases were male 97 percent of the time. All but one of the adult harassers were male.[40]

I've been sexually harassed for almost 3 years now, and it really hurts me, and it makes me feel like I'm a bad person, or that I'm no good and deserve what I get. One guy kept trying to feel me up and go down my pants in class. He'd also rub his leg up and down my leg and I hated it! He'd also asked me to have sex with him. . . . I really felt low and he called me a slut and a bitch when I said "NO". It shouldn't be happening to anyone, it breaks your soul and brings you down mentally and physically. (14 year old)[41]

The most common types of sexual harassment experienced by 89 percent of the young women were sexual comments, jokes, and suggestive looks and gestures; 83 percent reported being touched, pinched, or grabbed.[42] Respondents reported that the sexual harassment is sometimes curtailed by school authorities, but more often than not teachers tolerate it and consider it flirting or a normal part of adolescence.[43]

Sexual harassment often happens behind closed doors, but in schools it is a public event. The harassment these students spoke of happened in the presence of others 92 percent of the time, and almost all of the harassment that went on in the classroom was observed by others.[44] A fifteen year old related being trapped under a table in Industrial Arts while four guys "would grab my breasts and touch my butt. They thought it was all fun and games. It wasn't."[45] Thirty-nine percent of the girls and young women reported being harassed on a daily basis

---

36 Stein *et al.*, *supra* note 11 at 7.
37 *Ibid.*
38 Stein *et al., supra* note 11. The findings were reported in Adrian Nicole LeBlanc, "Harassment at School: The Truth Is Out," *Seventeen* (May 1993) 134.
39 Stein *et al., ibid.* at 6.
40 *Ibid.*
41 *Ibid.* at 3.
42 *Ibid.* at 2.
43 *Ibid.* at 1.
44 *Ibid.* at 7.
45 *Ibid.* at 5–6.

and 29 percent reported being sexually harassed on a weekly basis. Rarely did it happen only once.[46]

According to the survey, thirteen- to sixteen-year-old girls were almost one-and-a-half times as likely as nine- to twelve-year-old girls to be pressured to do something sexual.[47] Being forced to do something sexual rose in frequency among seventeen- to nineteen-year-old young women.[48]

> I was in summer school on the last day, I was wearing a silk black tank top and jeans (very baggy). Three guys cornered me and said, "You know if we raped you right now we could get away with it because your [*sic*] dressed like a slut." That alone made me feel so ashamed and embarrassed because I thought I looked nice, to have someone say you look like a slut just crushes your feelings. As if that weren't enough, when I yelled to my teacher she said, "You know you ask for it—you get what you deserve," and she wouldn't help me.[49] (17 year old)

The vast majority of girls do not receive the harassment without protesting. Sixty-five percent told the harasser to stop, over 40 percent walked away, and 35 percent resisted the harasser with physical force.[50]

The impact of this type of abuse takes its toll. Students spoke about their declining marks, their lack of self-confidence,[51] and an omnipresent fear of physical and sexual violence.[52] Not surprisingly, the young women expressed a "deep resentment toward their male peers, their apparently carefree lives and their violence."[53]

Sexual harassment is sometimes hard for girls and women to identify because it is considered a normal part of growing up or is simply attributed to raging hormones.[54] One young woman stated that a guy in one of her classes "thought

---

46 *Ibid.* at 4.

47 *Ibid.* at 5.

48 *Ibid.*

49 *Ibid.* at 9–10.

50 *Ibid.* at 8. The authors reported that the girls were more likely to do nothing or to walk away without telling the harasser to stop if the harasser was a teacher, administrator, or other staff member than if the harasser was a fellow student.

51 Lack of self-confidence is a trait found too often in young women. The Canadian study, *We're Here, Listen to Us! supra* note 8, reported that "[y]oung women are less likely (than young men) to feel they have good qualities, to feel self-confident, and to feel good about themselves" (at 25). The young women expressed feelings of powerlessness in relationships with boys. The feelings of powerlessness were tied to their feelings of low self-esteem, which in turn made "them all the more vulnerable to risks that particularly affect young women: sexual violence and unwanted pregnancy" (at 41).

52 *A Cappella, supra* note 7 at 14.

53 *Ibid.* at 21.

54 *Time* magazine noted that "hormones get blamed for just about every adolescent foible," in "Latest Teen Excuse" *Time* (8 May 1993) 12.

it was his privilege to grab my butt whenever he wanted. Like a fool, I thought it was just '*flirting*' or '*teasing*' but it made me feel dirty and violated."[55] Another girl said that at first she liked the attention: "[F]or me, being harassed made me feel like those boys were interested in me. . . . [A]s it continually went on, I really started hating them grabbing my ass."[56]

Some writers place sexual harassment on a continuum of violent sexual behaviour ranging from the "everyday normal" leering, whistling, and sexual comments to sexual assault and date rape.[57] No matter how sexual harassment is classified, if it is left unchecked it violates the rights of girls to an education, and it allows schools to become training grounds for sexual violence. Rix Rogers, special advisor to the minister of National Health and Welfare on child sexual abuse, discussed the intolerable acceptance of this type of behaviour:

> One of the most disturbing discoveries for me has to do with the impact of underlying social attitudes and values related to male and female sexuality. More than I ever realized, these tend to condition males to be sexual predators and females to be sexual victims. Our patriarchal society has set the conditions for sexual assaults and harassment, including the sexual abuse of children. I am increasingly uncomfortable with the realization that such behavior has for too long been tolerated in our society. In my opinion, one of the most significant tasks ahead of us is to make major changes in the underlying deeply rooted attitudes of sexism.[58]

One young woman stated poignantly: "I think that boys should not do what they do to us."[59] The sexual harassment perpetrated by boys on girls is a systemic barrier that impairs the girls' right to enjoy an education. So too is the sexual harassment, often fuelled by jealousy and homophobia, that girls do to girls and boys do to boys. This type of harassment is both discriminatory and illegal.[60]

Enforcement

Canadian employers are liable for the actions of their supervisors, employees,[61]

---

55 Stein *et al.*, *supra* note 11 at 7–8.
56 *Ibid.* at 7–8.
57 Elizabeth Stanko, *Intimate Intrusions* (London: Routledge and Kegan Paul, 1985), referred to in Helen Lenskyj, "Sexual Harassment: Female Athletes' Experiences and Coaches' Responsibilities" (1992) 12:6 Sports Science Periodical on Research and Technology in Sport.
58 Rix Rogers, *supra* note 27 at 9.
59 *A Cappella, supra* note 7 at viii.
60 See *Janzen, supra* note 23.
61 *Robichaud v. Canada (Treasury Board)*, [1987] 2 S.C.R. 84.

customers,[62] and students.[63] The liability can be costly both in financial terms and in terms of damage to an institution's reputation. In 1993, a Quebec human rights tribunal ordered a school board to pay $10,000 to a teacher for failing to protect him from students' racial harassment. The tribunal ruled that the employer had an obligation to respond appropriately to the racial harassment to ensure that the harassment did not recur.[64] In 1994, the Saskatchewan Indian Federated College paid a former student $3,000 after she filed a complaint with the Saskatchewan Human Rights Commission alleging that one of the instructors had sexually harassed her.[65] In 1991, the Minnesota Department of Human Rights ordered a school division to pay a student $15,000 after the school division was found to have violated the state's sexual harassment clause. Sexually explicit graffiti about the student had been written on the boys' washroom walls and left there for eighteen months.[66] In a more recent American case, a jury awarded $500,000 to a fourteen-year-old girl after they found that school authorities had ignored her complaints of sexual harassment.[67]

The issue of sexual harassment and employer liability was given careful consideration by the Canadian Supreme Court in 1987. The case of *Robichaud v. Canada (Treasury Board)* established a number of important principles.

First, human rights legislation is concerned with remedying the effects of discrimination and not with finding fault. The court reasoned that it was not necessary to prove an intention to discriminate, for to try and prove ill-will misses the remedial intent of the legislation. One objective found in human rights laws is the eradication of "anti-social conditions without regard to the motives or intention of those who cause them."[68] A Quebec human rights tribunal has ruled that simply disciplining students who harass others will not eradicate systemic

---

62 *Saskatchewan Human Rights Commission and Sandra Nixon v. Greensides* (28 May 1993) Sask. Court of Queen's Bench, discussed in "Are Employers Liable for Harassment by Customers?" (Nov. 1993) Lancaster Labour Law Reports, Charter Cases/Human Rights Reporter 4.

63 *Quebec Human Rights Commission v. Board of Education of Deux-Montagnes* (8 April 1993) Quebec Human Rights Tribunal, discussed in "School Board Ordered to Pay $10,000 to Teacher for Failure to Protect Him From Students' Racial Taunts" (May 1993) Lancaster Labour Law Reports, Charter Cases/Human Rights Reporter 2.

64 *Ibid.*

65 "Sexual Harassment Complaint Settled" *The [Saskatoon] StarPhoenix* (10 November 1994) D13.

66 Susan Strauss, *Sexual Harassment and Teens* (Minneapolis: Free Spirit, 1992) at 5; "Harassment in the Halls," *supra* note 3.

67 "Girl, 14, awarded $500,000" *The [Saskatoon] StarPhoenix* (4 October 1996) D10. "A Grade 6 boy subjected her to an almost daily barrage of vulgarities, lewd insults and threats to beat her up and even kill her." She was eleven years old at the time.

68 *Robichaud, supra* note 61 at 91.

anti-social conditions.[69] And the Supreme Court has ruled that a "poisoned" school environment requires a positive duty on the part of the school board to eliminate it.[70] It is not sufficient for school boards to remain passive, they must act with diligence in taking prompt, effective, and proportional measures to deal with problems.[71] The implication for educational administrators is that they have a duty to work at erasing the anti-social behaviour of students. It is not enough to rely on statements or even anti-harassment policies that condemn the behaviour, substantive action must be taken to expunge the behaviour from schools.

Second, the court, building on its first point, opined that the remedial objectives of human rights legislation, which include the removal of undesirable working conditions, would be stultified if the employer were not made responsible for the actions of his or her employees. The court said:

> Indeed, if the *Act* is concerned with the effects of discrimination rather than its causes (or motivations), it must be admitted that only an employer can remedy undesirable effects; only an employer can provide the most important remedy—a healthy work environment.[72]

Similarly, a 1992 Saskatchewan case relying on *Robichaud* stated that "only the employer is in a position to effectively curtail this anti-social behaviour."[73]

Thus, responsibility for a work environment poisoned by sexual harassment is placed squarely "on those who control it and are in a position to take effective remedial action to remove undesirable conditions."[74] Educational decision-makers control what happens in schools, thus the responsibility to take effective action to remove sexually harassing behaviour is on them. Indeed, administrators are compelled by education acts to maintain proper order and discipline.[75]

---

69 *Deux-Montagnes, supra* note 63 at 3. The tribunal found that disciplining students without addressing the issue of racial harassment was insufficient to meet its obligation under the Quebec Charter.

70 *Ross v. School District No. 15,* [1996] 1 S.C.R. 825 at 860. The court ruled that the continued employment of a teacher who disseminated anti-Semitic material contributed to an invidiously discriminatory or "poisoned" educational environment, contrary to New Brunswick's *Human Rights Act.*

71 *Ibid.* at 861, quoting with approval from the Human Rights Commission's board of inquiry decision.

72 *Robichaud, supra* note 61 at 94.

73 *Thessaloniki Holdings Ltd. v. Saskatchewan (Human Rights Commission)* (1992), 15 C.H.R.R. D/333 at D/334.

74 *Robichaud, supra* note 61 at 95.

75 In the case of *R. v. J.M.G.* (1986), 56 O.R. (2d) 705, the Court of Appeal in Ontario argued that administrators have a duty to maintain proper order and discipline. The court ruled in favour of the actions of an administrator who was accused by a student of having violated his right to be free from an unreasonable search and seizure. For

One of the duties of a principal, as written in the *Saskatchewan Education Act,* is to "give direction to members of his staff and to pupils as may be necessary to maintain the good order, harmony and efficiency of the school."[76] Good order, harmony, and efficiency in schools are absent in the presence of sexual harassment. The legal duties placed on administrators under education acts support the principle enunciated in *Robichaud* that employers, in this case educational administrators, are liable for the inactions of staff and students in stopping the harassment.

Third, the court ruled that an employer who responds "quickly and effectively to a complaint by instituting a scheme to remedy and prevent recurrence will not be liable to the same extent, if at all, as an employer who fails to adopt such steps."[77] However, employers cannot claim that they did nothing about harassment because no one complained to them directly. Employers are still liable for the actions or inactions of their employees if the employers knew of the harassing environment or if they ought to have known.[78]

The impact of the latter point will reverberate through those policies that deal with harassment only when a formal complaint has been made. Relying solely on the formal process of reporting a complaint places an unfair onus on the harassed to start the process in motion, when it is the responsibility of the decision-makers to develop a school climate void of such discrimination.

Conclusion

Sexual harassment in schools impedes the educational opportunities of girls and young women. The effect, as always, depends on each student, but generally harassment affects self-confidence and marks. Some students drop out of school altogether and every one of them must endure an added burden.[79]

Sexual harassment in schools between students is sex discrimination and as such is illegal under human rights legislation.[80] Educational administrators are obliged to take steps to eradicate it. If educational administrators, the majority of whom are male, do not act promptly and decisively, they face the prospect of litigation brought by the harassed students, the majority of whom are female. The sex difference between educational decision-makers and victims of sexual harassment is informative as recent case law has determined that because men

a discussion of this case, see. A. Wayne MacKay, "Students as Second Class Citizens Under the Charter" (1987) 54 C.R. (3d) 390.

76 *The Saskatchewan Education Act*, *supra* note 14.

77 *Robichaud, supra* note 61 at 96.

78 *Robichaud, ibid.; Greensides, supra* note 62; *Deux-Montagnes, supra* note 63; *Thessaloniki Holdings Ltd., supra* note 73.

79 *Supra* note 51 and accompanying text.

80 *Janzen, supra* note 23.

and women perceive sexually harassing behaviour differently, it is the victim's perspective (that is to say, the woman's perspective) that determines whether the conduct is sexual harassment.[81] Should legal action be taken against a school, the courts have ruled that the decision-makers are liable for the harm caused by sexual harassment and that they are also liable for the actions or inactions of their staff in curtailing it.[82] Employers and educational decision-makers who act quickly and effectively lessen their liability.[83]

As a means of reducing liability, some school divisions have developed policies on sexual harassment. According to the girls and young women who responded to the *Seventeen* survey, only 8 percent of their schools had a policy on sexual harassment that they enforced, even though the survey found that a school policy against sexual harassment was the most important factor in the school's response.[84]

It is advisable for school administrators to adopt a sexual harassment policy but, at the same time, they should be cautious about relying on formal procedures to the extent that these procedures impede the policy's effectiveness. The initial sexual harassment policy of one urban school division serves as an example here. The sexual harassment policy placed the responsibility on the harassee to report the sexual harassment as soon as possible. This placed the entire burden of initiating an investigation on the harassee and appeared to exonerate school staff who knew harassment was going on but were not directly affected by it and did nothing. The director of education was to inform the respondent (the alleged harasser) of the investigation and was to advise the alleged harasser to seek supportive counselling through the Employee Assistance Program. No such invitation was made to the complainant. These issues have since been corrected in a revised policy, but one statement from the earlier policy has been retained:

> Every effort will be made to ensure that everything is done that is fair and reasonable in the circumstances, to protect staff against complaints or accusations made by other staff members that are trivial, frivolous or made in bad faith. Individuals that have filed a complaint that is found to be in bad faith may be subject to disciplinary action.[85]

The tone of this statement offers cold comfort. Indeed, it could be seen by harassees as a barrier rather than as an aid to eradicating sexual harassment from

---

81   *A. v. E., supra* note 18; *Robinson, supra* note 33.
82   *Robichaud, supra* note 61.
83   *Ibid.*
84   Stein *et al., supra* note 11 at 11.
85   The Board of Education: Saskatoon School Division No. 13, Policy 7190 (June 22, 1999). The revised policy deals only with employee harassment. Pupil-to-pupil harassment is addressed through a February 1997 protocol.

schools. Such policies should leave no doubt that the norm is "zero tolerance."[86]

Researchers asked young women: "If your school were declared a harassment free zone tomorrow, how would your life be different?"[87] Here are some of their responses.

> A lot more girls would excel in their school work. . . . [W]e wouldn't limit ourselves, and we could then freely express how we feel about a subject and not have to face any oppression of any sort from our male classmates. . . . [W]omen would excel a lot more in academics simply because they wouldn't have to face the intimidation factor.

> If [girls] had the restraints taken off and they knew they were taken off then I think that it would have a very big bearing on their performance in class and in sports.

> People wouldn't be afraid about walking down certain halls at the school, walking past a certain bunch of guys that you know are going to say something or . . . that someone's going to reach out and grab your butt and everyone's just going to stand there like nothing happened.[88]

The powerful consequences of a learning environment poisoned by sexual harassment are manifested in educational inequity. Everyday school life for many girls and young women is akin to a war zone. Human rights laws and the *Charter* compel educational decision-makers to use their authority to ensure that girls and young women can learn in an environment free from sexual harassment.

---

86   The term "zero tolerance" is associated with the 1991 report on the sexual abuse of patients commissioned by the College of Physicians and Surgeons of Ontario. The report states that zero tolerance is a concept to be applied to the abuse of power— that is, that it must be recognized that there is an imbalance in the power situation between, in this case, men and women, boys and girls. *The Final Report of the Task Force on Sexual Abuse of Patients* (Toronto: College of Physicians and Surgeons of Ontario, 1991).

87   Pat Staton & June Larkin, *Sexual Harassment the Intimidation Factor* (Toronto: Green Dragon, 1993) at 20.

88   *Ibid*. at 20–21.

Chapter 9 ■
Group Punishment, Suspensions, and Expulsions

The rights proclaimed in section 7 of the *Charter* under the heading "Legal Rights" guarantee the right not to be deprived of life, liberty, and security of the person except in accordance with the principles of fundamental justice. Within these legal rights, the courts have considered whether students have a constitutional right to an education, the rights of parents to educate their children "as they see fit,"[1] and the principles of fundamental justice as they apply to educational matters.[2] One important matter yet to be decided by the courts concerns the constitutionality of suspensions and expulsions.[3]

Marvin Zucker, a judge with the Ontario Court of Justice (Provincial Division), stated that legal rights have two important elements. First, they encapsulate the capacity of one individual to demand and require another to behave in a certain way. Second, they make this capacity and requirement enforceable under the law.[4] A legal right "is a genuine entitlement or a valid claim, that one person makes of another."[5] Section 7 of the *Charter* entitles students to fairness.

Interpretation

Section 7 affects the procedures employed in disciplinary matters, and it may also be used to challenge the forms of discipline employed. Section 7 states:

7. Everyone has the right to life, liberty and security of the person and the right not

---

1   *R. v. Kind* (1984), 50 Nfld. & P.E.I. R. 332.

2   *R. v. Jones,* [1986] 2 S.C.R. 284. The Supreme Court ruled that although parents have certain rights regarding the education of their children, their rights do not include the right to educate their children "as they see fit." The public has a compelling interest in the education of children, making it necessary to ensure that their education is acceptable to the public.

3   In 1971 parents unsuccessfully challenged a board's decision to suspend their son from school. The matter was heard prior to the *Charter* coming into effect. See *Ward v. Blaine Lake School Board*, [1971] 4 W.W.R. 161 (Sask. Q.B.).

4   Marvin A. Zuker, *The Legal Context of Education* (Toronto: OISE Press, 1988) at 156.

5   *Ibid.*

to be deprived thereof except in accordance with the principles of fundamental justice.[6]

A section 7 challenge begins with "a finding that there has been a deprivation of the right to 'life, liberty and security of the person.' " It continues with "a finding that that deprivation is contrary to the principles of fundamental justice."[7] In order to understand the implications of section 7, it is necessary to consider what the terms "liberty and security of the person" include, and what the phrase "except in accordance with the principles of fundamental justice" means. For the purpose of this discussion, only the terms "liberty" and "security of the person" will be discussed since they are more germane to education than "life." There is no doubt that the term "life" will be of interest, but it is unlikely that it will affect, to any great extent, the educational setting.

Liberty

The word "liberty" potentially covers an enormous area of rights, including a right to education. Some scholars have argued that the term "liberty" refers only to physical restraint.[8] However, the Supreme Court has ruled that "liberty does not mean mere freedom from physical restraint,"[9] rather it includes "freedom from the threat of physical punishment or suffering";[10] the freedom of parents to make decisions for their children;[11] the right to make fundamental personal decisions that are rooted in the basic concepts of human dignity, personal autonomy, and privacy;[12] and the enjoyment associated with a free and democratic

---

6   *Canadian Charter of Rights and Freedoms,* Part 1 of the *Constitution Act, 1982,* being Schedule B to the *Canada Act 1982* (U.K.), 1982, c. 11.

7   *R. v. Beare,* [1988] 2 S.C.R. 387 at 401 (the respondent argued unsuccessfully that relevant sections of the *Identification of Criminal Act* and the *Criminal Code,* which provided for the fingerprinting of a person charged with, but not convicted of, an indictable offence, infringed s. 7 of the *Charter*), aff'd in *Pearlman v. Manitoba Law Society Judicial Committee,* [1991] 2 S.C.R. 869 at 881 (the Supreme Court of Canada rejected a lawyer's argument that the section of the *Law Society Act* that allows the cost of an investigation into professional misconduct to be awarded against the lawyer was a violation of s. 7 of the *Charter*).

8   P.W. Hogg, *Constitutional Law of Canada* (Toronto: Carswell, 1985) at 744.

9   *B. (R.) v. Children's Aid Society of Metropolitan Toronto,* [1995] 1 S.C.R. 315 at 368 (the Supreme Court ruled that parental rights, a liberty right, do not include the right to determine the type of medical treatment a child receives when it may cause the child harm); *Re B.C. Motor Vehicle Act,* [1985] 2 S.C.R. 486 (affirmed that liberty protects the loss of physical liberty).

10 *Singh v. Minister of Employment and Immigration,* [1985] 1 S.C.R. 177 at 207.

11 *B. (R.), supra* note 9 at 374. Not all of the judges agreed with this interpretation. Four judges argued that, in this case, parental decision-making in regard to medical treatment was not a liberty right.

12 *R. v. Morgentaler,* [1988] 1 S.C.R. 30 at 166.

society.[13] Commercial interests[14] and economic interests[15] are not protected under section 7.

Chief Justice Lamer of the Canadian Supreme Court places a limit on "liberty" as he argues that legal rights come into play only when a person interacts with the justice system.[16] Other members of the Supreme Court do not agree, and Justice Lamer's view is not the view of the majority on the court. This is important, for if Justice Lamer's view held sway, it would limit the legal rights of students to matters that involve the police and would leave them with no recourse to these rights in interactions with school authorities.

The *American Bill of Rights*, under the Fifth and Fourteenth Amendments, includes similar wording to section 7. It guarantees that there will be no deprivation "of life, liberty or property without due process of law."[17] The Canadian Supreme Court has quoted, with approval, the American Supreme Court's definition of "liberty."[18] The American court defined "liberty" as including

not merely freedom from bodily restraint but also the right of the individual to contract, to engage in any of the common occupations of life, *to acquire useful knowledge*, to marry, establish a home and bring up children, to worship God according to the dictates of his own conscience and generally to enjoy those long recognized . . . as essential to the orderly pursuit of happiness by free men.[19] [Emphasis mine]

---

13 *Jones, supra* note 2 at 590.

14 *R. v. Pinehouse Plaza Pharmacy Ltd.* (1988), 67 Sask. R. 201, appealed (1991) 89 Sask. R. 47 (S.C.A.), upheld. The respondent believed a city by-law prohibiting him from erecting signage beyond a certain size violated his rights under s. 7. The court ruled that commercial interests are not protected under "life, liberty, security of the person." For a good summary of the case, see Felix Hoehn, *Municipalities and Canadian Law* (Saskatoon: Purich, 1996) c. 10.

15 *Weyer v. R.* (1988), 83 N.R. 272 (Fed. C.A.), leave to appeal refused (1988), 88 N.R. 397 (S.C.C.). The applicant was dismissed from the federal public service and argued that because he could not subpoena witnesses to testify before the appeal board, his rights under s. 7 were violated. The challenge was dismissed on the basis that the *Charter* does not protect economic interests.

16 *Reference re. ss. 193 & 195 1 (1) (c) of the Criminal Code (Man)*, [1990] 1 SCR, 1123.

17 United States Constitution, amendments V & XIV.

18 *Singh, supra* note 10. *Weinstein v. Minister of Education for B.C.* (1985), 20 D.L.R. (4th) 609 at 619 (the lieutenant-governor in council replaced an elected board of school trustees with an appointed official trustee according to the authority provided for in the British Columbia *School Act* 1979, c. 375. The B.C. Supreme Court ruled that the appointment did not infringe s. 7 of the *Charter* because the *Charter* does not bestow rights or freedoms on elected boards. Only persons or individuals are entitled to those rights and freedoms); *B. (R.), supra* note 9.

19 *Meyer v. Nebraska*, 262 U.S. 390 at 399 (1923).

The phrase "to acquire useful knowledge" hints at a right to education. This right was explicitly included as a liberty right in a 1971 American decision when the court said: "It would seem beyond argument that the right to receive a public school education is a basic personal right or liberty."[20]

Reference was made to education in another American Supreme Court decision in 1973. Justice Douglas, in his concurring opinion in *Doe v. Bolton,* expanded further on what "liberty" means. He said:

> First is the autonomous control over the development and expression of one's intellect, interests and personality.
>
> . . .
>
> Second is freedom of choice in the basic decisions of one's life respecting marriage, divorce, procreation, contraception, and *the education and upbringing of children.*
>
> . . .
>
> Third is freedom to care for one's health and person, freedom from bodily restraint or compulsion, freedom to walk, stroll or loaf.[21] [Emphasis mine]

In 1984, the Newfoundland District Court concluded that "a child's right to education is included in the liberty guaranteed to it in s. 7 of the *Charter.*"[22] The educational implications of education as a right means, for example, that suspensions or expulsions violate the student's right. However, this does not mean that such actions are immediately construed as violating students' constitutional rights; students can be suspended and expelled as long as these forms of discipline conform to "the principles of fundamental justice." The detention of students has also been ruled as interfering with a student's right to liberty. An Ontario court ruled that when a group of teachers stopped a student from leaving the school because they suspected him of smoking marijuana in a classroom, "the teachers did detain the accused in that they deprived him temporarily of his right to liberty and security of his person."[23] But again, such detentions may be legal as long as they are administered in accordance with "the principles of fundamental justice."

Security of the Person

The phrase "security of the person" is more ambiguous than the term "liberty." American case law is of no assistance in this matter, since it does not use the phrase. Some of the cases heard by Canada's Supreme Court have provided

---

20 *Ordway v. Hargraves,* 323 F. Supp. 1155 at 1158 (D.C. Mass, 1971).

21 *Doe v. Bolton,* 419 U.S. 179 at 211 (1973).

22 *Kind, supra* note 1 at 338.

23 *R. v. Sweet,* Ont. District Court, Vanninni D.C.J., 7th Nov., 1986 (unreported) at 4. However, the court ruled that the detention of a student suspected of using marijuana was not a "detention within the meaning of s. 9 and s. 10 of the *Charter.*"

insight into its meaning. One common thread is that the term has more to do with the interaction of an individual with the justice system than does the term "liberty."[24]

In the case of *Morgentaler,* the court said: "[S]ecurity of the person must include a right of access to medical treatment for a condition representing a danger to life or health without fear of criminal sanctions."[25] It included in its definition personal autonomy, "at least with respect to the right to make choices concerning one's own body, control over one's physical and psychological integrity, and basic human dignity."[26] Central to all of these definitions is that "security of the person" refers to the physical and personal integrity of an individual free from possible legal sanctions.[27]

In *Singh v. M.E.I.*, former Justice Wilson said that, at the very least, "security of the person must encompass freedom from the threat of physical punishment or suffering as well as freedom from such punishment itself."[28] Justice Wilson's definition of "security of the person" may provide a legal argument on the constitutional validity of corporal punishment. This topic will be discussed in chapter 11.

J.D. Whyte, a former law professor and current deputy minister of justice in Saskatchewan, took a more expansive interpretation of the term "security of the person." He pointed out that there is no reason to believe "security of the person" includes only those invasions of "personal integrity" inflicted by the criminal justice system. He suggested it may include "matters which are essential to a person's capacity to act as an autonomous being."[29] If Whyte is correct, this could include a wide range of possibilities from the right to adequate financial security, to comprehensive health care, to the right to an education.

Principles of Fundamental Justice

In 1985, the Supreme Court ruled that "at a minimum the concept of 'fundamental

---

24 *Rodriguez v. British Columbia (Attorney General),* [1993] 3 S.C.R. 519 at 584–85. Sue Rodriguez, a terminally ill woman, argued that the *Criminal Code* offence of assisting a terminally ill person to commit suicide impinged on her security interests under s. 7. In a split decision, the court agreed but said the deprivation of her right was not contrary to the principles of fundamental justice.

25 *Supra* note 12 at 90. In *Nisbett v. Manitoba (Human Rights Commission)* (1993), 14 Admin. L.R. (2d) 216, leave to appeal refused (1993), 14 Admin. L.R. (2d) 231. The court ruled that security of the person is not affected in a proceeding of a non-penal nature under human rights legislation and s. 7 does not apply to such proceedings.

26 *Rodriguez, supra* note 24.

27 *Byrt v. Saskatchewan,* [1987] 2 W.W.R. 475 at 480, quoting with approval from *Gerol v. Canada (Attorney General)* (1986), 53 O.R. (2d) 275.

28 *Singh, supra* note 10 at 207.

29 J.D. Whyte, "Fundamental Justice: The Scope and Application of Section 7 of the Charter" (1983) 13 Man. L. J. 455 at 473.

justice' as it appears in s. 7 of the *Charter* includes the notion of procedural fairness,"[30] as defined by Chief Justice Fauteux in the decision of *Duke v. The Queen:*

> Without attempting to formulate any final definition of those words [principle of fundamental justice], I would take them to mean, generally, that the tribunal which adjudicates upon his rights must act fairly, in good faith, without bias and in a judicial temper, and must give to him the opportunity adequately to state his case.[31]

By referring to Chief Justice Fauteux's statements, the court interpreted fundamental justice to include the primary rule of natural justice, that of a fair hearing heard by an unbiased adjudicator. But the court was careful to leave the door open to further expansion on its meaning.

The Supreme Court has stated on numerous occasions that the meaning of the phrase "principles of fundamental justice" is to be found in the basic tenets and principles not only of the Canadian judicial process but also of other components of the Canadian legal system.[32] The meaning of the principles of fundamental justice was expanded upon further when the court ruled that the principles of fundamental justice can strike down laws that have the potential to convict an innocent person.[33]

> It has from time immemorial been part of our system of laws that the innocent not be punished. This principle has long been recognized as an essential element of a system for the administration of justice which is founded upon the belief in the dignity and worth of the human person and on the rule of law.[34]

As will be discussed later, this basic tenet has implications for educational disciplinary practices that punish innocent students because of the misdemeanours of a few. Within the educational sphere this can be interpreted to mean that students are innocent until proven guilty, that the tendency to assume that students are "trouble" and to treat them as such is an affront to their dignity and worth.[35]

Application to Education

In 1986 the Supreme Court considered the meaning of "liberty" and the "principles of fundamental justice" in an educational setting. The case involved

---

30 *Singh, supra* note 10 at 62; *R. v. Lyons,* [1987] 2 S.C.R. 309 at 361.
31 *Duke v. The Queen,* [1972] S.C.R. 917 at 923.
32 *Re B.C. Motor Vehicle Act, supra* note 9.
33 *Ibid.*
34 *Ibid.* at 282; *Beare, supra* note 7; *B. (R.), supra* note 9.
35 *Re Peel Board of Education v. B. (W.)* (1987), 59 O.R. 654.

a pastor, Pastor Jones, who operated a school in the basement of his church. Because he chose not to send his children to school he was required by the Alberta education act[36] to apply for an exemption and to submit his course outline for departmental approval. He refused to do so, arguing that God, rather than the Government of Alberta, had final authority over the education of his children and that the requirements contravened "his religious beliefs and deprives him of his liberty to educate his children as he pleases contrary to the principles of fundamental justice."[37]

Justice LaForest, writing for the majority, rejected Pastor Jones's argument, saying that even if the term "liberty" included the right of parents to educate their children as they saw fit, Pastor Jones was not deprived of the liberty interest contrary to the principles of fundamental justice. Justice LaForest reasoned that if Pastor Jones had been able to show that the school authorities had imposed arbitrary standards (standards extraneous to educational policy under the education act) or that they had acted in a fundamentally unfair manner, such as failing to carefully examine the facts, then the courts would intervene. But this was not the case. The province's compelling interest in the quality of education requires a system of review by competent and credible personnel. Justice LaForest found that the review process did not violate the principles of fundamental justice.[38]

In a 1995 case the Supreme Court was asked to rule on the constitutionality of the *Ontario Child Welfare Act,* which had been used to override parents' wishes regarding the medical treatment of their child. Infant Sheena was born four weeks prematurely to parents of the Jehovah's Witness faith. At the request of the parents, the attending physicians avoided the use of blood transfusions because of the parents' religious beliefs. The parents also believed that blood transfusions were unnecessary. However, Sheena's condition worsened and according to the doctors she needed a blood transfusion. After a hearing, the Provincial Court granted the Children's Aid Society a seventy-two-hour wardship of Sheena. The wardship was later extended to twenty-one days to allow for exploratory surgery that would require a further transfusion. The doctors required an extended time in order to confirm a medical suspicion of infantile glaucoma.

The parents argued that the powers of the *Child Welfare Act,* which allowed for temporary wardship of children, denied them their parental right to choose medical treatment for their daughter contrary to section 7 of the *Charter*. The nine judges on the Supreme Court differed in their interpretations of the case, but the majority ruled that the right to liberty includes the right of parents to make decisions concerning the health, education, and well-being of their children. The Supreme Court ruled that the act deprived parents of their right to decide

---

36 *School Act*, R.S.A. 1980, c. S-3, s. 143.

37 *Jones, supra* note 2 at 290.

38 *Ibid.* at 303.

what medical treatment should be administered to their children, thus infringing upon their "liberty."[39] The deprivation, however, was made in accordance with "the principles of fundamental justice." The court noted that the parents had been given reasonable notice of a hearing; the hearing had allowed for an exchange of arguments and the cross-examination of witnesses before an impartial adjudicator/judge; the onus of proving the need to deprive the parental right had been placed on the government agent; and the order was to be reviewed before its expiry date.[40] The temporary wardship was reasonable and justified considering the state's interest in protecting children.

Section 7 constitutionalizes the notion of natural justice, sometimes referred to as "due process." Whenever an individual's liberty or security of the person is threatened by the power of the government or its agents (school authorities), those with the power must be fair. They have an obligation to prove the need to deprive a person of his or her rights under section 7. When these cases arise, school officials are required to advise the student of the charges against him or her; to inform the student of the nature of the evidence against him; and to give reasonable notice that there is to be a hearing before an impartial adjudicator. This allows for an exchange of arguments and allows the student to be heard in his own defence.

These principles are pertinent, especially when considering the process employed by educational authorities in administering three specific forms of discipline: group punishment, suspension or expulsion, and corporal punishment. American courts that have considered the constitutionality of suspensions and expulsions have not ruled their use unconstitutional, but the procedures followed prior to a student being suspended or expelled have been. The procedures employed before a student is suspended or expelled will also be open to *Charter* scrutiny and have implications for students charged under the *Young Offenders Act*. The use of general disciplinary measures that affect innocent individuals is open to *Charter* scrutiny as well. Corporal punishment will be discussed at length in chapter 11.

Group Punishment

It is common practice in schools and in prisons to punish a large portion of the population for the actions of a few. In the school setting, this is usually done only in those cases when the rules of the school have been broken by unidentified individuals. It is a common practice because it generally works in pressuring the rule breaker to confess. This form of discipline may also take the form of cancelling field trips, sports events, school dances, and other such school activities.

In *Re B.C. Motor Vehicle Act,* Justice Lamer said the principle that the innocent not be punished "has long been recognized as an essential element of a system

---

39 *B. (R.), supra* note 9.
40 *Ibid.* at 377 & 380.

for the administration of justice which is founded upon a belief in the dignity and worth of the human person and on the rule of law."[41] Disciplining innocent students does not fit within this system and may violate the "principles of fundamental justice."

One Canadian court has ruled that the police have the right to detain everybody in a group during an investigation if a serious or violent crime has been committed and letting people who fall under suspicion go would interfere with the police investigation.[42] This ruling would apply to schools only in those cases where a serious or violent crime has occurred.

Suspensions and Expulsions

Traditionally, Canadian courts have been reluctant to become involved in the decisions of educational administrators. This fact is well illustrated in the pre-*Charter* case of *Ward v. Blaine Lake School Board,* in which a grade 6 student was suspended from school because the length of his hair did not conform to the school board rules.[43] The case was taken to the Saskatchewan Court of Queen's Bench. The parents of the student asked the court to do three things: to invalidate the school board rule, to prohibit the school board from interfering with the right of the student to attend school, and to order the school board to readmit the student. The court ruled that since the student had only a conditional right to attend school, a decision to remove the privilege was administrative and not judicial. Therefore, since natural justice applied only to judicial or quasi-judicial decisions, the suspended student had no legal recourse to overturn the decision. If the case were heard today undoubtedly the outcome would be different.

Section 7 draws no distinction between administrative or judicial decisions,[44] it simply applies to governments and their agents, of which one is the school board. The decisions they make, which may deny an individual's right to life, liberty, or security of the person, must be applied fairly and in accordance with the principles of fundamental justice. Proceeding on the assumption that there exists a right to an education under the *Charter*[45] as there is under the American Constitution,[46] it may be helpful to examine some important American decisions

---

41 *Re B.C. Motor Vehicle Act, supra* note 9 at 34.
42 *R. v. Dupuis* (1995), 162 A.R. 197 (C.A.). The accused successfully argued that a police search violated his *Charter* rights under s. 8. The police conducted the search without reasonable grounds for their belief that the accused was in possession of a knife.
43 *Ward, supra* note 3.
44 See, for example, *Singh, supra* note 10; *Nisbett v. Manitoba (Human Rights Commission)* (1993), 14 Admin. L.R. (2d) 216; *Operation Dismantle v. The Queen,* [1985] 1 S.C.R. 441. The Supreme Court ruled that the agreement made by the Canadian government to allow the American military to test cruise missiles in Canada does not violate s. 7.
45 *Kind, supra* note 1.
46 *Meyer, supra* note 19; *Ordway, supra* note 20: *Doe, supra* note 21.

that have dealt with the procedural due process rights of students in the area of suspensions and expulsions. These cases have been heard by the American Supreme Court under the heading "due process of the law." *Black's Law Dictionary* defines procedural due process to include "reasonable notice and opportunity to be heard and present any claim or defence."[47] This definition is similar to its English counterpart "natural justice." As discussed earlier, the principles of natural justice are included in "the principles of fundamental justice." Therefore the American cases dealing with the constitutionally protected procedural due process rights of students are helpful in considering the same rights of Canadian students.

The American Supreme Court first considered procedural due process for students in the 1975 case of *Goss v. Lopez*.[48] The case involved two Ohio students who were suspended from school for up to ten days because of disruptive behaviour. Their suspension was in accordance with an Ohio statute and it occurred without a hearing. School officials argued that since there was no constitutional right to an education, there was no deprivation of life, liberty, or property. Thus they argued that the due process clause of the Fourteenth Amendment did not apply. The court disagreed, saying that the state of Ohio provided an education and compelled students to attend.[49] It further stated that since the suspensions would be entered on the students' records, there was a liberty interest because the suspensions would damage their reputations and interfere with later opportunities for higher education and employment.

The court ruled that since the suspensions were for ten days, procedural due process applied, although the principles of due process could be less formal than those generally prescribed:

> [T]otal exclusion from the educational process for more than a trivial period, and certainly if the suspension is for ten days, is a serious event in the life of the suspended child. . . . The student interest is to avoid unfair or mistaken exclusion from the educational process with all of its unfortunate consequences. . . . At the very minimum . . . students facing suspension . . . must be given some kind of notice and afforded some kind of hearing. . . . The due process clause will not shield him from suspensions properly imposed, but it disserves both his interest and the interest of the State if his suspension is in fact unwarranted. . . . The risk of error is not at all trivial, and it should be guarded against if that may be done without prohibitive cost or interference with the educational process.[50]

The court also said that this minimal and flexible procedure does not necessarily

---

47 H.C. Black, *Black's Law Dictionary* (Minneapolis: West, 1979) at 1083.
48 *Goss v. Lopez*, 419 U.S. 565 (1975).
49 All provincial and territorial education acts compel students to attend school.
50 *Goss*, *supra* note 48 at 576.

allow a student to be represented by counsel, to have witnesses, or to confront and cross-examine witnesses against him. However, "longer suspensions or expulsions for the remainder of the school term or permanently, may require more formal procedures."[51] It further recognized circumstances in which it is advisable to remove a student immediately from school when his or her presence poses a danger to students or property or disrupts the academic process. In such cases, the court warned, notice and hearing should follow as soon as possible.

The American court ruled that the principles of due process, which are similar to the principles of natural justice, apply to students, but that the procedures can be less formal than those generally prescribed. Courts in Canada have also stated that the principles of fundamental justice vary according to the context.[52] For example, the defining of the "liberty" interest "may affect the determination of the principles of fundamental justice."[53] The practice of suspensions and expulsions has not been ruled unconstitutional in American cases and it is unlikely Canadian courts will take a different tack. The issue that is of more concern to the courts is whether the process leading up to the suspension or expulsion has been fair.

In light of the courts' interpretations of the principles of fundamental justice, educational administrators would do well to ensure that the process leading up to any suspensions or expulsions follows the principles of fundamental justice. This means that the matter should be heard by an unbiased adjudicator—most likely the principal unless it is the principal who has been involved in the incident; the student should be given reasonable notice of the hearing; the student should be clearly informed of the case against him or her; the student should be given the opportunity to respond; and the onus for proving the need to suspend or expel the student is placed on the educational officials.

The *Young Offenders Act* makes it an offence to publish the name of a young person charged with a criminal offence.[54] The result has been some confusion over whether school authorities can suspend or expel a student based on facts that are relevant to a charge being laid under the *Young Offenders Act*.[55] The

---

51   *Ibid.* at 584.
52   *B. (R.), supra* note 9; *R. v. Lyons*, [1987] 2 S.C.R. 309; *Pearlman, supra* note 7.
53   *B. (R), ibid.* at 363.
54   *Young Offenders Act*, R.S.C. 1985.
55   S. 38 of the *Young Offenders Act* provides: "38(1) Subject to this section, no person shall publish by any means any report: (a) of an offence committed or alleged to have been committed by a young person, unless an order has been made under section 16 with respect thereto, or (b) of a hearing, adjudication, disposition or appeal concerning a young person who committed or is alleged to have committed an offence in which the name of the young person, a child or young person who is a victim of the offence or a child or a young person who appeared as a witness in connection with the offence, or in which any information serving to identify such young person or child, is disclosed."

matter was clearly answered in a 1994 Ontario Court of Appeal decision:[56]

> Conducting an expulsion hearing, does not, by itself, constitute publication of a report that an offence, or an alleged offence, has been committed by a young person. Neither does a decision . . . to expel a pupil, constitute a conclusion that the student is also guilty of an outstanding criminal offence, given two sets of proceedings, different burdens of proof and a different purpose and focus to each.[57]

An expulsion hearing does not mean the disclosure of a criminal offence or alleged criminal offence. In *F.G. and J.M. v. Board of Education of Scarborough*, the court suggested such hearings be held in camera, saying: "Where a hearing is held in camera confidentiality may be maintained."[58] In addition, the suspension or expulsion of a student does not imply guilt but rather differing levels of proof, purpose, and focus, depending on whether the suspension or expulsion is a school disciplinary matter or a criminal offence. The court also stated that it was never the intent of the *Young Offenders Act* to shield against the enforcement of school discipline.[59] One of the most interesting aspects to this case is the fact that even students who have been found not guilty may be expelled or suspended. It must be noted, however, that the challenge before the court in this case was not a *Charter* challenge.

Students in a school in Saskatchewan were charged with sexual assault of other students at the school. The students appeared in Youth Court and entered pleas of not guilty. While the charges were pending, the board of education placed the students on "short bounds." This meant that the students' movements within the school were restricted. The purpose of the action was "to enforce a separation between the alleged offenders and the alleged victims in the matter of the charges of sexual assault."[60]

The students challenged the board's decision on the grounds that the board had exceeded its powers under the education act. Justice McLellan ruled that the

---

56 *F.G. and J.M. v. Board of Education of Scarborough* (1994), 68 O.C.A. 308. By its decision, the Ontario Court of Appeal overturned a lower court decision that ruled that the provisions of the *Young Offenders Act* precluded an expulsion hearing. See *Re Peel Board of Education v. B. (W.)* (1987), 59 O.R. 654. In *Re Peel Board of Education*, the Ontario Supreme Court had ruled that the expulsion of six youths charged with kidnapping, unlawful confinement, and sexual assault would breach the provisions of the *Young Offenders Act* and its prohibition on the publication of the youths' identities.
57 *F.G. and J.M., ibid.* at 312.
58 *Ibid.*
59 *Ibid.*
60 *G.H. v. Shamrock School Division No. 38 (Sask.) Board of Education*, [1987] 3 W.W.R. 270 at 272, quoting from a letter sent from the school board to the parents of each of the students charged.

board had exercised its power appropriately and that the applicants had failed to meet their burden of proof to show that the action taken was not correct. However, the judge also noted that although he had been asked to determine whether the board possessed the authority under the act to impose the restrictions, he had not been asked to determine whether the restrictions violated the *Charter* or to determine if there had been a denial of natural justice.

The alleged perpetrators were not denied their right to an education, but it could be argued that other liberty rights had been violated. The students might also have argued that they were assumed guilty, which violates a basic tenet to be upheld within the principles of fundamental justice. If the students had successfully made such arguments, it would then have fallen to the school board to justify the need to take these measures, as outlined under section 1 of the *Charter*. In other words, the school division would need to show that restricting the rights of students charged with sexually assaulting other students is reasonable and demonstrably justified in a free and democratic society.

The argument is an intriguing one, especially when looked at from the perspective of equality rights. Research has shown that sexual abuse of women and children is prevalent,[61] and that 80 to 95 percent of the perpetrators are men.[62] The majority of perpetrators are heterosexual.[63] Therefore, the right of females and children to an education without discrimination based on sex or age,[64] as provided for in provincial human rights legislation and the *Charter*, will most certainly be impeded if the student charged with sexually assaulting another student is allowed back into the classroom or even the school.

---

61 Rix Rogers, chair, *Reaching for Solutions: The Summary Report of the Special Advisor to the Minister of National Health and Welfare on Child Sexual Abuse in Canada* (Ottawa: Minister of Supply and Services, June 1990); Pat Freeman Marshall & Marthe Asselin Vaillancourt, co-chairs, *Final Report of the Canadian Panel on Violence Against Women* (Ottawa: Minister of Supply and Services, 1993); The Daily Statistics Canada: The Violence Against Women Survey (18 November 1993).

62 Judith L. Alpert, "Introduction to Special Section on Clinical Intervention in Child Sexual Abuse" (1990) 21:5 Professional Psychology: Research and Practice 323. See also David Finkelhor & D. Russell, "Women as Perpetrators," in David Finkelhor, ed., *Child Sexual Abuse: New Theory and Research* (New York: Free Press, 1984). Finkelhor & Russell report that sexual abuse by women occurs in approximately 20 percent of the cases with male victims and 5 percent of the cases involving females.

63 See G.G. Abel *et al.,* "Self-Reported Sex Crimes of Nonincarcerated Paraphiliacs" (1987) 3 Journal of Interpersonal Violence 2. Their research showed that non-incarcerated sex offenders do not subscribe to the myths about child molesters; instead, they are married, come from varying socio-economic backgrounds, claim religious affiliations, and appear respectable.

64 An argument could be made on this basis under a provincial human rights act or under s. 15 of the *Charter*. S. 15 guarantees the right to equal benefit of the law, in this case, the laws providing for public education.

In the fall of 1994 two students complained about the insensitivity of school officials in dealing with their fears over being placed in the same classroom as a boy who had been charged with sexually assaulting them.[65] It seems the school policy on violence and discipline was inadequate. School officials erroneously believed that they could not remove the male student because he had not yet been found guilty. Donna Greschner, chief commissioner of the Saskatchewan Human Rights Commission, stated that school officials are not prevented from removing an accused sex offender from a class. *The Saskatchewan Human Rights Code* states that every person has a right to the use of educational institutions without discrimination and that "the school board has an obligation to provide an equal educational opportunity for the young women."[66] A professor of criminal law said that pulling someone out of class is not a presumption of guilt, it is merely an assessment that, "given the accusations against you by these other students, it's not appropriate for you to be together."[67]

The cases of suspension and expulsion discussed in this section do not deal with *Charter* arguments. However, considering the disparate impact of sexual assault cases on the equal educational opportunities of females and children, it seems unlikely that *Charter* challenges to the decisions of the school administrators in these types of cases would succeed—especially if the objective to be gained in limiting the liberty of one student is to ensure that all students have the same opportunity to acquire an education.

Conclusion

The legal rights under section 7 have been interpreted as procedural rather than substantive. In other words, a student's right to an education can be deprived through suspensions and expulsions as long as the process is fair. Students are entitled to be informed of the case against them and have it heard before an impartial adjudicator. The student is to be given adequate notice of the hearing and the opportunity to present his or her case. Students who have been charged under the *Young Offenders Act* and whose charges affect the rights of other students can be dealt with in school—by, for example, a suspension or by other means—as long as the school hearing does not disclose the criminal offence or alleged criminal offence.[68] School disciplinary practices that punish an entire group of students in the hope of ensuring that a few "trouble-makers" will conform violate the basic tenet that the innocent not be punished and are thus counter to the principles of fundamental justice.

---

65 Bonnie Brayden, "School Board Reviews Discipline: Sex Assault Victim Angry That Attacker Placed in Same Class" *The [Saskatoon] StarPhoenix* (14 September 1994) A3.

66 Bonnie Brayden, "Rights Code Allows School to Pull Offender From Class" *The [Saskatoon] StarPhoenix* (15 September 1994) A8.

67 *Ibid.*, quoting Norm Zlotkin, criminal law professor, University of Saskatchewan.

68 See *F.G. and J.M.*, *supra* note 56.

Chapter 10 ■
Search, Seizure, and Detention

Sections 8, 9, and 10 of the *Charter*, like section 7 discussed in chapter 9, fall under the heading of "legal rights" and affect a number of educational issues such as the right to freedom from unreasonable searches of students or their property, locker searches, and the detention or restraining of students. Some of these matters have been considered by the courts; others have yet to be challenged.

Charter rights are rules governing the limitations of the state's powers. These legal rights are usually used by those who have been charged with a crime. Legal commentators Alan Gold and Michelle Fuerst make no apologies for this, saying that "complete success against crime involves methods and rules that would create a state that is not worth living in."[1] Likewise complete success against criminal activities in schools would create an educational environment not worth learning in. Complete success against criminal activities in schools could mean and indeed has meant that students have no expectation of privacy, which is a right society takes for granted, unless of course you are in prison.[2]

Historically courts have been reluctant to uphold the legal rights of students in issues of "law and order." This has diminished the capacity of students to require others to behave in certain ways and to have that requirement enforceable by law.[3] In other words, the courts, through their decisions, have diminished the capacity of students to require school authorities to behave towards them in the manner that these authorities are required to behave towards others, or alternatively, in the manner police officers are required to behave towards students. Too often it is the students who must adhere to the questionable demands of school authorities to behave in certain ways. If they do not, the sympathy of the courts often seems to lie with the school authorities rather than with the students.

---

1   Alan D. Gold & Michelle Fuerst, "The Stuff That Dreams Are Made Of! Criminal Law and the Charter of Rights" (1992) 24 Ottawa L. Rev. 13 at 16.
2   There has been a move recently to install surveillance cameras in Canadian schools. Some parents, students, and teachers approve of them. Is this intrusive equipment a necessary tool to combat criminal activity or an example of an educational environment not worth learning in? See Kim McNairn, "Constant Surveillance: Cameras Set Up to Track Vandalism, Theft Insulting to Some Marion Graham Students" *The [Saskatoon] StarPhoenix* (24 September, 1998) A1; Ailsa M. Watkinson, "Cameras Show Board's View of Young People" *The [Saskatoon] StarPhoenix* (22 October 1998) A5.
3   Marvin A. Zuker, *The Legal Context of Education* (Toronto: OISE, 1988) at 156.

Search and Seizure

Section 8 states:

> 8. Everyone has the right to be secure against unreasonable search or seizure.[4]

The Supreme Court has ruled that section 8 is "to protect individuals from unjustified state intrusions upon their privacy."[5] The issue in section 8 has been described as a moral one based on the standards and expectations operating within a society.[6] Section 8 can be compared to the Fourth Amendment of the American Constitution, which protects the rights of people to be secure in their persons, houses, papers, and effects against unreasonable search and seizure.[7] Although the Canadian Supreme Court made it clear in *Hunter v. Southam* that the Fourth Amendment is not identical to section 8, it has been relied upon in developing the meaning of section 8.[8]

The Fourth Amendment has been the subject of many constitutional challenges regarding the rights of students to be secure against unreasonable search and seizure. The issues that come up in many of these cases are the balance between the constitutional right to be secure from unreasonable search and seizure and the legitimate obligation of school officials to provide a safe and secure educational environment; the criteria that must be met in order for a search to be considered reasonable; the status of school officials when conducting a search of a student, that is, whether they are acting *in loco parentis* (in the place of parents) or as agents of the state; and the legality of strip searches, locker searches, and the search of personal property.

Interpretation

In 1984 the Canadian Supreme Court considered the first case brought forward under section 8. The case of *Hunter v. Southam*[9] challenged the constitutionality of section 10 of the *Combines Investigation Act*.[10] Under this act, the director of investigations and research of the Combines Investigation Branch authorized the entry and examination of documents and other items of the *Edmonton Journal*, a division of Southam Inc. Southam Inc. alleged that sections 10(1) and 10(3) of

---

4   *Canadian Charter of Rights and Freedoms,* Part 1 of the *Constitution Act, 1982,* being Schedule B to the *Canada Act 1982* (U.K.), 1982, c. 11, s. 8.
5   *Hunter v. Southam,* [1984], 2 S.C.R. 145 at 160.
6   R.T.H. Stone, "The Inadequacy of Privacy: *Hunter v. Southam* and the Meaning of 'Unreasonable' in Section 8 of the Charter" (1989) 34 McGill L. J. 685 at 689.
7   American Constitution, amendment IV.
8   *Supra* note 5 at 155, 159, & 161.
9   *Ibid.*
10 *Combines Investigation Act,* R.S.C. 1970, c. C-23.

the *Combines Investigation Act* were inconsistent with the right to be secure against unreasonable search and seizure. The Supreme Court referred to balancing competing interests when it said:

> This limitation on the right guaranteed by Section 8 . . . indicates that an assessment must be made as to whether in a particular situation the public's interest in being left alone by the government must give way to the government's interest in intruding on the individual's privacy in order to advance its goals, notably those of law enforcement.[11]

The court stressed the need to examine the impact of a search and seizure on the individual and not simply to rely on the government's interest:

> [A]n assessment of the constitutionality of a search and seizure . . . must focus on its reasonable or unreasonable impact on the subject of the search or the seizure, and not simply on its rationality in furthering some valid government objective.[12]

In addition to its directive stating that section 8 protects individuals from intrusions on their privacy and that any constitutional assessment of the search must focus on the impact of the search, the court ruled that a warrant is a precondition for a valid search and seizure and thus warrantless searches are prima facie "unreasonable."[13] The court also stated that when balancing the need for crime control with the need to protect privacy, the balance is achieved when "credibly-based probability replaces suspicion."[14]

Unfortunately these treatises were not applied when the Supreme Court of Canada, following the lead of the Ontario Court of Appeal[15] and the Nova Scotia Court of Appeal,[16] considered the constitutionality of student searches.[17] Rather the court was swayed by the rationale of furthering "a valid [school] objective."[18]

The first *Charter* case dealing with the search and seizure of students was *R. v. J.M.G.* The case was heard two years after the American Supreme Court had considered a similar fact case.[19] Twelve years later, the case of *R. v. M. (M.R.)*[20]

---

11 *Supra* note 5 at 159–60.
12 *Ibid.* at 157.
13 *Ibid.* at 161. The court recognized there may be instances where it is not feasible to obtain a warrant, but in such instances the government must be able to present arguments as to why it was impossible to do so.
14 *Ibid.* at 167.
15 *R. v. J.M.G.* (1986), 56 O.R. (2d) 705 (O.C.A.).
16 *R. v. M. (M.R.)* (1998), 7 C.R. (5th) 1 (N.S.C.A.).
17 *R. v. M. (M.R.),* [1998] 3 S.C.R. 393. The case was an appeal of *R. v. M. (M.R.), ibid.*
18 *R. v. J.M.G., supra* note 15.
19 *New Jersey v. T.L.O.,* 105 S. Ct. 733 (1985).
20 *Supra* note 17.

was heard by the Supreme Court of Canada. Both of these decisions referred extensively to the American case of *New Jersey v. T.L.O.*, heard under the Fourth Amendment. The facts of the cases—one American and two Canadian—are outlined below.

The case of T.L.O. began when a teacher at a New Jersey high school discovered two girls smoking in the lavatory, one of whom was the respondent, fourteen-year-old T.L.O.[21] Smoking in the lavatory was a violation of school rules. The girls were taken to the administration office and questioned. T.L.O. denied she had been smoking and claimed that she did not smoke at all. The vice-principal demanded to see her purse and found a package of cigarettes. As he reached into the purse for the cigarettes he also noticed a package of cigarette-rolling paper. He suspected that the rolling paper meant drugs were involved, and he proceeded to search the purse thoroughly, whereupon he found a small amount of marijuana, a pipe, a number of empty plastic bags, a substantial quantity of money in $1 bills, an index card that appeared to be a list of students who owed T.L.O. money, and two letters that implicated T.L.O. in marijuana dealing. T.L.O. confessed that she had been selling marijuana and on the basis of the confession and the evidence seized by the vice-principal delinquency charges were laid against her. T.L.O. contended that the search of her purse violated the Fourth Amendment and moved to suppress the evidence found in her purse. She also argued that her confession should not have been considered since it was tainted by the allegedly unlawful search. The American Supreme Court was asked to determine whether the Fourth Amendment's prohibition against unreasonable search and seizure applied to searches conducted by public school officials and, if so, whether the search was reasonable. The court ruled that the Fourth Amendment applied to searches conducted by public school officials but that in this case the search was a reasonable one.

Two years after the American decision, the Ontario Court of Appeal heard the case of *R. v. J.M.G.*[22] The case dealt with the search and seizure of a grade 7 student who was seen outside the school yard placing drugs in his sock. The principal and vice-principal summoned the student to the principal's office and asked him to remove his footwear. The student took something out of his pant cuff and ate it. After some time, the principal obtained what he considered to be suspicious matter and called the police. The student was charged with possession of marijuana. At trial the student argued that his right to be secure against unreasonable search or seizure, as guaranteed under section 8, had been violated. The student also argued that since he was detained by the principal and subsequently charged with an offence, he had the right to retain and instruct counsel and to be informed of that right according to section 10(b) of the *Charter*. The judge dealt with J.M.G.'s section 8 argument with extensive reference to the

---

21 *Supra* note 19.
22 *Supra* note 15.

American case of *T.L.O.* and ruled that the search was a reasonable one. Leave to appeal the case was refused by the Supreme Court of Canada.[23] The impact of this case has been substantial.[24] It is a decision firmly ensconced in the traditional paradigm of school governance, one that diminishes student empowerment and dignity.

The disturbing legacy of the decision was reaffirmed by the Supreme Court in the 1998 case of *R. v. M. (M.R.).*[25] In this case the Supreme Court upheld the search of a student that was conducted by a vice-principal while a Royal Canadian Mounted Police officer sat by and observed. The search of the student was conducted without a warrant, the consequences for the student were subsequent criminal charges, and the search was deemed "reasonable" by the court based on reasonable suspicion rather than on the court's own test of a "credibly-based probability."[26] The Supreme Court's decision was a major setback for students and those who advocate on their behalf. It had been hoped that the court would take the opportunity to affirm that students are to be afforded the same level of respect as is offered to the rest of society in issues of unreasonable state intrusion.[27] The issues of concern here are the presence of the police officer during the search, the justification for the search, the consequences of the search on the student, and the limiting of the student's rights void of a section 1 discussion.

The case began when the vice-principal was informed by other students that M. was selling drugs. The vice-principal was told by one of the informants that M. would be carrying drugs in the evening to a school dance.[28] When the vice-principal saw M. at the dance he called the RCMP and asked M. and a friend to come with him to his office. He then asked them if they were in possession of drugs and informed them that he was going to search them. At that time the RCMP officer arrived dressed in plain clothes and introduced himself to the students.[29] The vice-principal asked each student to empty out his pockets. M.

---

23 I have come to expect that when I talk about the *Charter* and student rights with educators, much of the information will be new to them. The exception is this case. Educators are aware of the leeway given to them and how it differs from that of the police.

24 *R. v. J.G.M.* has been used to overturn lower court rulings that the search of a student's locker was unreasonable; *R. v. Samms*, 1985, C.B. 573 (unreported); *R. v. J.J.W. & A.D.B.* (1990), 83 Nfld. and P.E.I. R. 13. See also *R. v. Sweet*, Ont. Dist. Ct., Vanninni D.C.J., 7th Nov, 1986 (unreported); *R. v. M. (M.R.), supra* note 17.

25 *Supra* note 17.

26 *Ibid.*

27 See, for example, A. Wayne MacKay, "Don't Mind Me, I'm from the R.C.M.P.: *R. v. M. (M.R)*—Another Brick in the Wall Between Students and Their Rights" (1998), 7 C.R. (5th) 24.

28 *Supra* note 17 at 402.

29 *Ibid.* The trial judge made note of the fact that the RCMP officer and the vice-principal met outside the office door before the officer entered. He concluded that they met to

was asked to pull up his pant leg, whereupon the vice-principal noticed a bulge in M.'s sock and removed a cellophane bag. He handed the bag to the RCMP officer, who identified the contents as marijuana and advised M. that he was under arrest. M. was told he could retain counsel and that he had the right to contact a parent or adult. He attempted to reach his mother by phone. He stated that he did not wish to contact anyone else. The officer and M. then went to M.'s locker and searched it as well. No more drugs were found.[30]

In *Hunter v. Southam*, the Canadian Supreme Court had noted that limiting a right guaranteed under section 8 requires balancing the public's interest in being left alone against the government's interest in intruding on a person's privacy to advance legitimate government interests and, in particular, law enforcement.[31] The court reiterated some of these observations when Justice Cory, speaking for the majority in *R. v. M. (M.R.)*, said:

> On one hand, it is essential that school authorities be able to react swiftly and effectively when faced with a situation that could unreasonably disrupt the school environment or jeopardize the safety of the students. . . . Yet schools also have a duty to foster the respect of their students for the constitutional rights of all members of society. Learning respect for those rights is essential to our democratic society and should be part of the education of all students. These values are best taught by example and may be undermined if the students' rights are ignored by those in authority.[32]

Despite the court's acknowledgement that schools have a duty to foster the value of respect by example, it moved in an irreconcilable direction by contradicting its earlier dictum in *Hunter*. In *Hunter* the court had directed that whenever the constitutionality of a search is challenged, an assessment must be made not simply of the rationality of a government objective,[33] but also of its "reasonable" or "unreasonable" impact on the subject of the search. In *Hunter*, the court had affirmed that section 8 acts "as a limitation on whatever powers of search and seizure the federal or provincial government already and otherwise possess."[34] In *R. v. M. (M.R.)*, however, the Supreme Court paid no heed to its own dictates and placed more weight on the rationality of a government (school)

---

discuss how to conduct the search, thus making the vice-principal an agent of the state. Justice Major of the Supreme Court in his strongly worded dissent stated: "I agree with the trial judge that it stretches credulity to suggest that their meeting related to anything other than the reason for calling the police and how the search should be conducted" (at 433).

30 *Ibid.* at 403.
31 *Hunter, supra* note 5 at 160.
32 *Supra* note 17 at 401–02.
33 *Hunter, supra* note 5 at 157.
34 *Ibid.* at 156.

objective "to maintain proper order and good discipline in the school and to attend to the health and comfort of students."[35]

The decision in *R. v. M. (M.R.)* was justified in part by misconceptions. Justice Cory introduced the reasoning behind the court's decision by saying:

> Schools today are faced with extremely difficult problems which were unimaginable a generation ago. Dangerous weapons are appearing in schools with increasing frequency. There is as well the all too frequent presence at schools of illicit drugs. These weapons and drugs create problems that are grave and urgent.[36]

Justice Cory did not provide evidence that this is indeed true; many think it is not. Sociology professor Bernard Schissel points out "that there has been little real increase in serious youth crimes [and] that participation rates in criminal activities are relatively stable."[37] Recent statistics bear this out, showing that in Canada the rate of youths charged with an offence dropped by 4 percent in 1996, with decreases reported across all crime categories.[38] And in 1997–98 youth courts handled 4 percent fewer cases than in 1992–93.[39]

---

35 *Supra* note 17 at 423.

36 *Ibid.* at 401. He repeated similar sentiments later in the decision (at 415). Sadly there were no intervenors in this case to dispel youth stereotypes and myths.

37 Bernard Schissel, *Blaming Children: Youth Crime, Moral Panics and the Politics of Hate* (Halifax: Fernwood, 1998) at 10. The author notes that Canada's war on crime is directed at youth. The author submits that the perception of increased youth crime is fuelled by the increased visibility of youth due to their idle time and the images of youth in the media—most notably the American media. See also W. Rod Dolmage, "One Less Brick in the Wall: The Myths of Youth Violence and Unsafe Schools" (1996) 7 Education Law Journal 185 at 188. The author challenges the widely held belief that youth crime is increasing as is evidenced in a quote from a judge who presided over a case involving three young female offenders charged with the assault of another. In sentencing the youths, the judge said, "Youth crime and violence are increasing across Canada." See also Nicholas Bala, *Young Offenders Law: Essentials of Canadian Law* (Ontario: Irwin Law, 1997), who notes that "the media, by focusing on relatively rare instances of serious youth violence, may distort public perceptions. Fears about youth crime may also be fuelled by the aging make-up of the population and by the insecurity felt by many in the face of accelerating social and economic change" (at 11).

38 R. King, "Canadian Crime Statistics" 17:8 Juristat (Ottawa: Statistics Canada, 1997).

39 "Vital Statistics" *The Globe and Mail* (26 March 1999) A9. The 1999 tragic school shootings in Littleton, Colorado, and Taber, Alberta, may tempt some to use these incidents as evidence of increased youth crime and the resultant dangers posed for schools, especially considering the extensive media coverage they received. It is to be hoped that these incidents will not be used to justify the need for more restrictions on students' rights. The facts of both cases show that they would not have been prevented by more surveillance cameras, student searches, or increased police presence in schools. See Brian Bergman, "Tragedy in Taber" *Maclean's* (10 May 1999) 20.

With the erroneous perception that youth crime is increasing across the country and that increased "problems which threaten the safety of students and the fundamentally important task of teaching,"[40] the Canadian Supreme Court ruled on a number of issues that had been raised in earlier Canadian and American cases concerning the constitutionality of student searches.

In *R. v. M. (M.R.)*, the court first affirmed that the *Charter* applies to schools.[41] It then considered whether the vice-principal in this case was acting as an agent of the police. The court ruled that he was not an agent of the police, saying "[t]he mere fact that there was cooperation between the vice-principal and the police and that the officer was present during the search is not sufficient to indicate that the vice-principal was acting as an agent of the police."[42] After all, the justices reasoned, the search would have been conducted in the same manner by the vice-principal had the police officer not been there. And, "it cannot be forgotten that on occasion a secondary school student may be larger and more powerful than the teacher who must in the interests of the safety of other students conduct the search"[43] In his dissent, Justice Major said: "It is disingenuous for the respondent to suggest that the presence of the police officer had no effect on the appellant's perception of the interrogation and subsequent search."[44] The impact of the court's decision is that school personnel are exempt from the criteria police officers must follow when searching students and any other members of society— criteria that were considered so fundamental to public interest in a democratic society as a shield against the powers of governments and their agents that they were enshrined in the Constitution.

A third issue considered by the court was whether the student had a reasonable expectation of privacy. This is an important first step in considering a violation of section 8 because if there is no expectation of privacy there can be no violation of section 8.[45] The court concluded that a student's expectation of privacy at school is certainly less that it would be in other circumstances.[46] Justice Cory used, by way of example, the diminished expectation of privacy individuals expect at border crossings.[47] It is an odd comparison. It raises the spectre of "illicit drugs and dangerous weapons,"[48] a notion that appears to support the court's *a priori* view of youth.[49] In explaining the court's deliberations on the standard to

---

40 *Supra* note 17 at 415.
41 *Ibid.* at 410.
42 *Ibid.* at 411.
43 *Ibid.* at 426.
44 *Ibid.* at 432.
45 *Ibid.* at 412–13.
46 *Ibid.* at 414.
47 *Ibid.*
48 *Ibid.* at 415. The quote comes from Justice Cory's discussion of the state of the environment in schools today.
49 In one case, Justice Cory made reference to "swarmings" by youth gangs even though the case involved a single youth. See *R. v. M. (J.J.)*, [1993] 2 S.C.R. 421 at 423.

be applied to searches conducted by school authorities, Justice Cory again made reference to the increase in drugs and weapons in schools. He stated that "[c]urrent conditions make it necessary to provide teachers and school administrators with the flexibility required to deal with discipline problems in schools."[50] Therefore the court ruled that a warrant was not a requirement prior to a search. The court followed closely the reasoning in the American case of *T.L.O* and said, "When a school official conducts a search of or seizure from a student, a warrant is not required. The absence of a warrant in these circumstances will not lead to a presumption that the search was unreasonable."[51]

The court also rejected the "credibly-based probability" test that it had articulated in *Hunter.*[52] The court reasoned that "teachers and principals must be able to react quickly to protect their students and to provide the orderly atmosphere required for learning."[53] The court also reasoned that the need to "protect students" and their reduced expectation of privacy support the need for a more lenient and flexible approach to searches conducted by teachers and administrators.[54] A search by school officials can be undertaken, the court said, if there are "reasonable grounds" to believe that a school rule has been broken. Reasonable grounds are to be determined in their context and include information received from students considered to be credible or from the observations of teachers or principals.[55]

The court adopted the *T.L.O.* test of determining whether the search of a student is "reasonable." The test is two fold. First there is the consideration of whether the action was justified at its inception and second, whether the search was reasonable under the circumstances.[56]

The court summarized the factors to be considered in determining whether a search is reasonable as including, first, a determination of whether the teachers or principals are authorized, by statute, to conduct searches of students.[57] In this case the court ruled that the vice-principal had the authority within the scope of his duty to maintain order and discipline in the school.[58] This is a strange turn of events considering that the *Charter,* as part of the supreme law of Canada, governs the scope of provincial legislation rather than provincial legislation governing the scope of the *Charter.* Thus the rationality in furthering some valid objective (in this case, order and discipline) has been used to justify limiting the student's

---

50 *Supra* note 17 at 415–16.
51 *Ibid.* at 420.
52 *Hunter, supra* note 5 at 167.
53 *Supra* note 17 at 421. Once again, the reference to the need to protect students portrays a violent educational environment but is void of any evidence.
54 *Ibid.*
55 *Ibid.* at 422.
56 *Ibid.* at 419.
57 *Ibid.* at 424.
58 *Ibid.* at 426.

right to be free from an unreasonable search and seizure. Second, the search is to be conducted in a sensitive manner and to be minimally intrusive.[59] In this case the court ruled that it was minimally intrusive. Finally the court said that in order to determine if the search was reasonable, all the surrounding circumstances had to be considered,[60] including the age and gender of the student.

In summary, the search of M. was ruled not to have been unreasonable and in the circumstances there was no violation of section 8.[61] The justifications for the decision included unsubstantiated assumptions about youth and the prevalence of drugs and weapons in schools. Platitudes were given to the need to respect the rights of students[62] but no substantive weight was given to the legitimate and fundamental argument that society has an interest in the development of democratic values, which clearly involves upholding legal rights in a non-discriminatory manner. The opinion of one legal commentator on the case of *R. v. J.M.G.* applies equally to this case: "The Court took a very relaxed view of the principal's action here, since it is hard to believe that in any other context a non-consensual search inside a person's clothing would be so easily justified."[63]

There are a number of disconcerting elements to this case, not the least of which is the ominous possibility of police officers advising school authorities to conduct searches that they themselves cannot do either in schools or on the street. As the dissenting judge noted:

> Our society calls upon its peace officers to ensure our safety; theirs is a dangerous occupation. The use of shortcuts by law enforcement officials will frequently be efficient but just as frequently may offend *Charter* rights as occurred here.[64]

In his commentary of the case of *R. v. J.M.G.*, legal scholar Wayne MacKay pointed out that "the consequences for the student . . . are the same regardless of who conducts the search."[65] The impact of Justice Cory's interpretation is that a student's right to be secure against an unreasonable search and seizure is diminished by virtue of being in school. The consequences, however, are not.

It is worth noting that the court in *R. v. M. (M.R.)* did not turn to section 1 to justify limiting the student's rights. Instead it limited the scope of section 8 at its

---

59 *Ibid.* at 424.

60 *Ibid.*

61 *Ibid.* at 428.

62 *Ibid.,* for example, the court noted that "it should not be forgotten that the manner in which students are treated in these situations will determine their respect for the rights of others in the future" (at 424).

63 Stone, *supra* note 6 at 689.

64 *Supra* note 17 at 433.

65 A. Wayne MacKay, "Principles in Search of Justice for the Young: What's Law Got to Do With It?" (1995) 6 Education and Law Journal 181 at 193.

origin or, more to the point, in the context of the school. As I have argued elsewhere, section 1 of the *Charter* is the appropriate place for limiting rights and freedoms. It is after all "the balancing provision."[66] The discussion as to whether it is appropriate to limit the rights of students regarding searches in schools should be placed within the guidelines of section 1.

In *R. v. M. (M.R.)* the Supreme Court's response to the student's section 8 argument was to rely on the American case of *T.L.O.*[67] and to apply the American two-fold test to determine the reasonableness of the search. The application of the American test, conceived under the *American Bill of Rights*, effectively circumvented the justification stage of a section 1 analysis. Under the American constitution, there is no equivalent to the *Charter*'s section 1 and so by applying the American test, the court usurped the principle of reverse onus, which would have required school authorities to justify the search within the values and principles of a democratic society. Under section 1, school officials would have had to provide cogent and persuasive evidence of the need, considering the nature of schools, to limit a student's expectation of privacy and to show that other means of meeting the objective of a safe learning environment had been considered. A section 1 analysis would have safeguarded the rights of students by ensuring that decisions were not made about them based on stereotypical assumptions and would have ensured that the courts had evidence on the impact of such a search on the student.[68]

In the 1984 case of *Hunter*, the Canadian Supreme Court ruled that limiting a right guaranteed under section 8 requires a balance between the public's interest in being left alone and the government's interest in intruding on a person's privacy in order to advance legitimate government interests and, in particular, law enforcement.[69] The court warned against setting the balance of a reasonable search too low and allowing for "fishing expeditions of considerable latitude,"[70] effectively tipping the balance strongly in favour of the state. Yet in the 1998 case of *R. v. M. (M.R.)* this is effectively what the court did—it tipped the balance strongly in favour of school officials.

Strip Searches, Locker Searches, and Private Possessions

Within weeks of the Supreme Court's decision in *R. v. M. (M.R.)*, nineteen grade

---

66 *B. (R.) v. Children's Aid Society of Metropolitan Toronto*, [1995] 1 S.C.R. 315 at 367.

67 *Supra* note 17 at 419.

68 There were no intervenors in the case of *R. v. M. (M.R.)* to counter the stereotypical views of the court. Clearly children and youth are not well represented in their encounters with the justice system.

69 *Supra* note 5 at 159–60.

70 *Ibid.* at 167.

9 boys from Kingsville, Ontario, were strip searched.[71] They were told to strip after one boy complained to his gym teacher that $90 had been taken from his gym bag. The boys were taken, one at a time, into an office and told to remove their pants and to bend over as the vice-principal and the gym teacher conducted a cavity search for the money.[72] In spite of the M. case, it appears that this case will not pass constitutional muster. In its decision, the Supreme Court noted that "a student attending school would have a subjective expectation that his privacy, at least with respect to his body, would be respected."[73] And even though M. was searched on his body, his search was deemed not to have been intrusive (he was asked to turn up the cuff of his pants). The same cannot be said in this case (the students were asked to remove their pants and bend over so that a cavity search could be done).

In order to determine if a search is reasonable, the circumstances must be assessed. It may be appropriate, the court ruled, to undertake swift and extensive searches if student safety is at risk.[74] There was no threat of danger to any student in this case. In addition the search was not carried out in a sensitive and minimally intrusive manner and it could be argued that strip searching anyone in order to recover $90 is disproportionate to the overall goal.[75] The students have launched a court action against the school district.[76]

One of the most extensive searches of students occurred in 1979 at a high school in Indiana. School officials and police worked together to search for illicit drugs. They inspected the entire student body of 2,780 students with the help of dogs and dog handlers. As a result of the search, four junior high students, all girls, were removed from their class, stripped nude, and interrogated.[77] Not one of them was found to possess any illicit material.

The United States Court of Appeal, Seventh Circuit, rejected the argument that the search violated the Fourth Amendment right to be secure from unreasonable search and seizure, but, even though they found the search not to

---

71 "Staff Regrets Strip Search of Students" *The [Saskatoon] StarPhoenix* (9 December 1998) A13.

72 In response to the incident that made the papers all across Canada, Ontario premier Mike Harris said: "I personally think back to teenage years and Grade 9 and the challenges of puberty and of a very sensitive age and I can't imagine that there is a teacher or vice-principal anywhere in Ontario that would have been party to anything like this. I find it abhorrent" (*ibid.*).

73 *R. v. M. (M.R.), supra* note 17 at 413.

74 *Ibid.* at 423–24.

75 Limiting a student's right to be free from an unreasonable search has to meet the requirements of s. 1. It is unlikely that a search of this nature could be justified as the deleterious effects overwhelm any salutary effects.

76 "Stripped-Searched Students Launch Suit" *The [Saskatoon] StarPhoenix* (21 January 1999) A10. It is not clear whether they are using s. 8 of the *Charter* in their action.

77 *Doe v. Renfrew*, 631 F. 2d 91 (7th Cir., 1980), cert. denied, 451 U.S. 1022 (1981).

be unreasonable, the court did permit one of the students who was strip searched to seek damages from those school officials responsible. The court rejected a lower court decision that had said the school officials were immune from liability because they had acted in "good faith," saying:

> It does not require a constitutional scholar to conclude that a nude search of a thirteen year old child is an invasion of constitutional rights of some magnitude. More than that: it is a violation of any known principle of human decency. Apart from any constitutional readings and rulings, simple common sense would indicate that the conduct of the school officials in permitting such a nude search was not only unlawful but outrageous under "settled indisputable principles of law." . . . We suggest as strongly as possible that the conduct herein described exceeded the "bounds of reason" by two and one half country miles.[78]

The dissenting judge in this case noted that "at the time of the raid, [school authorities] possessed no specific information as to the particular drugs or contrabands, transactions or events, or drug suppliers or abusers."[79] Further, it could be argued that subjecting all 2,780 students to this type of search when school officials had acknowledged that no more than 21 students[80] were known to have been involved in drug-related incidences exceeded the scope permissible and affronted the principle that all are innocent until proven guilty. The measures adopted were an excessive intrusion in light of the age and sex of the students and the vagueness of any knowledge of the infraction.

In 1983, another American strip search for drugs was ruled reasonable.[81] The student in this case was fifteen years old at the time and admitted giving two fellow students prescription medicine and two female students a quantity of marijuana. After he had told the school administration that he had smoked marijuana, had possession of it, and had transferred it to another student, he was subjected to a search. The student was requested to lower both his trousers and undershorts. The court found he was not offensively touched and it was necessary to lower his trousers and undershorts because "under-clothing [is a] prime hiding place for controlled substances."[82] The court refused the student's demand for both damages and injunctive relief, saying that the school officials had reasonable grounds for the search, considering the appellant's age, history, and record within the school system.

Because of the severity of strip searches and the absolute affront to a person's dignity, bodily integrity, and self-respect, the best advice is not to use strip searches

---

78 *Ibid.* at 92.
79 *Ibid.* at 93.
80 *Ibid.*
81 *Rone v. Davies County Board of Education*, 655 S.W. 2d 28 (Ky., 1983).
82 *Ibid.* at 29.

at all.[83] At the same time we must work to ensure that students know when it is appropriate to refuse the orders of those with authority. One commentator noted that "incidents like the one in Kingsville point to the need to pass on to our children the ability to think for themselves, and the gumption to stand up to authority that is abusing its powers."[84]

American students have challenged the use of specially trained dogs to sniff for drugs. Some school officials in the United States tried to argue that using dogs to sniff students was not a search as contemplated by the Fourth Amendment. Justice Brennan of the American Supreme Court said, "I cannot agree that the . . . school officials' use of the trained police dogs did not constitute a search."[85] Subsequently, a distinction was made between the sniffing of persons and the sniffing of objects. A lower American court ruled that the use of trained dogs to sniff objects, such as backpacks, lockers, or cars, is not a search and therefore is not subject to the Fourth Amendment, but that using dogs to sniff students is a search. There is something profoundly inhuman about bringing in dogs to sniff students. School authorities who rely on dog searches are advised to be prepared to articulate clearly why such measures are necessary.

American courts have been divided on the question of whether a student can expect privacy in matters relating to the content of his or her locker. In one such challenge, the court distinguished between school property and other property. The court ruled that a student does not have exclusive control of his or her locker because a locker is deemed school property. Therefore school officials can search it, saying the right of inspection of the student lockers "is inherent in the authority vested in school administrators and that the same must be retained and exercised in the management of our schools if their educational functions are to be maintained and the welfare of the student body preserved."[86] In *People v. Overton,* the court said: "[N]ot only have the school authorities the right to inspect but this right becomes a duty when suspicion arises that something of an illegal nature may be secreted there."[87] But, in another case, a student's expectation of privacy in the contents of his locker was deemed to be protected by the Fourth Amendment. In *State v. Engerud,* the court said:

> We are satisfied that in the context of this case the student had an expectation of privacy in the contents of his locker. . . . For the four years of high school, a school

---

83   The minister of education in Ontario, in an attempt to clarify that strip searches were not acceptable, said: "Searches are limited to serious matters that involve weapons and drugs, not money." See "Stripped-Searched," *supra* note 76.

84   John Bird, "When is 'No' Okay" (1999) 62 The United Church Observer 22 at 22.

85   *Doe, supra* note 77 at 1025.

86   *State v. Stein*, 456 P. 2d 1 at 3 (Kan. S.C., 1969).

87   *People v. Overton*, 249 N.E. 2d 366 at 367 (N.Y.C.A., 1969).

locker is a home away from home. In it the student stores the kind of personal effects protected by the Fourth Amendment.[88]

In *People v. Overton* the search of a student's locker by police officers was upheld, even though the warrant that directed the search of the locker was defective. The court reasoned that since the consent to search the locker came from the vice-principal, the search was considered legal. The police locker search revealed four marijuana cigarettes. Wayne MacKay noted that if the reasoning in *People v. Overton* were adopted by Canadian courts, "school administrators could legitimate any search of a locker or a desk by simply extending to the police the school's consent, thus negating any rights of freedom from search."[89] Even the American Supreme Court, in *T.L.O.,* affirmed the students' right to privacy under the Fourth Amendment, when it said: "[A]lthough this court may take notice of the difficulty of maintaining discipline in the public schools today, the situation is not so dire that students in the schools may claim no legitimate expectation of privacy."[90]

In the case of *R. v. M.(M.R.)* the Supreme Court commented on the issue of locker searches to say that while the student may have an expectation of privacy with respect to his person, the student can expect a lesser degree of privacy in a school environment.[91] An ominous sign, perhaps, that the court would be more cavalier in its view of locker searches. A judge in a 1990 Canadian case involving the search of a student's locker raised the issue of whether the search was unreasonable and thus a violation of section 8 of the *Charter*. The case was subsequently overturned by the Newfoundland Supreme Court, Trial Division, partly through applying *R. v. J.M.G.* and partly because it was the judge who raised the *Charter* issue and not the student. The lower court judge had ruled:

> [T]here has to be some standard of evidence that have [*sic*] to protect the young person, whether they be children in a home or children in a school. . . . [C]hildren in school must have some minimum level of protection of their rights and in the school situation it seems to me that at least there should be a reasonable suspicion before students should be subject to searches.[92]

The judge's affirmation that students have a right to expect some level of

---

88 *State v. Engerud,* 463 A. 2d 934 (N.J.S.C., 1983).

89 A. Wayne MacKay, *Education Law in Canada* (Toronto: Emond-Montgomery, 1984) at 222.

90 *T.L.O., supra* note 19 at 742. The court in *T.L.O.* did not deal with locker searches but noted by way of footnote that the lower courts were divided on whether the contents of a student's locker were subject to the Fourth Amendment.

91 *Supra* note 17 at 415.

92 *R. v. J.J.W. & A.D.B., supra* note 24 at 15.

protection from the unfettered searching of their lockers and his allusion to the spectre of a *Charter* violation are encouraging. His argument acknowledges that regardless of some maneuvering by school administrators and legal scholars to ensure administrative access to locker searches, such actions should be viewed suspiciously by the judiciary.[93]

One writer has advised school officials that their "rules should state that assigned lockers are for student 'use' only and are not student property. Such initiatives will limit potential arguments that an illegal search has taken place should an educator be required to conduct a locker search."[94] But if society takes the position that all individuals, including students, are to be protected from unreasonable search and seizure by governments and their agents, it is indeed lamentable to plot ways to overcome this unquestionable democratic freedom. If a search is necessary to ensure that the educational environment is free of illegal drugs and weapons—a laudable goal—then it is up to those who believe that the search is necessary to demonstrate that it is reasonable. If they are unable to demonstrate that the search is reasonable, they are given the second chance of demonstrating that an unreasonable search is justifiable in a democratic society. It must be remembered that the purpose of the *Charter* is to ensure that Canada is free and democratic, and that includes protecting its citizens and its students from the unfettered power of the powerful.

In the case of searches, it is suggested that a more advisable approach would be for school officials to differentiate between disciplinary matters that can be dealt with in the school and those that could have criminal consequences. Once school officials have decided that a matter deserves tougher sanctions than the school can administer, the matter should be handed to the police to investigate. This would include all instances involving the possibility of illegal substances such as drugs, alcohol, and weapons, and other criminal offences. As MacKay noted:

> The clear division of school rules into those with criminal consequences and those without is a desirable starting point. Students should have the same rights as adults

---

93 Jonathan L. Black-Branch, *Making Sense of the Canadian Charter of Rights and Freedoms: A Handbook for Administrators and Teachers* (Toronto: Canadian Education Association, 1995) at 10. Black-Branch argues for, among other things, the use of metal detectors in schools and the "development of a rapport between police officers and the school. . . . If there has been previous contact, the police may have been in a position to offer informal advice and suggestions on what the school should do" (at 11). This is in sharp contrast to the concerns of MacKay, which I support, see *supra* note 27. See also Louis Fischer, David Schimmel, & Cynthia Kelly, *Teachers and the Law,* 3rd ed. (New York: Longman, 1991), who note that "many courts are concerned that such collaboration between administrators and the police undermines the relationship between administrators and students" (at 232).

94 Black-Branch, *ibid.*

unless school authorities can make a reasonable limits argument to the contrary.[95]

It is hoped that, despite the Supreme Court's decision in *R. v. M. (M.R.)*, school officials will be wary of acting for the police or of working too closely with the police, as this could be seen as undermining the educators' relationship with students.[96] Such behaviour also sets the tone, in schools, of a "police state" rather than "a free and democratic society."

It would be in keeping with the spirit and purpose of the *Charter* for the courts to give a broad and liberal meaning to the rights of students in all areas, and if circumstances warrant restricting those rights, the school authorities should do so after first justifying the need for the restriction under the requirements of section 1.

Detention

Section 9 of the *Charter* states:

9. Everyone has the right not to be arbitrarily detained or imprisoned.[97]

A person is considered detained or arrested when an element of compulsory restraint is involved.[98] Once a person has been arrested or detained, he or she must be given certain information and resources. Section 10 states:

10. Everyone has the right on arrest or detention

(a) to be informed promptly of the reasons therefor;

(b) to retain and instruct counsel without delay and to be informed of that right; and

(c) to have the validity of the detention determined by way of *habeas corpus* and to be released if the detention is not lawful.[99]

---

95 A. Wayne MacKay, "Students as Second Class Citizens Under the Charter" (1987) 54 C.R. (3d) 390 at 399.

96 Fisher *et al., supra* note 93 at 232. Justice Cory for one thinks the use of more police officers in schools is a good idea, hindered only by a lack of resources. He said: "No doubt in these circumstances, if financial resources permitted it, a security officer might be employed by the school and would, unless violence was threatened, be present and sit passively in the office" (*R. v. M. (M.R.), supra* note 17 at 426–27).

97 *Canadian Charter of Rights and Freedoms,* Part 1 of the *Constitution Act, 1982,* being Schedule B to the *Canada Act 1982* (U.K.), 1982, c. 11, s. 9.

98 *Chromiak v. The Queen* (1980), 12 C.R. (3d) 300; according to the decision of *Re B.C. Motor Vehicle Act,* [1985] 2 S.C.R. 486, arbitrarily detaining or imprisoning an individual is another example of depriving an individual of his or her right to liberty, in breach of the principles of fundamental justice found in s. 7.

99 *Supra* note 97, s. 10.

Section 10 comes into play as soon as a student is detained and interrogated on any matter that could result in criminal charges. It appears that the everyday matters of school discipline involving detention would not be subjected to section 10 considerations. In the 1985 case of *R. v. H.*,[100] the judge of the Provincial Court of Alberta, Youth Division, said:

> I think it is unlikely that parliament intended that the rights prescribed by Section 10 of the *Charter* would extend to the type of detention imposed as a normal disciplinary measure upon a school student. An ordinary school detention usually does not involve any legal consequences.[101]

The Supreme Court, in *R. v. M. (M.R.)*, said that section 10 did not apply to the student's detention because section 10 "was not meant to apply to relations between students and teachers, but rather to relations between individuals and the state, usually focused upon the investigation of a criminal offense."[102] The logic is confounding since the case of M. was just that: a relationship between an individual and the state with a focus on a criminal investigation.

In 1991 the British Columbia Youth Court ruled that a student's right under section 10 had been infringed when a student was detained by school officials and later charged with possession of marijuana.[103] The student was suspected of possessing drugs and had been advised to talk to the school counsellor as a person who could be trusted. During the discussion, the student handed over to the counsellor a cigarette package containing marijuana. School officials then contacted the police without informing the student of his right to counsel. The court ruled that the accused was detained at the time of his conversation with the counsellor and since his right to counsel was never made clear to him, his rights under section 10(b) of the *Charter* had been infringed. As a result, the evidence was not allowed to be entered in court because it had been obtained illegally.[104]

The court noted that the school officials had two options open to them. They could have handled the matter under the *Schools Act* or they could have involved the police. Since they chose the latter course of action, section 10 came into effect. The court warned that school officials cannot take advantage of their positions to do for the police what the police cannot do themselves. The distressing legacy of *R. v. M. (M.R.)* is just that, school officials can take advantage of their positions and do for the police what the police cannot do themselves.

The case of *R. v. H.*[105] also considered the rights of a student under section 10

---

100 *R. v. H.* (1985), 43 Alta. L.R. (2d) 250 (Prov. Ct. Youth Div.).
101 *Ibid.* at 256.
102 *Supra* note 17 at 429.
103 *R. v. J.R.G.* (1991), 22 Charter Rights Decisions, 800-02 (B.C. Youth Ct.).
104 See s. 24 of the *Charter* in the appendix.
105 *Supra* note 100.

of the *Charter*. In this case, a thirteen-year-old student was charged with stealing $65 from his teacher's purse. When the teacher realized that the money was missing, she reported the incident to the vice-principal. The next morning she spoke to her class about the theft and told them that if the money was returned that would be the end of the matter. Some boys came forward, admitted the theft, and returned some of the money. The names of the boys were brought to the attention of the principal by another teacher, whereupon they were told to report to the principal's office, where they were interrogated. The principal, unaware of the agreement the teacher had made with her class, called the police after obtaining an admission from the boys.

The first issue the court had to decide was whether a detention in a principal's office was a detention within the meaning of section 10 of the *Charter*. It ruled that it was, saying: "The word 'detention' conjures up one meaning: the restraint imposed by a teacher or a principal as a disciplinary measure in relation to a student's behaviour at school."[106] The accused in this case was complying with a demand to attend at the principal's office concerning a criminal offence. The court said:

> It is reasonable to believe that a thirteen year old would believe that he had no other choice but to attend [the principal's office]; it is also reasonable to believe that the accused felt compelled to attend because of the possible consequences if he failed to attend. It would not be reasonable to expect a young person to question such a direction or to refuse to comply. *He was aware that he was being investigated by the Principal in respect of his participation in a criminal offence.* Just as most adults would comply with a similar direction by a peace officer in a similar situation, so too would most young persons comply with the direction of a school principal.[107] [Emphasis mine]

The counsel for the accused argued that the rights of the accused under section 10 of the *Charter* had been infringed because the accused had not been informed of his right to counsel. Counsel asked the court to exclude the evidence of the principal and the accomplices under the provisions of section 24 of the *Charter*. Section 24 allows for the exclusion of evidence if it is obtained in a manner that infringes or denies any rights or freedoms guaranteed by the *Charter* and if "the admission of [the evidence] in the proceedings would bring the administration of justice into disrepute."[108] The court agreed and ruled the evidence inadmissible.

The two cases discussed above are in sharp contrast to the Supreme Court's ruling in *R. v. M. (M.R.)*. In *M.* the court ruled that the detention of a student in the principal's office was not a detention within the meaning of section 10. In

---

106 *Ibid.* at 256.
107 *Ibid.* at 257.
108 See s. 24 of the *Charter* in the appendix.

that case, the court ruled that the detention of a student is not the type of detention considered under section 10 since "the accused was already under detention of a kind throughout his school attendance."[109] The analogy of schools to jail cannot be lost. By attending school, it seems, students can be detained without being informed of their rights and face possible criminal justice consequences.

A particularly tragic outcome to the detention and questioning of students was played out on December 11, 1997, when Kenneth Au Yeung, a Toronto student, committed suicide. Au Yeung was questioned about a school yearbook prank in which a passage was altered to link a longtime choir director at the school with a recent sex scandal at Maple Leaf Gardens, the home of the National Hockey League team the Toronto Maple Leafs. The principal called in an off-duty police officer to question Au Yeung. The student asked to contact his parents but was told that the meeting was informal. Hours later Au Yeung killed himself. A coroner's inquest recommended that

the principal, or acting staff member in charge, must notify parents of students under the age of 18 whenever a serious breach of discipline occurs, when a criminal investigation is commenced, when extremely unusual situations arise, or when in doubt about a situation.[110]

The Supreme Court said:

[A] detention within s. 10 of the *Charter* [occurs] when a police officer or other agent of the State assumes control over the movement of a person by a demand or direction which may have significant legal consequence and which prevents or impedes access to counsel.[111]

Once a decision has been made not to handle a possible criminal matter under the *School Act* but to call in the police, parents or guardians are to be notified. The important thing to remember is that once the police are involved section 10 comes into force. In such cases, the interrogation of students and the collection of evidence are best handled by the justice system, not by the school.

Conclusion

Extending legal rights to students tests our resolve and commitment to empowering students. Perhaps it is the empowerment that these rights represent that causes their development to move forward in fits and starts. But it must not

---

109 *J.M.G., supra* note 15 at 712.
110 "Dissecting a Tragedy: The Jury Rules on the Suicide of a Choirboy" *Maclean's* (20 July 1998) 15.
111 *R. v. Therens,* [1985] 1 S.C.R. 613 at 641–42.

be forgotten that the legal rights discussed here are the very same rights we as adults demand for ourselves.

One of the testiest areas in student rights involves upholding the rights of students who may have drugs or other illegal substances at school. But protecting the rights of everyone, regardless of their status in society, is exactly what human rights laws are all about. As one writer noted, "Human rights is not an abstract field of study. It is a field of work."[112] And there is no doubt that upholding student rights makes more work for educational administrators.

The courts have been unpredictable in granting students their rights to be protected from unreasonable search and seizure and from unreasonable detention. But, as I have argued above, it is only fair to grant to students the same protection we all expect for ourselves. If a student is suspected of being in possession of an illegal substance and it is deemed necessary to conduct a search, school authorities have two choices: they can conduct the search themselves and deal with the discipline themselves, or they can call in the police and leave the search to them. The important question to be asked is whether the police would be brought in if an illegal substance were to be found. If the answer is yes, the advice is to let the police do the search. It is to be hoped that the decision to call in the police and let the wheels of criminal justice roll will only be put into effect once school authorities have reflected on the student's history, circumstances, and the long-term consequences of their decision.

112 Richard Pierre Claude & Burns H. Weston, eds., *Human Rights in the World Community: Issues and Action,* 2nd ed. (Philadelphia: University of Pennsylvania Press, 1992) at xii.

Chapter 11 ■
Corporal Punishment

Corporal punishment has been a means of disciplining students since the inception of formal education. Its roots lie in the doctrine of original sin. One scholar wrote:

> To a large extent, it has been the social and religious views of the time which have helped to determine the nature of school discipline. . . . Under theological auspices the doctrine of original sin cast over childhood and the schools a shadow not to be dispelled until this century.[1]

Today it is generally thought that corporal punishment is no longer used in schools. This is not the case. In Canada, only the provinces of British Columbia, Quebec, and New Brunswick and the territory of the Yukon prohibit its use by way of statute.[2] As well, a few school boards across the country have taken the initiative and banned its use, while some are debating its usefulness. In general, though, corporal punishment is still used across Canada to punish students. The belief that corporal punishment is a thing of the past may be due to the fact that the term is so closely associated with the strap, but corporal punishment includes a wide variety of other controlling and painful methods of discipline.

Corporal punishment is defined as "the use of physical force with the intention of causing a child to experience pain but not injury, for purposes of correction or control of the child's behaviour."[3] The definition describes a number of behaviours and includes

---

1   Charles E. Philips, *The Development of Education in Canada* (Toronto: Gage, 1957) at 527.
2   The Saskatchewan Department of Education considered amending the *Education Act* by stating "no principal, teacher, or other person who has the authority to discipline students shall strike at the pupil or use a strap, cane, or other object for the purposes of administering discipline by way of corporal punishment" (Jason Warick, "Corporal Punishment in Schools on Way Out" *The [Saskatoon] StarPhoenix* (19 February 1997) A1). The amendment did not proceed because the government's polling found that adults were split in their support for such an amendment. Despite the banning of corporal punishment in other provinces, judges, as will be discussed below, have found ways around these laws.
3   M.A. Straus & D.A. Donnelly, "Corporal Punishment of Adolescents by American Parents" (1993) 24 Youth and Society 419 at 420, cited in Joan E. Durrant & Linda Rose-Krasnor, *Corporal Punishment: Research Review and Policy Recommendations* (Winnipeg: University of Manitoba Press, 1995).

1) spanking or slapping administered to the hand, clothed buttocks, or leg; 2) grab-bing or shoving with more force than is needed; 3) shaking or pulling hair; 4) hit-ting or slapping of the head, face, or bare buttocks; and/or 5) hitting with belts, paddles, hair brushes, sticks and other objects.

Other forms of corporal punishment include confinement, deprecation of food, forcing a child to stand or kneel for a long period of time, forcing a child to maintain an uncomfortable or painful position or to hold weights, and forcing a child to eat noxious substances.[4]

The definition includes a variety of forceful practices, including taping a child's mouth shut;[5] taping a child to a desk;[6] and applying karate chops to the face of a student.[7] Restraining a student, however, is not corporal punishment if it is done for the protection of the student or of others.[8] The central factor in defining corporal punishment is that it inflicts discomfort for the purpose of correction.[9] Its utility is "historically justified by the desired outcome of degradation."[10]

---

4   Durrant & Rose-Krasnor, *ibid.* at 1–2.

5   "Teacher Gets Suspended Sentence" *The [Saskatoon] StarPhoenix* (4 January 1996) A8. A Newfoundland teacher was convicted of assault after an eleven-year-old girl, diagnosed with attention-deficit disorder, had her mouth taped shut on two separate occasions. The teacher was placed on six months' probation; see also "Teacher Granted Discharge" *The [Saskatoon] StarPhoenix* (7 May 1996) A12. The Newfoundland teacher was given an absolute discharge for taping a child's mouth shut. The child had Downs syndrome.

6   "School Board Admits Teacher Taped Girl to Desk" *The [Saskatoon] StarPhoenix* (24 April 1996) C15. A Newfoundland teacher taped an eight-year-old girl to her desk. This was the third case involving Newfoundland teachers using tape to control students, see *ibid.*

7   "Ban on Strapping Urged" *The [Saskatoon] StarPhoenix* (10 June 1996) A1. A high school principal in New Brunswick disciplined a group of male students with karate chops.

8   For example, s. 37 of the *Criminal Code* states: "Everyone is justified in using force to defend himself or any one under his protection from assault, if he uses no more force than is necessary to prevent the assault or the repetition of it" (*Criminal Code, R.S.C. 1985*). Teachers have argued in support of s. 43 of the *Criminal Code* because they are worried that if it is removed they will not be protected from charges of assault when they break up fights (see Bonnie Braden, "Stopping Fights Legally Risky, Say Principals" *The [Saskatoon] StarPhoenix* (April 1995) A10). However, they have that defence under s. 37.

9   There have been some tragic results arising from educational disciplinary actions. For example, American Michael Waechter, a grade 5 special education student with a congenital heart defect, died after being ordered to sprint a 350-yard " 'gut run' for talking in line . . . during recess." See *Waechter v. School Dist. No. 14-030*, 773 F. Supp. 1005. 1007 (W.D. Mich. 1991).

10   Anne McGillivray, "'He'll Learn It on His Body: Disciplining Childhood in Canadian Law" (1997) 6 The International Journal of Children's Rights 1 at 1.

The rationale for using corporal punishment is explained by Canadian legal scholar Jeffery Wilson, who noted:

> [T]he underlying basis rests in the common law principle of the parent's rights to discipline and the child's duty to submit. . . . [C]onduct which otherwise might constitute assault is an accepted part of parent/child dynamics.[11]

The authority of school officials to administer corporal punishment is passed on to them through the common-law doctrine of *in loco parentis,* which means "in the place of a parent." The classic statement of this doctrine comes from eighteenth-century legal scholar Sir William Blackstone:

> [A parent] may also delegate part of his parental authority during his life, to the tutor or school master of his child; who is then *in loco parentis*, and has such a portion of the power of the parent committed to his charge, viz.: that of restraint and correction, as may be necessary to answer the purposes for which he is employed.[12]

Corporal punishment has been referred to by some scholars as "legalized assault by adults against children."[13] Normally if a person applies intentional force on another without his or her consent, he or she is guilty of assault. The victim can charge the perpetrator with assault under the *Criminal Code* and/or pursue a civil action and sue for monetary damages. However, students do not have the same recourse. The use of corporal punishment by school personnel has been accepted through common law practice and is condoned by Canada's *Criminal Code.*[14]

Criminal Code

The purpose of the *Criminal Code* is to

> contribute to the maintenance of a just, peaceful and safe society through the establishment of a system of prohibitions, sanctions and procedures to deal fairly and appropriately with culpable conduct that causes or threatens serious harm to individuals or society.[15]

The *Criminal Code* prohibits such actions as theft, defamation, and physical assault. Yet within the *Code* is section 43, an anomaly that allows for the use of

---

11 Jeffery Wilson, *Children and the Law* (Toronto: Butterworth, 1978) at 241.
12 William Blackstone, *Commentaries on the Laws of England* (Baton Rouge: Claitors, 1915) at 453.
13 J.C. Holt, *Escape From Childhood* (New York: E.P. Dutton, 1974).
14 *Supra* note 8, c. C-46.
15 *The Criminal Law in Canadian Society* (Ottawa: Government of Canada, 1982).

force on children. The effect of section 43 is to expose students to harm and to the threat of harm, thus depreciating the *Code*'s purpose of maintaining a just, peaceful, and safe society. Section 43 states:

> Every school teacher, parent or person standing in the place of the parent is justified in using force by way of correction toward the pupil or child, as the case may be, who is under his care, if the force does not exceed what is reasonable under the circumstances.[16]

Section 43 is crucial in maintaining the use of physical force on students because, by its very existence, it portrays this behaviour as acceptable. This section is almost always employed as a defence whenever a teacher is charged with assault and it is extremely successful. For example, in the past few years, section 43 has been used to defend a teacher who hit a student on the head with a hammer;[17] a teacher who hit a nine-year-old girl on her buttocks in front of the class, which according to her mother, left a "bright red hand mark on her left side" about two hours after the incident;[18] and a teacher who forcefully removed

---

16 *Supra* note 8, s. 43.

17 *R. v. Swanson* No. 2945 (Prov. Ct. B.C., 23 June 1993). The hit was hard enough to cause the student to cry out and grab his head. The judge remarked that "[i]n this case no damage or injury worth talking about resulted" (at 6). The judge took time at the beginning of his decision to make reference to other cases that had successfully used s. 43 as a defence but which he believed would not be viewed as acceptable today. Even so, he dismissed any concerns relating to the harm caused the student and commented that "there's no large element of humiliation associated with the punishment, It was not something that was dragged out over a long period of time, and the force of the blow in question was delivered not in anger but in what the evidence has made out to be a measured fashion" (at 6).

18 *R. v. Graham* (15 August 1994) (N.B. Prov. Ct.) [unreported], referred to in Ian Fellows, "Spare the Rod and Spoil the Child" (1995) 6 Education and Law Journal 203. The judge commented that he failed to understand why the case was brought forward in the first place. He quoted the passage "spare the rod and spoil the child" in his decision and justified its use with reference to the *Charter*'s preamble, which states: "Whereas Canada is founded upon principles that recognize the supremacy of God and the rule of law." The judge said: "It is difficult to recognize His supremacy without giving import to His words." The phrase "spare the rod and spoil the child" does not come from the Bible but from Samuel Butler's poem "Hudibras" (1664); see Ian Gibson, *The English Voice, Beating, Sex and Shame in Victorian England and After* (London: Duckworth, 1978) at 49. See also *R. v. Plourde* (1993), 140 N.B.R. (2d) 273 (Prov. Ct.). A charge of assault was laid by two students against their teacher. The judge ruled against them and said, "[T]he defendant had to deal with the insolent behaviour of two students in order to maintain his authority and order in the classroom." The judge relied on s. 43, saying the force did not exceed what was reasonable under the circumstances.

two students from the classroom, shoving one student against the blackboard ledge and bruising his back.[19]

In addition, the law has been used to defend a father who "repeatedly slapped, punched and kicked his 8-year-old son while imprisoning his hands above his head, with sufficient force to leave a sweater imprint on the child's arm and severely bruise his back."[20] In 1995 section 43 was successfully used as a defence in a case involving an allegation of child sexual abuse,[21] and to acquit a father who hit his five-year-old daughter on her bare buttocks after he "thumped" her across the trunk of his car in a public parking lot.[22]

One of the major issues for judges when they are considering cases of assault on children is to determine whether the force used exceeded what was reasonable under the circumstances. The criteria to be considered include the nature of the offence calling for correction; the age and character of the child and the likely effect of the punishment on this particular child; the gravity of the punishment; the circumstances under which it was inflicted; and the injuries, if any, suffered.[23] If the injuries endanger life, limbs, or health, or cause disfigurement, "that alone would be sufficient to find that the punishment administered was unreasonable under the circumstances."[24]

The test itself is an obstacle in that it eclipses the fundamental and substantive

---

19 *Plourde, ibid.*

20 Anne McGillivray, "*R. v. K. (M.)*: Legitimating Brutality" (1993) 16 Criminal Reports 125 at 126, commenting on the case of *R. v. K. (M.)* (1993) 16 Criminal Reports 121.

21 *R. v. W.F.M.* (1995), 169 A.R. 222 (Court of Appeal). A stepfather was accused of sexually assaulting his twelve-year-old stepdaughter. One incident involved the stepfather ordering his stepdaughter to remove her pants and underwear and to lie across his knee so that he could spank her on her bare buttocks. In a split decision, Justice McClung of the three-person Court of Appeal ruled that "s. 43 of the *Criminal Code* . . . [does not dissolve] as a matter of law when a child reaches his or her twelfth birthday." The dissenting judge said that the trial judge's assumption that as long as the spanking was for a disciplinary purpose it could not be a sexual assault was "an incorrect one" (at 234). For a discussion of this case and others, see Mark Carter, "Sexual Assault and the Correctional Force Defense (C.C. s. 43): Relationships of Status in Canadian Criminal Law." Paper presented to the Congress of the Social Sciences and Humanities, Sherbrooke, June 1999.

22 *R. v. Peterson* (1995), 98 C.C.C. (3d) 253 (Ont. C.J. Prov. Div.). In the summer of 1995, an American couple visited Canada with their two children. The oldest child, a five-year-old girl, slammed the car door on her brother's hand. The father administered corporal punishment on the bare buttocks of the girl after placing her across the trunk of the car. He was charged with assault and eventually acquitted because the judge ruled that the assault was not excessive.

23 *R. v. Dupperon* (1985), 43 C.R. (3d) (C.A.) 70 at 78. The accused strapped his thirteen-year-old son on the bare buttocks with a leather belt approximately ten times. He was convicted of assault.

24 *Ibid.*

issue of whether children and students have the right to physical and bodily integrity. In other words, does physical punishment as a means of discipline uphold regard for the personal dignity and integrity of children and students? Also missing from almost all of these cases is an examination of the good, if any, that arises from the use of physical force on children and students. With the advent of the *Charter* and other human rights documents these questions are now being asked. A *Charter* challenge will be heard in the Ontario Court (General Division) in the fall of 1999.[25] The challenge is directed at section 43 of the *Criminal Code* and if successful it will mean that section 43 is of no force or effect. The consequence will be that teachers, parents, and others acting in the place of parents cannot use section 43 as a defence when charged with assaulting a child.

The use of corporal punishment on children and students raises a number of intriguing *Charter* arguments, some of which are being used in the challenge to the constitutionality of corporal punishment. First, does section 43 of the *Criminal Code* discriminate on the basis of age and a child's status, contrary to section 15 of the *Charter*, because it does not provide either equal protection or benefit of the law to children? Second, if it can be shown that corporal punishment is administered in a discriminatory manner, does it infringe section 15 of the *Charter*? Third, is corporal punishment contrary to section 12 of the *Charter*, which prohibits the use of "cruel and unusual punishment"? Fourth, can corporal punishment be ruled unconstitutional because it interferes with a person's right to "liberty" and "security of the person" as protected under section 7 of the *Charter*? If it can be ruled unconstitutional under section 7 of the *Charter*, must it be administered only in accordance with the principles of fundamental justice? Finally, can corporal punishment be justified under section 1 of the *Charter* because it meets a sufficiently important objective?

Equality Rights and Discrimination

Section 15 of the *Charter* provides that every individual has the right to equal protection and equal benefit of the law without discrimination because of age. However, section 43 of the *Criminal Code* uses age as a marker in permitting

---

25   The case was instigated by the author and is currently being argued by the Canadian Foundation for Children, Youth and the Law (Justice for Children and Youth). The case is referred to as *Canadian Foundation for Children, Youth and the Law v. The Attorney General in Right of Canada*. When my *Charter* challenge to s. 43 of the *Criminal Code* became public there was strong reaction all around. See, for example, Jason Warick, "Ex-teacher Fights Ottawa Over Spanking" *The [Saskatoon] StarPhoenix* (23 December 1997) A3; Les Macpherson, "Tax Money Wasted on Costly Court Fights" *The [Saskatoon] StarPhoenix* (3 January 1998) A3; Verne Clemence, "Reform Would Deny Equal Charter Access" *The [Saskatoon] Sun* (7 January 1998) 6; and numerous letters to the editor.

physical force to be exerted upon a person. It approves the use of force as a means of correction to be used on children but not on adults.[26] The *Criminal Code* does not provide a definition of "child" but according to the *Convention on the Rights of the Child,* "a child means every human being below the age of eighteen years unless, under the law applicable to the child, majority is attained earlier."[27] Is the distinction in the *Criminal Code* a violation of section 15?

The first step of a section 15(1) analysis is determining whether the distinction denies "equal protection" or "equal benefit" of the law as compared with some other person. There can be little doubt that the effect of section 43 is that it denies children equal protection and equal benefit of the *Criminal Code.* In fact, in 1984, the Canadian Supreme Court ruled that section 43 denies "equal protection" of the law to some groups.[28] This case was not a *Charter* case—it examined the purpose and effect of section 43—but it is worth considering because it provides insight into the Supreme Court's opinion at that time on the use of corporal punishment.

Mr. Ogg-Moss, a mental retardation counsellor at the Rideau Centre in Ontario, unsuccessfully appealed a conviction of common assault imposed by a lower court. Mr. Ogg-Moss had hit a twenty-one-year-old, developmentally handicapped resident five times on the forehead with a large metal spoon to punish him for spilling his milk. The defence argued unsuccessfully that Mr. Ogg-Moss was protected from a charge of assault under section 43 of the *Criminal Code.* Former Chief Justice Dickson stated:

> [T]he overall *effects* of that section are clear, no matter how its terms are defined. It exculpates the use of what would other-wise be criminal force by one group of persons against another. It *protects* the first group of person, but, it should be noted, at the same time it *removes* the protection of the criminal law from the second.[29] [Emphasis in original]

The court acknowledged that the effect of section 43 is "to deprive a specific individual or groups of the equal protection we normally assume is offered by the criminal law."[30] The use of the phrase "equal protection" is significant because

---

26 Laws used to allow for the use of force on criminals, servants, and wives. Today the only group who can legally be beaten are children.

27 *Convention on the Rights of the Child,* U.N. Doc. A/RES/44/25 (1989). The age of eighteen is a common marker in defining who is a "child." It is used as the age of majority in Canada for purposes of voting. In addition, Saskatchewan legislation establishing the Children's Advocate defines children as being under the age of eighteen. See *The Ombudsman Act,* R.S.S. 1978, c. 0-4; name changed to *The Ombudsman and Children's Advocate Act,* S.S. 1994, c. 7. S. 9.

28 *Ogg-Moss v. The Queen,* [1984] 2 S.C.R, 173 at 183.

29 *Ibid.* at 182.

30 *Ibid.*

this same phrase is used in section 15 of the *Charter.*

Children, including students, are a specific group denied equal protection of the *Criminal Code,* while parents and school personnel are protected in "the use of what would other-wise be criminal force." Section 43 condones unequal treatment between children and adults, which ultimately results in unequal outcomes. The equality rights of students and children are limited or diminished.

Justice McIntyre of the Canadian Supreme Court commented that when considering the concept of equality it may not always be necessary to treat everyone the same, but having said that, he cautioned:

> [T]he main consideration must be the impact of the law on the individual or the group concerned. Recognizing that there will always be an infinite variety of personal characteristics, capacities, entitlements and merits among those subject to a law, there must be accorded, as nearly as may be possible, an equality of benefit and protection and no more of the restrictions, penalties or burdens imposed upon one than another.[31]

Section 43 does not treat everyone the same, nor does it accord equality of benefit or protection. In fact, it exposes children and students to penalties and burdens that could not legally be imposed on another.

The second part of a section 15(1) analysis asks if the distinction constitutes discrimination. That is, does the denial rest on one of the grounds enumerated in section 15(1) or on an analogous ground? Age is an enumerated ground in section 15 of the *Charter.* Unlike some human rights statutes, there is no restricting definition of age in the *Charter.*[32] Therefore, students and children, people between the ages of zero and eighteen years, as well as adults, have the right to equal protection and equal benefit of the law without discrimination on the basis of age.[33]

The distinction provided for under section 43 of the *Criminal Code* constitutes discrimination on the basis of age and the disadvantaged status of children. The historical treatment of children has fed a stereotypical view that using force as a means of correcting their behaviour is appropriate.[34] However, current research

---

31 *Andrews v. Law Society of British Columbia,* [1989] 1 S.C.R. 143.
32 For example, *The Saskatchewan Human Rights Code* defines age as being between the ages of eighteen and sixty-four.
33 I have argued elsewhere that by their historical status children are a "disadvantaged group" as contemplated under s. 15(1) of the *Charter.* Their lack of power, their disenfranchisement, and their historical status as "chattel" expose them to serious abuse and disadvantage. See Ailsa M. Watkinson, "Prohibiting Corporal Punishment: In the Name of the *Charter,* the Child and Societal Values," in Samuel M. Natall & Robert P. Hoffman, eds., *Business Education and Training: A Value-Laden Process: Corporate Structures, Business, and the Management of Values* (Boston: University Press of America, 1998) at 301.
34 See, for example, Samuel X. Radbill, "Children in a World of Violence: A History of Child Abuse," in Ray E. Helfer & Ruth S. Kempe, eds., *The Battered Child,* 4th ed.

demonstrates that using force on children does more harm than good and can no longer be justified.[35] Its continued use and the protection afforded those who use force on children is not based on objective fact but rather on a stereotypical assumption. As will be discussed below, there is scant evidence to support the view that corporal punishment is beneficial and overwhelming research to counter it.

Justice McIntyre of the Supreme Court said:

> Discrimination is unacceptable in a democratic society because it epitomizes the worst effects of the denial of equality, and discrimination reinforced by law is particularly repugnant. The worst oppression will result from discriminatory measures having the force of law. It is against this evil that s. 15 provides a guarantee.[36]

Section 43 of the *Criminal Code* discriminates against children on the basis of their age and status. It is repugnant and oppressive because, as will be discussed below, the harm it causes outweighs any possible good and "the impact of the impugned legislation is to disadvantage the group or individual in a manner which perpetuates the injustice which s. 15(1) is aimed at preventing."[37] Laws or acts of governments or their agents, including school officials, which discriminate against individuals because of their race, national or ethnic origin, colour, religion, sex, age, or mental or physical disability will be ruled unconstitutional unless they can be justified under section 1.

In 1972 the American Supreme Court ruled, in what is considered to be a landmark decision, that capital punishment was unconstitutional.[38] The case was not decided on whether capital punishment constituted cruel and unusual punishment but on whether capital punishment violated the Constitution because it was applied in a discriminatory manner. Justice Douglas, quoting from a President's Commission on Law Enforcement and Administration of Justice, said:

(Chicago: The University of Chicago Press, 1987) c. 1; I. Hyman & J. Wise, eds., *Corporal Punishment in American Education* (Philadelphia: Temple University Press, 1979); Alice Miller, *For Your Own Good: Hidden Cruelty in Child-Rearing and the Roots of Violence,* translated by Hildegarde & Humter Hannum (Toronto: McGraw-Hill Ryerson, 1980); Philip Greven, *Spare the Child: The Religious Roots of Punishment and the Psychological Impact of Physical Abuse* (New York: Alfred A. Knopf, 1991); Michael Freeman, "Whither Children: Protection, Participation and Autonomy" (1994) 22 Man. L. J. 307; Murray A. Straus, *Beating the Devil Out of Them: Corporal Punishment in American Families* (Toronto: Maxwell Macmillan, 1994) and other references used throughout this chapter.

35 See Durrant & Rose-Krasnor, *supra* note 3. The authors surveyed the research on corporal punishment and its effects. They concluded that corporal punishment "is likely to foster, rather than inhibit, the development of aggressive behaviour" (at 10).

36 *Andrews, supra* note 31 at 172.

37 *Miron v. Trudel,* [1995] 2 S.C.R. 418 at 493.

38 *Furman v. Georgia*, 92 S. Ct. 2726 (1972).

[T]here is evidence that imposition of the death sentence and the exercise of dispensing power by the courts and the executive follow discriminatory patterns. The death sentence is disproportionately imposed and carried out on the poor, the Negro, and the members of unpopular groups.[39]

There is evidence to show that boys account for 70 percent of children under the age of twelve who are corporally punished.[40] Children with disabilities also receive more corporal punishment.[41] If it can be shown that corporal punishment is applied in a discriminatory manner—that is, that it is used more often on boys, minorities, or those with disabilities than on others guilty of similar misconduct—it is conceivable that corporal punishment could be ruled discriminatory and thus unconstitutional.

Cruel and Unusual Punishment

Section 12 of the *Charter* states:

> 12. Everyone has the right not to be subjected to any cruel or unusual treatment or punishment.[42]

The Canadian Supreme Court has ruled that corporal punishment is cruel and unusual treatment.[43] It stated:

> [P]unishments must never be grossly disproportionate to that which would have been appropriate to punish, rehabilitate or deter the particular offender or to protect the public from that offender.
>
> . . .
>
> [W]hen a punishment becomes so demeaning that all human dignity is lost, then the punishment must be considered cruel and unusual. At a minimum, the infliction of corporal punishment . . . will not be tolerated.[44]

---

39 *Ibid.* at 2732.

40 Statistics Canada, *Children As Victims of Violent Crime* (Ottawa: Minister of Supply and Services, 1991).

41 Sharon Lohrmann-O'Rourke & Perry Zirkel, "The Case Law on Aversive Interventions for Students with Disabilities" (1998) 65 Exceptional Children 101.

42 *Canadian Charter of Rights and Freedoms,* Part 1 of the *Constitution Act, 1982,* being Schedule B to the *Canada Act 1982* (U.K.), 1982, c. 11, s. 12.

43 *R. v. Smith,* [1987] 1 S.C.R. 1045 at 1074. The accused challenged the constitutional validity of the seven-year minimum sentence for importing narcotics as being cruel and unusual punishment contrary to the *Charter* because of the potential disproportionality of the sentence. The majority of the Supreme Court ruled that the minimum sentence violated s. 12 and could not be justified using s. 1.

44 *Kindler v. Canada,* [1991] 2 S.C.R. 779 at 815, paraphrasing from *Smith, ibid.* The

In coming to this conclusion, the court directed that a central consideration in determining whether a form of punishment is cruel and unusual "is the principle of human dignity which lies at the heart of s. 12. It is the dignity and importance of the individual which is the essence and the cornerstone of democratic government."[45]

Defining whether a treatment or punishment demeans human dignity rests in societal standards, and there are indications that the use of corporal punishment is falling into disrepute. A survey of Canadian adults found that only about 20 percent believed that corporal punishment results in obedience, learning acceptable behaviour, and increased respect.[46] Despite these findings, Canada lags behind many countries by permitting the use of corporal punishment on students. A United Nations document reported that, out of the twenty-seven countries listed in the report, Canada stands as one of only three that still permit corporal punishment in their schools.[47]

The United Nations Committee on the Rights of the Child criticized the Canadian government for permitting the use of force on children.[48] As a signatory to the *Convention on the Rights of the Child*, Canada is to submit a report on the welfare of children to the committee every five years. In June 1995 the committee indicated clearly that physical punishment of children is not compatible with article 19 of the convention, which calls for the protection of children from all forms of physical or mental violence. In addition the committee made reference to article 28, which recognizes the right of the child to an education and assures that appropriate measures will be taken "to ensure that school discipline is administered in a manner consistent with the child's human dignity."[49] The

---

Supreme Court was asked to rule on whether an extradition order could be carried out when the person being extradited faced the death penalty. The court was deeply divided on the issue. The majority ruled that the extradition was allowable using s. 7 of the *Charter.*

45 *Kindler, ibid.* at 812.

46 Joan Durrant, "Public Attitudes Toward Corporal Punishment in Canada." (Paper presented at the International Symposium on Violence in Childhood and Adolescence, Research Centre on Prevention and Intervention in Childhood and Adolescence, University of Bielefeld, Bielefeld, Germany, September 1994).

47 UNICEF, *The Progress of Nations* (New York: United Nations, 1994), cited in Durrant & Rose-Krasnor, *supra* note 3 at 31. Durrant & Rose-Krasnor report that "by 1900 corporal punishment had already been abolished in the schools of Poland, the Netherlands, Luxembourg, Italy, Belgium, Austria, Finland, and France. It has now been abolished in the state-supported schools of every Western European country, including Britain. Other countries that forbid corporal punishment in their schools include China, Cyprus, Ecuador, Hong Kong, Israel, Japan, Jordan, Mauritius, New Zealand, Philippines, Qatar, and Turkey" (at 31).

48 "Canada's Failure to Protect Children's Rights Criticized" *The [Saskatoon] StarPhoenix* (29 May 1995).

49 *The Convention on the Rights of the Child,* U.N. Doc. A/RES/44/25 (1989), art. 28. The committee also made reference to article 37, which commits state parties to

committee expressed its concern over the use of corporal punishment and the ill treatment of children in schools and institutions. The committee recommended that Canada

> examine the possibility of reviewing the penal legislation allowing corporal punishment of children by parents, in schools and in institutions where children are placed [s. 43 of the Criminal Code] . . . [and] consider the possibility of introducing new legislation and follow-up mechanisms to prevent violence . . . and that educational campaigns be launched with a view to changing attitudes in society on the use of physical punishment . . . and fostering the acceptance of its legal prohibition.[50]

A number of widely publicized cases of corporal punishment have been reviewed by the European Court of Human Rights. These cases came forward under the *European Convention on Human Rights*.[51] This convention is binding on the countries of Europe, who are signatories. The *European Convention on Human Rights,* as well as other international conventions, is important in interpreting the meaning of the *Charter*.[52]

Article 3 of the convention states: "[N]o one shall be subjected to torture or to inhuman or degrading treatment or punishment."[53] Under this article, the European Court of Human Rights ruled, in a unanimous decision, that English law failed to protect a boy, who was nine at the time, from ill treatment by his stepfather.[54] The case was brought forward by a British boy who was beaten with a garden cane by his stepfather. The cane-inflicted injuries required the boy to spend some time in hospital. The courts in Britain cleared the stepfather of causing "actual bodily harm." The European Court of Human Rights said: "Children and other vulnerable individuals, in particular, are entitled to State protection, in the form of effective deterrence, against such serious breaches of personal integrity." The court awarded the boy £10,000 (approximately $23,500 Cdn.) and reasonable legal costs. [55] In 1982, the parents of two Scottish schoolboys challenged the

---

ensure that "[n]o child shall be subjected to torture or other cruel, inhuman or degrading treatment or punishment."

50 Concluding Observations of the Committee on the Rights of the Child: Canada. U.N. CRC 9th Sess., 233rd Mtg., U.N. Doc. CRC/C/15/Add. 37 (1995) at 5.

51 *European Convention on Human Rights,* Euop. T.S. No. 5, 213 U.N.T.S. 221.

52 See, for example, A.F. Bayefsky & M. Eberts, eds., *Equality Rights and the Canadian Charter of Rights and Freedoms* (Toronto: Carswell, 1985); F.G. Jacobs, "Non Canadian Constitutional Experience Relevant to The Fundamental Freedoms Provisions of the Charter: The European Convention on Human Rights" (1983) Man. L. J. 13 at 599–604.

53 *Supra* note 51, art. 3.

54 *A. v. United Kingdom* (23 September 1998) (European Crt. of Human Rts.).

55 EPOCH Worldwide (25 September 1998) European Court of Human Rights Case Concerning Parental Corporal Punishment—"*A. v. U.K.*" The full judgement is

authority of school officials to administer corporal punishment, even though neither child had been subjected to it. The court rejected the argument that the possible threat of corporal punishment was "torture" or "inhuman" treatment under article 3 because the applicants' two sons were not in any real or immediate danger. The court did acknowledge, however, that a sufficiently real or immediate threat of conduct prohibited by article 3 may be in conflict with its provisions.[56] In another case, the court ruled that judicial corporal punishment, imposed on a fifteen-year-old child convicted of assaulting another schoolboy, constituted degrading punishment contrary to article 3.[57] In 1993 the English government settled a case for £20,000 (approximately $47,000 Cdn.) and a guarantee that no further suits would be instigated by the plaintiff.[58] The case involved the caning of a schoolboy that had caused severe swelling and bruising,

The courts' interpretations of section 12 of the *Charter* and article 3 of the convention, plus changing attitudes, provide a strong argument that corporal punishment is cruel and unusual treatment, making its use a prime target of a constitutional challenge. The continued use of physical force on students enfeebles society's commitment to the principle of human dignity.

Liberty and Security of the Person

Section 7 of the *Charter* prohibits the government or its agents from depriving a person of "life, liberty, or security of the person, except in accordance with the principles of fundamental justice." A section 7 challenge begins with first, "a finding that there has been a deprivation of the right to 'life, liberty and security of the person' and second, that that deprivation is contrary to the principles of fundamental justice."[59] According to the courts' interpretation of section 7,

---

available on the court's web site at www.dhcour.coe.fr. The British government has banned the use of corporal punishment in schools but seems determined to maintain its use by parents. See " 'Smacking' Here to Stay in Britain" *Ottawa Citizen* (30 September 1998). The article notes that "the landmark decision last week [23 September 1998] sparked an uproar in England where spankings are as traditional as roast beef and Yorkshire puddings" (*supra* note 51).

56 *Campbell and Cosans v. United Kingdom* (1982), 4 European Human Rights Reporter 293 (European Crt. of Human Rts.). The court also ruled that the parents had the right to prohibit school authorities from administering corporal punishment on their children and that the refusal of the school authorities to give assurances that their children would not be subjected to corporal punishment violated their rights under article 2, protocol no. 1 of the *European Convention on Human Rights,* which states in part: "In the exercise of any functions which it assumes in relation to education and to teaching, the state shall respect the right of parents to ensure such education and teaching in conformity with their own religious and philosophical views."

57 *Tyrer v. United Kingdom* (1978), 21 Yearbook 612 (European Crt. of Human Rts.).

58 *Y. v. U.K.* (1993), cited in McGillivray, *supra* note 10 at 31.

59 *R. v. Beare,* [1988] 2 S.C.R. 387 at 401. The respondent argued unsuccessfully that relevant sections of the *Identification of Criminal Act* and the *Criminal Code,* which

corporal punishment appears to be a violation of a person's right to liberty and security of the person.

The Canadian Supreme Court has ruled that liberty includes the right to make fundamental personal decisions that are rooted in the basic concepts of human dignity, personal autonomy, and privacy,[60] and the enjoyment associated with a free and democratic society.[61] In the case of *Ingraham v. Wright*,[62] the American Supreme Court acknowledged that the use of corporal punishment in public schools "implicates a constitutionally protected liberty interest."[63] Former Justice Wilson of the Canadian Supreme Court stated that the term "security of the person" under section 7 "must encompass freedom from the threat of physical punishment or suffering as well as freedom from punishment itself."[64] Security of the person also includes personal autonomy, "at least with respect to the right to make choices concerning one's own body, control over one's physical and psychological integrity, and basic human dignity."[65]

It seems clear from the interpretation given to section 7 that if corporal punishment in a school setting were subjected to a *Charter* challenge under section 7, it would be considered an affront to the liberty right of a student as well as to a student's security and personal integrity. This position is supported by the Supreme Court's ruling that found that section 43 of the *Criminal Code* interferes with a person's right to be free from invasions on his or her physical security that he or she does not consent to.[66]

Perhaps the most telling comment on the Supreme Court's opinion about corporal punishment comes in the judicial rebuttal to the argument, raised in *Ogg-Moss*, that a mentally retarded adult is to be considered a "child" within the meaning of section 43. Former Chief Justice Dickson said this would amount to

> a life sentence, and the consequent attenuation of his right to dignity and physical security is permanent. I cannot believe that it is the intention of the *Criminal Code* to create such a category of permanent second class citizens on the basis of a mental or physical handicap.[67]

provided for the fingerprinting of a person charged with, but not convicted of, an indictable offence, infringed s. 7 of the *Charter*; aff'd in *Pearlman v. Manitoba Law Society Judicial Committee*, [1991] 2 S.C.R. 869 at 881. The Supreme Court of Canada rejected a lawyer's argument that the section of the *Law Society Act* that allows the cost of an investigation into professional misconduct to be awarded against the lawyer was a violation of s. 7 of the *Charter*.

60 *R. v. Morgentaler*, [1988] 1 S.C.R. 30 at 166.
61 *R. v. Jones*, [1986] 2 S.C.R. 284 at 318.
62 *Ingraham v. Wright*, 430 U.S. 651 at 664 (1977).
63 *Ibid.* at 672.
64 *Singh v. M.E.I.*, [1985] 1 S.C.R. 177 at 207.
65 *Rodriguez v. British Columbia (Attorney General)*, [1993] 3 S.C.R. 519.
66 *Ogg-Moss, supra* note 28 at 183.
67 *Ibid.* at 187.

The implication to be drawn for educational purposes is that the rights of students and children to dignity and physical security is attenuated by section 43 of the *Criminal Code* and, as a result, their status is second class.

Once an argument has been made that corporal punishment impedes an individual's right to liberty and security of the person, the second stage of the section 7 analysis comes into force. The second stage is concerned with the possible limiting of these values in accordance with the principles of fundamental justice.[68] However, the principles of fundamental justice cover not only procedural matters but also a substantive interpretation of the principles. The court said that the principles are found in "some consensus that they are vital or fundamental to our societal notion of justice."[69] The court noted that one point that has gained public consensus is the prohibition against capital punishment. This prohibition is supported "on the basis that allowing the state to kill will cheapen the value of human life and thus the state will serve in a sense as a role model for individuals in society."[70] Statistical data show an increasing public consensus for the elimination of corporal punishment.[71] Allowing the state to hit the weakest members of society, children, cheapens the value of children. This has serious consequences because the state is a role model for individuals in society.

The procedural scope of the principles of fundamental justice raises questions about the process used in the administration of corporal punishment. The substantive scope of the principles of fundamental justice supports the elimination of corporal punishment.

In the 1975 case of *Baker v. Owen,* the American Supreme Court affirmed a lower court decision concerning the due process rights of students prior to the administration of corporal punishment.[72] The lower court had set forth minimal due process procedures that accommodated "as best as possible the child's interest with the state's unquestioned interest in effective discipline."[73] The lower court had said that corporal punishment should never be employed before other means of discipline have been tried, and that students must be informed of the specific behaviours that may lead to corporal punishment before it is used. The court also said that the punishment must be administered in the presence of another school official, who must be informed, in the student's presence, of the reasons for the punishment. This would "allow a student to protest, spontaneously, an egregiously arbitrary or contrived application of punishment."[74] Finally, the court had said that the school official who administers the punishment must provide

---

68 *Rodriguez, supra* note 65.
69 *Ibid.* at 590.
70 *Ibid.* at 608.
71 Durrant & Rose-Krasnor, *supra* note 3.
72 *Baker v. Owen*, 395 F. Supp. 294 (M.D.N.C., 1975), aff'd, 423 U.S. 907 (1975).
73 *Ibid.* at 302.
74 *Ibid.*

the child's parent, upon request, with written reasons for the corporal punishment and with the name of the other school official who was present.[75]

In 1977, the Supreme Court considered a second case, *Ingraham v. Wright,*[76] but here the court appeared to contradict its earlier decision. One of the petitioners, who claimed he was innocent of any wrongdoing, was subjected to a "paddling" that was so severe that he required medical treatment and missed eleven days of school due to the injuries. The question before the American Supreme Court was whether the administration of corporal punishment upon public school students, absent a notice of the charges for which the punishment was inflicted and absent an opportunity to be heard, violated the due process clause of the Fourteenth Amendment, which is comparable to section 7 of the *Charter.* The Supreme Court, in a five to four split decision, ruled that procedural due process does not apply to the administration of corporal punishment, since the traditional common-law remedies of laying a charge of assault or seeking damages are fully adequate to afford due process.

This was a surprising turn of events, considering that only two years previously the court had upheld a student's right to procedural due process prior to the administration of corporal punishment by affirming the decision of *Baker v. Owen*[77] and that the court had also ruled that students have a right to procedural due process in matters concerning expulsion and suspension.[78] The court justified its decision by saying:

> Were it not for the common-law privilege permitting teachers to inflict reasonable corporal punishment on children in their care, and the availability of the traditional remedies for abuse, the case for requiring advance procedural safeguards would be strong indeed.[79]

A five to four split decision is an indication of disparate opinions and is often viewed as setting a weak precedent. For this reason, it is worth noting the comments of Justice White, one of the dissenting American Supreme Court judges, who reminded the court:

> The reason that the Constitution requires a state to provide "due process of law" when it punishes an individual for misconduct is to protect the individual from erroneous or mistaken punishment that the state would not have inflicted had it found the facts in a more reliable way.[80]

---

75 *Ibid.*
76 *Supra* note 62.
77 *Supra* note 72.
78 *Goss v. Lopez,* 419 U.S. 565 (1975).
79 *Ingraham, supra* note 62 at 674.
80 *Ibid.* at 692.

Justice White noted that "[i]n this case the record reveals beatings so severe that if they were inflicted on a hardened criminal for the commission of a serious crime, they might not pass constitutional muster."[81] He also denounced the argument that an abused child can later sue the teacher and recover damages, saying:

> The infliction of physical pain is final and irreparable; it cannot be undone in a subsequent proceeding. . . . A student, punished for an act he did not commit, cannot recover damages from a teacher proceeding in utmost good faith . . . on the reports and advice of others; the student has no remedy at all for punishment imposed on the basis of mistaken facts, at least as long as the punishment was reasonable from the point of view of the disciplinarian, uninformed by any prior hearing.[82]

In 1970, the Saskatchewan Court of Appeal did not consider a hearing necessary prior to the infliction of corporal punishment.[83] In this case, Mr. Haberstock, a vice-principal, had been charged with assaulting a student. Mr. Haberstock believed that three students on a school bus had called him names while he was supervising schoolyard activities. When the students returned to school on the following Monday he approached them in the schoolyard and slapped each of them across the face, breaking one boy's tooth. One student alleged he was innocent, as was later confirmed by the courts.[84] However, the judge acquitted Mr. Haberstock of assault, saying:

> The appellant, in punishing [the student], did so in the honest belief that he had participated in the name-calling. Therefore, in my opinion, . . . the appellant was entitled to use force by way of correcting . . . a pupil under his care at the time.[85]

Subjecting a student to corporal punishment because of an "honest belief" that the student has been misbehaving will most certainly not pass a *Charter* challenge. In a recent case, a judge commenting on *Haberstock* opined: "I suspect that today the court would insist that the teacher had embarked upon a reasonable course of inquiry to ascertain if his or her impression was correct before even slapping a student."[86]

The Supreme Court stated that the principles of fundamental justice are based on judicial tenets and practices, one of which is "that the innocent not be

---

81 *Ibid.* at 685.
82 *Ibid.* at 693.
83 *R. v. Haberstock* (1970), 1 C.C.C. (2d) 433 (Sask. C.A.).
84 *Ibid.* at 434.
85 *Ibid.* at 435.
86 *Swanson, supra* note 17 at 2.

punished."[87] In *Singh v. M.E.I.*, former Justice Wilson said:

> If "the right to life, liberty, and security of the person" is properly construed as relating only to matters such as death, physical liberty, and physical punishment, it would seem, on the surface at least, that these are matters of such fundamental importance that procedural fairness would invariably require an oral hearing. . . . Where a serious issue of credibility is involved, fundamental justice requires the credibility be determined on the basis of an oral hearing.[88]

Clearly, procedural fairness in matters relating to life, liberty, and security of the person will be the rule. The courts may decide that the informal "give and take" hearings allowed for in *Goss v. Lopez*[89] are adequate for school settings. Former Justice Wilson acknowledged that less formal procedures may be used in some circumstances when she said, "I am prepared, nevertheless, to accept for present purposes that written submissions may be an adequate substitute for an oral hearing in appropriate circumstances."[90] These comments, along with others made by the Supreme Court, make it clear that the major purpose of section 7 is to uphold the dignity and worth of the human person by ensuring that everyone has the right to a hearing before an unbiased adjudicator so that the innocent are not punished.

Necessary Justification

If the courts agree that the use of force on children violates the *Charter*, the government will have to justify its use under section 1. The government must demonstrate, using empirical, objective evidence, that the use of force on children meets the objective of correcting their behaviour. The government may argue that the sufficiently important objective to be gained by allowing teachers to use force on students is to ensure that they learn correct behaviour, which will facilitate an environment in which learning can take place.

One judge, when considering the legitimacy of corporal punishment, cited with approval the following passage:

> It is important for the teacher to make sure that there is respect for authority; this is part of his responsibility as teacher and educator. The teacher represents authority and it is his duty to make sure he is shown respect. This is part of the duty he owes to the student who lacks respect for him and especially the duty he owes to the rest of the class. . . . If corporal punishment is used, it is necessary to make it effective

---

87   *Re B.C. Motor Vehicle Act*, [1985] 2 S.C.R. 486 at 513.
88   *Singh, supra* note 64 at 213.
89   In *Goss, supra* note 78 at 576, the American Supreme Court ruled that students have the right to a hearing prior to being expelled or suspended from school.
90   *Singh, supra* note 64 at 213.

to a certain degree. Otherwise, far from being a measure salutary to the child, it will become on his part, a cause of indifference, even more than that, of independence and defiance; hence the fault for which the punishment was intended will be repeated to satiety, since his chastisement is lenient.[91]

The judge did not offer any evidence to support his contention that corporal punishment is an appropriate form of discipline, and there is overwhelming evidence to show that he is wrong. Corporal punishment is likely to increase adverse behaviour, as well as endanger students physically and psychologically.

Corporal punishment teaches its victims to obey authority out of fear rather than out of respect. Evidence shows that incidents of violence are more prevalent in schools that use corporal punishment.[92] This correlates with studies that have shown "one of the most consistently shown side effects of corporal punishment is that its victims will more often engage in physically aggressive behaviour than those people who were never subjected to such punishment."[93] This is explained in part because children tend to imitate adults, especially "when the adult's actions are seen as effective in getting what the adult wants."[94]

Ralph Welsh, a clinical psychologist who has worked with thousands of juvenile delinquents for over ten years, has constructed a behavioural model referred to as the "Belt Theory of Juvenile Delinquency." His research found that "nearly all of [his] patients had been struck with a belt or its equivalent in their formative years." And that "the recidivist male delinquent who was never struck with a belt, extension cord, fist, or an equivalent is virtually non-existent."[95]

Studies have also shown a negative and statistically significant relationship between the use of corporal punishment and academic achievements,[96] and that

---

91 *Plourde, supra* note 18, also cited in *Graham, supra* note 18 at 205.

92 Cynthia P. Cohen, "Beating Children Is As American As Apple Pie" (Spring 1978) Human Rights 24 at 26.

93 A. Herman, "A Statutory Proposal to Prohibit the Infliction of Violence Upon Children" (1985) 19 Family L.Q. 1 at 32, cited in David J. Messina, "Corporal Punishment v. Classroom Discipline—Mistaken Identity" (1988) 34 Loyola Law Review 35 at 67.

94 Herman, *ibid.* at 34–35.

95 Ralph S. Welsh, "Spanking: A Grand Old American Tradition?" in (1986) *National Association of Social Workers, Spare the Rod?! A Resource Guide: Alternatives to Corporal Punishment* 14 at 15, cited in Messina, *supra* note 93 at 68–69. Welsh has suggested that every belt manufacturer be required to stamp a warning on the back of the belt: "*Danger!* The Surgeon General Has Determined That the Use of This Implement on Your Child is Dangerous to His Mental Health, and May Contribute to Delinquency, Wife Abuse, and Heart Disease—and Regret You Ever Had Children in the First Place" (Messina at 69, footnote 173).

96 Varghese I. Cherian, "Corporal Punishment and Academic Achievement of Xhosa Children from Polygamous and Monogamous Families" (1994) 134 The Journal of Social Psychology 387.

high school dropouts "were more likely to have experienced moderate to severe corporal punishment than were college students or professionals."[97] Other studies have found a positive association between the frequency of corporal punishment and both psychological distress and depression.[98]

Research among samples of preschoolers, school-aged children, and adolescents on the use of corporal punishment in the home has found that there is a linear relationship between frequency of spanking and frequency of aggression towards siblings and parents;[99] that children who have received physical punishment are more than twice as likely to repeatedly and severely attack a sibling than are those who have not been physically punished;[100] that juveniles who received physical punishment as children are three times as likely to assault non-family members than those who did not receive this form of discipline; that people who were frequently physically punished have a higher likelihood of assaulting their spouses;[101] and that theft rates are higher among juveniles who have been physically punished than among those who have not been so disciplined.[102] Longitudinal studies confirm the correlation between the use of physical punishment on children and violent/aggressive behaviour when they become adults.[103]

Philip Greven, author and cofounder of EPOCH-USA, asserts that one of the most enduring consequences of physical punishment is "the stifling of empathy and compassion for oneself and others."[104] In a more recent study, researchers found that when parents use corporal punishment to reduce anti-social behaviour, the long-term effect tends to be the opposite regardless of the parents' socio-economic status, their ethnicity, the gender of the child, or whether the parents

---

97   Durrant & Rose-Krasnor, *supra* note 3 at 6.

98   Heather A. Turner, "Corporal Punishment as a Stressor Among Youth" (February 1996) 58 Journal of Marriage and the Family 155.

99   L. Eron, "Parent-Child Interaction, Television Violence, and Aggression of Children" (1982) 37 American Psychologist 197; R.E. Larzelere, "Moderate Spanking: Model or Deterrent of Children's Aggression in the Family?" (1986) 1 Journal of Family Violence 27, referred to in Durrant & Rose-Krasnor, *supra* note 3.

100   Murray Straus, "Ordinary Violence, Child Abuse, and Wife Beating: What Do They Have in Common?" in D. Finkelhor, R. Gelles, G. Hotaling, & M. Straus, eds., *The Dark Side of Families: Current Family Violence Research* (Beverly Hills, CA: Sage, 1983), referred to in Durrant & Rose-Krasnor, *ibid.*

101   Data from a National Family Violence Survey reported in Durrant & Rose-Krasnor, *ibid.* at 6.

102   Murray Straus, "Discipline and Deviance: Physical Punishment of Children and Violence and Other Crime in Adulthood" 38 Social Problems 133, referred to in Durrant & Rose-Krasnor, *ibid.*

103   See Durrant & Rose-Krasnor, *ibid.* at 7, for a discussion of these studies and their findings.

104   *Supra* note 34 at 127.

provide a satisfactory social and emotional environment.[105]

A seventeen-member commission of leading childcare experts and lawyers, set up to look into the killing of a toddler by two young boys in Britain, concluded that physical punishment is a significant factor in the development of violent attitudes and actions by children. The commission recommended a ban on corporal punishment and stated that "violent tendencies begin in childhood and are made worse by the 'macho male attitudes' in society."[106]

Recently, lawyers for a father charged with assaulting his daughter[107] canvassed more than twenty experts, hoping to find one who would say that the accused's act was not harmful to the child. None would testify to this effect because "professionals who study child abuse and corporal punishment are unanimously against spanking because it is violent, its effectiveness is based on fear and it sends the wrong message."[108]

Joan Durrant, a professor and child clinical psychologist, and Linda Rose-Krasnor, a psychology professor, concluded from their extensive review of the literature concerning the impact of corporal punishment that "the use of physical force by parents [and educators] serves as a model, rather than an inhibitor of aggression in children"[109] and that "the degree to which a society legitimizes the use of physical force through . . . corporal punishment the higher will be its rate of criminal violence."[110]

One writer has commented:

> [N]othing is a clearer statement of the position that children occupy in society, nor a clearer badge of childhood, than the fact that children are the only members of society who can be hit with impunity. There is probably no more significant step

---

105 Murray A. Straus & David B. Sugarman, "Spanking by Parents and Subsequent Anti-Social Behaviour in Children" (1997) 151(8) Archives of Pediatrics and Adolescent Medicine 761. See also (1997) 7:4 Children's Legal Rights Journal (Special Issue: Corporal Punishment).

106 Glenda Cooper, "Experts Urge Ban on Smacking Children" *The [U.K.] Independent* (9 November 1995) 3. The article was reporting the findings of the Commission on Children and Violence (Gulbenkian Foundation, London, England, November 1995). Sir William Utting, chairperson of the commission, said: "We must develop a culture which disapproves of all forms of violence to children. . . . All the lessons of my working life point to the fact that violence breeds misery; it does not resolve it."

107 *Peterson, supra* note 22.

108 Robert Hercz, "Bum Rap" *Saturday Night* (November 1995) 20. The trial and publicity had an effect on the parents who reported that they have not spanked their children since.

109 *Supra* note 3 at 8.

110 *Ibid.* at 10.

that could be taken to advance both the status and protection of children than to outlaw the practice of physical punishment.[111]

In its decision in *Ogg-Moss,* the Supreme Court said that "unless the force is 'by way of correction' that is, for the benefit of the education of the child, the use of force will not be justified."[112] According to the extensive research conducted by Durrant and Rose-Krasnor, there is no study that shows a child benefits from the use of corporal punishment.

Conclusion

Removing section 43 of the *Criminal Code* would take away a societal standard that tolerates physical force on children and, as research has shown, contributes to the abuse of children. One of the main factors contributing to the maltreatment of children is cultural acceptance of corporal punishment.[113] The inclusion of section 43 in the *Criminal Code* is Canada's cultural statement that using physical force on children is acceptable.

It is important to note that the removal of section 43 would not remove all defences to an assault already provided for in the *Criminal Code.* Sections 34, 35, 37, 38, 39, and 41 of the *Criminal Code* protect persons using physical force in response to violent or dangerous behaviour directed at themselves or others. Restraint is not a form of corporal punishment and therefore if section 43 were removed, it would not prevent a parent or teacher from using force to restrain another if it were done for the purposes of protection.

The continued reliance on corporal punishment as a means of correcting a child's behaviour is an anomaly. As a society we have agreed to protect children, the most vulnerable among us, yet we use adult strength to hit them for their own good! Not only is such behaviour an absolute affront to a child's personal security and dignity—a violation of his or her rights—but in the long term it does more harm than good.

---

111 Michael Freeman, "The Convention: An English Perspective" in Michael Freeman, ed., *Children's Rights: A Comparative Perspective* (Brookfield, USA: Dartmouth Publishing Company, 1996) 93 at 100.

112 *Supra* note 28 at 193.

113 J. Kaufman & E. Zigler, "The Prevention of Child Maltreatment: Programming, Research and Policy" in D.J. Willis, E.W. Holden, & M. Rosenberg, eds., *Prevention of Child Maltreatment: Development and Ecological Perspectives* (New York: John Wiley, 1992).

Chapter 12 ■
Conclusion

In Mordecai Richler's classic children's story *Jacob Two-Two Meets the Hooded Fang*, Jacob Two-Two finds himself charged with insulting behaviour to a big person. His misdemeanour was asking the store clerk for a bag of tomatoes, twice. Jacob Two-Two always repeated his sentences because he was the youngest in a family of seven and was often ignored. He was brought before Mr. Justice Rough, who, it must be said, had little or no patience with children. Justice Rough considered the matter before him to be extremely serious, and he had no intention of letting Jacob Two-Two get away with anything because leniency could lead to more monstrous crimes:

> Mr. Justice Rough paused and knit his fierce brows. "Once and for all, children must be taught—"
>
> "THAT BIG PEOPLE ARE NEVER NEVER WRONG," all the big people in the court shouted back.
>
> . . .
>
> "Jacob Two-Two," [the judge] continued, turning to the accused, "I should warn you that in this court, as in life, little people are considered guilty, unless they can prove themselves innocent, which is just short of impossible."[1]

The tale of Jacob Two-Two is both endearing and poignant. It illustrates the all-too-prevalent lack of respect accorded children and youth. If a class of persons such as women, Aboriginal people, or religious minorities were treated in the same manner, we would have no problem identifying the treatment as wrong and perhaps labelling the treatment as sexist or racist. We don't even have a word to describe the lack of regard for children and youth. It is so commonplace.

The protection of the rights of children and youth is based on the assumption that every person is endowed with an inherent dignity. This dignity empowers people and it protects them. The Supreme Court said: "It is the dignity and importance of the individual which is the essence and the cornerstone of democratic government."[2] Human dignity is not a status to be earned, it is an inherent right. The purpose of the *Charter* and other human rights documents is

---

1   Mordecai Richler, *Jacob Two-Two Meets the Hooded Fang* (Toronto: Puffin Books, 1975) at 19–21.
2   *Kindler v. Canada,* [1991] 2 S.C.R. 779 at 812.

to affirm and protect society's recognition of the inherent dignity of each person.[3] The rights and freedoms entrenched in the *Charter* extend to "everyone" and to "every person."[4] There are no exceptions for slaves, wives, children, or students.[5]

Students have rights. The sorts of rights referred to as student rights include the fundamental freedom to practice one's religion, to be free from religion, and not to be forced to practise another's religion; freedom of thought, opinion, and expression; and the right to gather in groups. Students have the legal right to life, liberty, and security of the person, and the right not to be denied these rights without first being granted a fair hearing; a limited right to be secure against unreasonable search and seizure; the right not to be arbitrarily detained and the right to be informed of the reason for the detention; as well as the right not to be subjected to any cruel and unusual treatment or punishment. The equality rights provision in the *Charter* means that students are protected from discrimination in education.

The idea of student rights is not new. It has been evolving, somewhat fitfully, since the American decision of *Tinker v. Des Moines*.[6] Progress has been slow for two reasons. First, those who advocate for the advancement of student rights have relied, perhaps too heavily, on the courts to pave the way, only to find that the courts in cases of "law and order" have tended to defer to educators. But judges change and they bring with them their own life experiences, impressions, interpretations, and ideologies.[7] In Canada, as in the United States, there have been important ideological changes in the decisions arising from the Supreme Court.

The first *Charter* cases heard by the Supreme Court created a climate of interpretation that promoted empathy and caring in decisions. Their trail-blazing decisions have had and will continue to have a lasting effect on the *Charter*'s interpretation. In subsequent years, however, there was a tempering of this trail-blazing attitude. Although recent decisions have returned to a more expansive interpretation of the *Charter,* it is clear that courts on their own cannot be relied

---

3   For example, the objectives of *The Saskatchewan Human Rights Code,* C.S. 24.1 as amended, are (a) to promote recognition of the inherent dignity and the equal inalienable rights of all members of the human family; and (b) to further public policy in Saskatchewan that every person is free and equal in dignity and rights and to discourage and eliminate discrimination.

4   These words are used throughout the *Charter* in its listing of who is entitled to the rights and freedoms listed in it.

5   Historically these groups were denied status as persons endowed with rights.

6   *Tinker v. Des Moines,* 393 U.S. 502 (1969).

7   See, for example, *R. v. K. (M.)* (1993), 16 C.R. 121, in which the judge deemed the case before him, a charge of assault against a parent who had kicked his son, a waste of time. He said, "The discipline adminstered to the boy in question . . . was mild indeed compared to the discipline I received in my home" (at 122). See also *Vriend et al. v. Alberta* (1996), 181 A.R. 16, and Judge McClung's comments on gay rights.

upon to provide substantive and continuous change.[8] Second, educational theory and practice continue to follow the authoritarian model, and it is the democratic model that is a prerequisite for the recognition of student dignity and the promotion of student rights.

The willingness of educational professionals to promote student rights is encumbered by the conflicting values of teacher professionalism and democracy. Amy Gutmann, a professor at Princeton, described the conflict as a tension between the professional autonomy of teachers and the perceived erosion of their competence when students influence the form or content of their own education.[9] But things are changing. More writers and practitioners in the realm of education are promoting and realizing a caring and community-oriented democratic school environment.[10] Perhaps with the help of both progressive court decisions and changing educational paradigms student rights will be fully realized.

The Impact of the Courts

The courts have played an important role in providing an impetus to transform education and its administration. The courts have interpreted the equality rights and fundamental freedoms in the *Charter* in a manner that is contextual. Their decisions have underscored the need to listen carefully to others, the need to strive for a more equitable and humane society, and if necessary, the need to upset the status quo. As a result of recent court decisions, empathy, passion, and sympathy—an ethic of care response—have begun to play a major role in educational decision-making. The importance placed on listening carefully to

---

8   Examples of tempered decisions include *Thibaudeau v. Canada*, [1995] 2 S.C.R. 627. In a split decision the court ruled that sections of the *Income Tax Act*, which requires that a separated or divorced parent include any amounts of money received in alimony as income for taxation purposes while allowing the parent who pays alimony to claim it as a deduction, did not infringe the equality rights section of the *Charter; Egan v. Canada*, [1995] 2 S.C.R. 513; *Eaton v. Brant County Board of Education*, [1997] 1 S.C.R. 241. More recent expansive decisions include *Eldridge v. British Columbia (Attorney General)*, [1997] 3 S.C.R. 624, and *Vriend v. Alberta* (1998), S.C.J. No. 25285.

9   Amy Gutmann, *Democratic Education* (New Jersey: Princeton University Press, 1987) at 88.

10 See, for example, *The Adaptive Dimension in Core Curriculum* (Regina: Saskatchewan Department of Education, 1992); David Purpel, *The Moral and Spiritual Crisis in Education: A Curriculum for Justice and Compassion in Education* (Massachusetts: Bergin and Garvey, 1989); Thomas J. Sergiovanni, *Leadership for the Schoolhouse: How Is It Different? Why Is It Important?* (San Francisco: Jossey-Bass, 1996); Lynn G. Beck, *Reclaiming Educational Administration As a Caring Profession* (New York: Teachers College Press, 1994); Thomas B. Greenfield, "The Decline and Fall of Science in Educational Administration" (1986) 17:2 Interchange 57.

others, on allowing those who historically have been left out a place and a say, is democratizing because it "challenges the politics of elites and masses."[11] The courts' interpretation of the *Charter* has an impact on all members of the educational community.

On Students

In order to clearly understand the scope of student rights under the *Charter* it is necessary to consider once again the *Charter*'s purpose. The Canadian Supreme Court has stated that purpose of the *Charter* is to ensure that Canadian society is free and democratic, and that the rights and freedoms enshrined within it are to be interpreted within the values and principles of a democratic society. The Supreme Court said that the values and principles include respect for the inherent dignity of all persons, a commitment to justice and equality, accommodation of a wide variety of beliefs, and respect for group and cultural differences.[12] The constitutional and democratic rights of students are framed by these values and principles. The limiting of student rights under section 1 of the *Charter* is to be accomplished within this same framework. Educators can limit the rights of students if the need to do so meets a sufficiently important objective and if the limit is cognizant of the students' inherent dignity and is concomitant with the principles of justice, equality, and the accommodation of beliefs.

The push for student rights in Canada over the past fifteen years has had many noteworthy successes. In addition, the decisions of the courts have expanded upon the *Charter*'s meaning to provide support for those advocating for student rights. For example, the courts are amenable to upholding the fundamental rights of students. They have recognized fundamental freedoms as being the cornerstone of a democracy and they have not been persuaded by educational rhetoric or administrative convenience of the need to limit these rights. *Charter* decisions have ruled school prayer and religious exercises to be unconstitutional.[13] These rulings have gone so far as to include the right of a student not to be "forced to act in a way contrary to his belief or his conscience"[14] by way of coercion.[15] This

---

11 Benjamin Barber, *Strong Democracy: Participatory Politics for a New Age* (Berkeley: University of California Press, 1984). Barber distinguishes between "thin democracy" and "strong democracy." Thin democracy is individualistic and for private ends. It lacks a firm foundation in citizenship, participation, public good, or civic virtue (at 4). Strong democracy is communal and "contrives to live together communally not only to [human] mutual advantage but also to the advantage of [human] mutuality" (at 118).

12 *R. v. Oakes,* [1986] 1 S.C.R. 103 at 136.

13 *Zylberberg et al. v. Sudbury Board of Education* (1988), 29 O.A.C. 23; *Russow v. British Columbia (A.G.)* (1989), 35 B.C.L.R. (2d) 29; *Canadian Civil Liberties Association v. Ontario (Minister of Education)* (1990), 71 O.R. (2d.) 341 (Ont. C.A.).

14 *R. v. Big M Drug Mart Ltd.,* [1985] 1 S.C.R. 295.

15 *Zylberberg, supra* note 13.

means that using the public school system to manifest Christianity, even though excusal clauses allow those who do not wish to participate to be excused, has a coercive effect and is unconstitutional.[16] In reaching their decisions the courts were particularly concerned with the effect of majoritarian power on minority students. One court expressed the need for educational decision-makers to stand in the shoes of the powerless before making their decisions.[17]

The Canadian Supreme Court has ruled that liberty includes the right to make fundamental personal decisions that are rooted in the basic concepts of human dignity, personal autonomy, and privacy,[18] and the enjoyment associated with a free and democratic society.[19] The implication to be drawn for educational purposes is that the rights of students and children to dignity and personal autonomy are attenuated by the use of many forms of physical force on students in school and by other abuses of power.

Suspensions or expulsions may violate students' right to an education if these forms of discipline do not conform to the principles of fundamental justice. The principles of fundamental justice oblige school authorities to give a student whose rights are abridged reasonable notice of a hearing into the matter; an opportunity for an exchange of arguments and the cross-examination of witnesses before an impartial adjudicator or judge; proof, presented by the school authority, of the need to deprive the right; and a review of the order before its expiry date.[20]

But the courts' interpretation of a student's legitimate right not to be subjected to unreasonable search and seizure has been limited. The Canadian Supreme Court ruled that "a student's reasonable expectation of privacy in the school environment is . . . significantly diminished" because of the expectation that teachers and school officials will ensure a safe environment in schools.[21] This decision, as it now stands, robs students of the rights they have elsewhere in the community. The effect is that student rights are more limited in the very institution that, in theory at least, is to prepare youth for democratic citizenship.[22]

Court decisions, especially in the area of equality, have underlined the true meaning of educational equality. Equal treatment or equal opportunity is not enough. In fact, treating everyone the same can exact inequality. The courts' interpretation of equality—an equality that includes equality of results—forces

---

16 The exceptions, as discussed in chapter 4, are Alberta and Saskatchewan.

17 *Zylberberg, supra* note 13 at 34.

18 *R. v. Morgentaler*, [1988] 1 S.C.R. 30 at 166.

19 *R. v. Jones*, [1986] 2 S.C.R. 284 at 318.

20 *B. (R.) v. Children's Aid Society of Metropolitan Toronto*, [1995] 1 S.C.R. 315 at 377 & 380.

21 *R. v. M. (M.R.)*, [1998] 3 S.C.R. 393 at para. 33.

22 See Ailsa M. Watkinson, "Suffer the Little Children Who Come into School," in Juanita Ross Epp & Ailsa M. Watkinson, eds., *Systemic Violence: How Schools Hurt Children* (London: Falmer Press, 1996).

educators to consider individuals and their particular circumstances and to reflect on whether the education presented to the students is meeting their individual needs.

Any limits placed on student rights and freedoms through policies, procedures, or regulations are to be justified within the values and principles of respect for the inherent dignity of students, a commitment to justice and equality, the accommodation of a wide variety of beliefs, and respect for group and cultural differences. The onus placed on educational decisions-makers to justify their actions provides students with an opportunity to carefully scrutinize and evaluate such decisions.

On Educators

A school is a communication for a whole range of values and aspirations of a society. In large part, it defines the values that transcend society through the education medium. The school is an arena for the exchange of ideas and must, therefore, be premised upon principles of tolerance and impartiality so that all persons within the school environment feel equally free to participate.[23]

"All persons within the school environment" most certainly includes students. And if schools are an arena for the exchange of ideas, then it is imperative that students be given the opportunity to participate in education in a way that is congruent with democratic principles. But respect for equality and fundamental freedoms on their own do not a democratic educational environment make. The educational setting must be infused with tangible evidence of respect for the dignity of everyone, and with justice, equality, and caring. These are required of "all persons within the school environment."[24]

The responsibility placed on educators to uphold the rights of students requires of educators some special personal characteristics: the ability to empathize with youth, a demonstrated regard for the inherent dignity of the human person, an ability to listen and put oneself in the shoes of another, and if necessary, a willingness to change. As the courts have noted, teachers play a vital role in the school system: "Teachers are inextricably linked to the integrity of the school system. Teachers occupy positions of trust and confidence, and exert considerable influence over their students as a result of their positions."[25] Their image, grounded in their character, sets the tone in a school. The French philosopher Albert Schweitzer is credited with having said, "Modeling is not the best way to teach. It is the only way to teach." Without a doubt, this is a heavy load for teachers to take on, but it is crucial in maintaining a credible and accessible education system.

---

23 *Ross v. School District No. 15,* [1996] 1 S.C.R. 825 at 856–57.
24 *Ibid.*
25 *Ibid.* at 857.

In *Ross,* the Supreme Court quoted with approval the following excerpt from a legal journal:

> Teachers are a significant part of the unofficial curriculum because of their status as "medium." In a very significant way the transmission of prescribed "messages" (values, beliefs, knowledge) depends on the fitness of the "medium" (the teacher).[26]

Teachers, administrators, and others who work with students in this day and age of rights and freedoms must be capable of analysis, visioning, and advocacy— all elements associated with reflection and caring.[27] These elements of reflection and caring are needed in order to meet the legal obligation placed upon educators to consider each student as an individual. The courts' interpretation of the *Charter* has been contextual, directing attention to the particular needs of individuals. These decisions have affirmed the promise of an ethic of care in education.

The reflective teacher is a caring teacher, one who is capable of critically analyzing the current state of education by asking who it works for and who it disadvantages. The reflective process also involves visioning—that is, stepping outside the status quo, to explore what needs to be done in the classroom, in the curriculum, within a school's culture, and within the organization of education to fully realize the educational and democratic potential of all students. Finally, the reflective and caring teacher is an advocate of the student. In that capacity, teachers act with and for students to ensure that the potential of all students is fulfilled and that students' inherent human dignity is maintained.

Educators are responsible for eliminating learning environments that are poisoned by sexual, racial, or homophobic harassment. This responsibility has been placed squarely "on those who control [the learning environment] and are in a position to take effective remedial action to remove undesirable conditions."[28] Educational decision-makers control what happens in a school, thus they are responsible for taking effective action to remove harassing behaviour. Administrators are compelled by education acts to maintain proper order and discipline.[29] In addition, the *Charter* has placed an important onus on educators

---

26 Allison Reyes, "Freedom of Expression and Public School Teachers" (1995) 4 Dalhousie Journal of Legal Studies 35.

27 John Dewey, *How We Think: A Restatement of the Relation of Reflective Thinking to the Education Process* (New York: D.C. Heath, 1933). Dewey proposed three elements of reflective teaching: open-mindedness, responsibility, and whole-heartedness.

28 *Robichaud v. Canada (Treasury Board),* [1987] 2 S.C.R. 84 at 95. Robichaud filed a complaint with the Canadian Human Rights Commission alleging that she had been sexually harassed by her supervisor. The court ruled that employers, in this case the Department of National Defence, are liable for the actions of their employees "in the course of employment."

29 In the case of *R. v. J.M.G.* (1986), 56 O.R. (2d) (O.C.A.) 705, the Court of Appeal in Ontario argued that administrators have a duty to maintain proper order and discipline.

by calling upon them to justify their actions. This onus has made the system more open so as to expose "less than worthy goals [which] may be cloaked in the rhetoric of justice and reason."[30] The ability to justify decisions in a cogent and objective manner is a useful practice no matter what the issue may be.[31]

On School Boards

School boards are responsible and thus liable for the actions of their staff. The threat of costly *Charter* challenges impels school boards to provide clear direction to their staff on their responsibility to uphold student rights and to ensure that students are treated with respect. This includes a duty to provide a learning environment free from discrimination.

The Supreme Court affirmed the public's "compelling interest in education,"[32] one that requires the assurance that every child is receiving efficient instruction approved by secular authorities in all educational establishments. This public interest places on school boards a number of obligations.

School boards must act with diligence in taking prompt, effective, and proportional measures to deal with the problems of harassment, inequality, and intolerance in schools.[33] Simply disciplining those who harass others will not eradicate systemic anti-social conditions. School boards must undertake proactive and effective tactics to eradicate systemic barriers. They must be able to show that the curriculum is unbiased, that it does not promote any view that might negatively impact on religious and cultural minorities or on the basis of gender or ability. The Supreme Court directed:

> It is not sufficient for a school board to take a passive role. A school board has a duty to maintain a positive school environment for all persons served by it and it must be ever vigilant of anything that might interfere with this duty.[34]

The court ruled in favour of the actions of an administrator who was accused by a student of violating his right to be free from an unreasonable search and seizure. For a discussion of this case, see A. Wayne MacKay, "Students as Second Class Citizens Under the Charter" (1987) 54 C.R. (3d) 390.

30 *Miron v. Trudel*, [1995] 2 S.C.R. 418 at 485.

31 See Ailsa M. Watkinson & Linda Holmes, "Reflections on the Closing of Our Children's School" (1996) 8:1 Our School Ourselves. We argue that since school closures are such an emotional issue, it is incumbent upon decision makers to carefully disclose the rationale for their decisions. We advocate that they follow the process and proportionality test employed in a section 1 analysis.

32 *Jones, supra* note 19 at 588.

33 *Quebec Human Rights Commission v. Board of Education of Deux-Montagnes* (April 8, 1993) Quebec Human Rights Tribunal, discussed in "School Board Ordered to Pay $10,000 to Teacher for Failure to Protect Him From Students' Racial Taunts" (May 1993) Lancaster Labour Law Reports, Charter Cases/Human Rights Reporter 2 at 3; *Ross, supra* note 23 at 864.

34 *Ross, ibid.* at 861.

School boards as well as educators must be able to justify decisions that limit the rights and freedoms of students and staff. The justification has to be clear and cogent and most certainly not based on administrative convenience.[35]

On Government and Community

The Supreme Court said:

> Discrimination is unacceptable in a democratic society because it epitomizes the worst effects of the denial of equality, and discrimination reinforced by law is particularly repugnant. The worst oppression will result from discriminatory measures having the force of law.[36]

Governments, as the drafters and enforcers of educational legislation, have a crucial role to play in promoting and upholding the democratic rights of students. They have the power, authority, and obligation to do so. They are also obliged to cull their education acts to ensure that their legislation does not interfere with the *Charter* rights of students. Two examples come to mind: the authority given to administrators to use corporal punishment, and provisions that allow for Christian practices in schools.

The former Saskatchewan minister of education challenged educators to seek justice as a means of constructing hope. She said:

> Our society is diverse. In the midst of our diversity, the public education system is the social institution with the greatest capacity to nurture tolerance, understanding and community among diverse groups and interests.[37]

The public education system is just that: the public's. If that is so, it follows that all citizens have a say in the education of youth. This education should be one that fulfills the *Charter*'s purpose and the promise of a democratic society and one that grants to all citizens the rights and freedoms we would want for ourselves.

The Education Transformation Impact

There are calls from within the educational community for systemic educational changes—changes that go to the heart of school governance, school organization, leadership, curriculum content and design, pedagogy, staffing, and teacher preparation.[38] The terms used to describe the transformational changes may vary

---

35 *Singh v. M.E.I.*, [1985] 1 S.C.R. 177.

36 *Andrews v. Law Society of British Columbia*, [1989] 1 S.C.R. 143 at 172.

37 The Honourable Pat Atkinson, former Minister of Education, Opening Remarks to the Canadian Association of School Administrators (Radisson Hotel, Saskatoon, 28 September 1997).

38 See, for example, Ailsa M. Watkinson & Juanita Ross Epp, "Addressing Systemic Violence in Education," in Juanita Ross Epp & Ailsa M. Watkinson, eds., *Systemic*

but the theme is generally the same. The proposals challenge educators, boards of education, and the government to practise democracy while preaching the virtues of democratic principles. There is a synergy between the democratizing of education and more humane and caring learning environments. They are dependent on one another and both are essential ingredients in the promotion of student rights. These changes call for systemic upheavals in school culture.[39]

Linda Darling-Hammond, an American educator, proposed the development of

communities of learning grounded in communities of democratic discourse. It is only in this way that communities can come to want for all their children what they would want for their most advantaged—an education for empowerment and an education for freedom.[40]

Thomas Sergiovanni envisioned schools as communities of caring, along the same lines proposed by many feminist and critical theorists.[41] He suggested that we change the metaphor. Educational institutions should be seen as communities rather than as bureaucratic organizations.[42]

Robert Carlson, an American professor of education, advocates for members of a school and its community to be guided by democratic values to permit the shaping and reshaping of a school's vision and values. He stated that one of the values in the democratic process is the protection it provides for those who are disadvantaged:

A democratic process built on open and full participation of all members of a community should safeguard against the creation of more restrictive visions that

---

Violence in Education: Promise Broken (New York: State University of New York Press, 1997) at 190.

39 The School Effectiveness Movement, for example, has been criticized as being ineffective in bringing about meaningful school reform. See, for example, Ailsa M. Watkinson, "Administrative Complicity and Systemic Violence in Education," in *Systemic Violence in Education, supra* note 38; David A. Squires & Robert D. Kranyik, "The Comer Program: Changing School Culture" (1996) 53:4 Educational Leadership 29.

40 Linda Darling-Hammond, "Reframing the School Reform Agenda: Developing Capacity for School Transformation" (1993) 74 Phi-Delta-Kappan 752 at 755.

41 See, for example, Nel Nodding, *The Challenge to Care in Schools: An Alternative Approach to Education* (New York: Teacher's College Press, 1992); Carol Gilligan, *In a Different Voice: Psychological Theory and Women's Development* (Cambridge: Harvard University Press, 1982); Purpel, *supra* note 10; Beck, *supra* note 10.

42 Thomas J. Sergiovanni, *Building Community in Schools* (San Francisco: Jossey-Bass, 1994) at 6. Sergiovanni uses German words to express Gilligan's notion of justice and care. Various school organizations are described as either *Gesellschaft,* meaning contractual (the ethic of justice), or *Gemeinschaft,* meaning kinship (the ethic of care).

are imposed on weaker or less represented members of the community. It is through the debates, so integral to the democratic process, that value conflicts, paradoxes, dualisms may be aired and resolved.[43]

These ideas are not new. In the 1940s John Dewey tirelessly promoted a more democratic education and conceptualized the school as the "laboratory" of democracy "where students and teachers could wrestle with the challenges of the democratic experiences."[44] He wrote:

> Just as democracy in order to live must move and move forward, so schools in a democracy cannot stand still, cannot be satisfied and complacent with what has been accomplished, but must be willing to undertake whatever reorganization of studies, of methods of teaching, of administration, including that larger organization which concerns the relation of pupils and teachers to each other, and to the life of the community. Failing in this, the schools cannot give democracy the intelligent direction of its forces which it needs to continue in existence.[45]

Dewey warned that if schools do not change, do not progress towards democratization, they risk taking refuge in an ark that "is not the ark of safety in a deluge. It is being carried by the deluge of outside forces, varying, shifting, turning aimlessly with every current in the tides of modern life."[46]

It has taken over half a century, fifty more years of modernity, for the deluge to hit home, and not everyone is convinced. But research on the democratizing of education within a caring learning environment demonstrates success for student learning, staff satisfaction, and challenges for educational decision-makers. The proposed, and in some cases actual, democratic changes in the administration and deliverance of public education affects all components of the education community.

On Students

A democratic and caring learning environment is characterized by a co-operative, nurturing, interdependent, and respectful learning community. It is defined as a student-centred environment with small classes, student input in decision-making, and attention to individual needs. It is an environment in which the experiences of students are elevated in importance.[47] In this learning environment, students

---

43 Robert V. Carlson, *Reframing and Reform: Perspectives on Organization, Leadership, and School Change* (New York: Longman, 1996) at 163.

44 Purpel, *supra* note 10.

45 John Dewey, *Philosophy of Education (Problems of Men)* (New Jersey: Littlefield, Adams and Co., 1946) at 48.

46 *Ibid.*

47 J.W. Murphy & J.M. Choi, "Decentering Social Relations," in J. Murphy & D. Pecks, eds., *Open Institutions* (Westpoint, CT: Praeger, 1993).

and teachers get to know each other well. It is a community of teachers, administrators, and students working co-operatively, nurturing "fundamental humane and creative educational thinking, enabling them to bestow upon their pupils the happiness of school life and the joy of exchanging ideas with the teachers."[48]

Darling-Hammond asserted that an environment of respect and trust assists learners to think critically, to synthesize, to transform, to experiment, and to create.[49] Studies show that learning opportunities for students are enhanced within a humane and co-operative learning environment;[50] that such an environment promotes social networking, co-operative behaviour, and creative and self-enhancing independence;[51] and that student academic performance improves when educators stress co-operation rather than competition.[52]

Likewise, efforts to create a caring community within each school and each classroom are linked to increases in students' social, moral, and intellectual development. The caring community atmosphere helped students "to improve in social competence, interpersonal behaviour in the classroom, interpersonal understanding, endorsement of democratic values and higher-level reading comprehension."[53] The authors credit "close, stable relationships with caring adults as being pivotal in student development of intellectual, social and moral growth."[54] In addition, the negative effects of poverty are largely or wholly ameliorated in schools that have a high sense of community.[55] Other studies have shown that violence is rare in such environments, that there are fewer suspensions, and that there is less deviant behaviour and better attendance.[56]

---

48 Shalva Amonashvili, "Non-directive Teaching and the Humanization of the Educational Process" (1989) 19 Prospects 581 at 585.

49 Linda Darling-Hammond, "The Quiet Revolution: Rethinking Teacher Development" (1996) 53:6 Educational Leadership 4.

50 Doris B. Matthews, "The Effect of School Environment on Intrinsic Motivation of Middle-School Children" (1991) 30 Journal of Humanistic Education and Development 30. Matthews reports that the intrinsic motivation in academic learning of girls and boys is increased in humanistic school settings as compared with students in more structural school environments; Edward W. Schultz *et al.*, "School Climate: Psychological Health and Well Being in School" (1987) 57 Journal of School Health 432.

51 Schultz, *ibid.* at 32.

52 Beck, *supra* note 10 at 44.

53 Eric Schaps & Daniel Solomon, "Schools and Classrooms As Caring Communities" (1990) 48 Educational Leadership 38 at 40.

54 *Ibid.*

55 Victor Battistich *et al.*, "Caring School Communities" (1997) 32:3 Educational Psychologist 137.

56 Squires & Kranyik, *supra* note 39 at 29. The Comer School Development Program employs a collaborative process that brings together teachers, principals, parents, and community members to create programs that foster the educational development of children.

Sara Lightfoot is an American scholar of education. In her detailed search for and description of the "good school," she remarked that "[g]ood schools are places where students are seen as people worthy of respect"[57] and where there is "the fearless and empathic regard of students."[58] These schools demonstrate interest in all students "but especially for saving lost souls and helping students who are most vulnerable."[59] She states that one way of judging institutional goodness for students is to "observe the regard and treatment of the weakest members."[60]

A national study of exemplary secondary schools in Canada attempted to identify and analyze successful practices in schools. The authors of the study found that the most frequently mentioned reason for schools being labelled "exemplary" was the quality of the social environment for students. They reported that "a successful school is one that feels like a home, a place where all feel equal and safe and where teachers care."[61]

On Educators

The benefits of a democratic educational environment are shared by both educators and students. Lynn Beck, an educational administrator, reported numerous studies that demonstrate that all who work and study within a caring education system "flourish under leadership that stresses co-operation, acceptance, nurturance and interdependence."[62] Other studies support the relationship between caring leaders and school effectiveness, suggesting "that effective schools tend to be led by administrators who have a deep concern for students' holistic personal development."[63] A supportive working atmosphere for teachers—one that stresses nurturing, positive interpersonal relationships—is linked to both teacher commitment and student achievement.[64] Teachers who feel enabled to succeed with students, due in part to shared decision-making and collegial work environments,

---

57 Sara Lawrence Lightfoot, *The Good High School: Portraits of Character and Culture* (New York: Basic, 1983) at 350.

58 *Ibid.* at 342.

59 *Ibid.* at 349.

60 *Ibid.* at 349.

61 Jane Gaskell *et al., Secondary Schools in Canada: The National Report of the Exemplary Schools Project* (Toronto: Canadian Education Association, 1995). The study selected twenty-one schools from across Canada that had a reputation for success.

62 Beck, *supra* note 10 at 44.

63 K.A. Leithwood & D.J. Montgomery, "The Role of the Elementary School Principal in Program Improvement" (1982) 52 Review of Educational Research 309, cited in Beck, *ibid.* at 49.

64 J.G. Maeroff, "Getting to Know a Good Middle School: Shoreham-Wading River" (1990) 71 Phi-Delta-Kappan, 504; L. Schorr, *Within Our Reach: Breaking the Cycle of Disadvantage* (New York: Doubleday, 1989), cited in Beck, *ibid.* at 46–47.

are more committed than those who feel unsupported in their practice.[65]

Educational consultants Robert Garmston and Bruce Wellman used the term "quantum" to describe a working environment that is an interconnected web of relationships.[66] The authors proposed that a quantum working environment is a self-renewing school, a collaborative place "where adults care about one another, share common goals and values . . . solve problems together, and fight passionately but gracefully for ideas to improve instruction."[67]

Those who have direct contact with students are central in fostering a caring learning environment. Darling-Hammond recognized the effect teacher practices have on enhancing student learning as well as on improving students' "higher-order thinking" and on educators' success in dealing with "at risk" children.[68] She described the caring teacher when she stated:

> Concerns about "at-risk" children—those who drop out, tune out and fall behind—cannot be addressed without teachers who are prepared to understand and meet the needs of students who come to school with varying learning skills, from diverse family situations, and with differing beliefs about themselves and about what school means for them.[69]

The language of community and caring is used in the case studies of exemplary schools to describe the types of relationships among staff as well as staff relationships with students.[70] A caring working environment enhances job satisfaction among educators, improves student satisfaction and achievement, and nurtures the democratic rights of students.

On School Boards

The selection of educators is extremely important. After all they set the tone, they are the central actors.[71] The selection process requires careful screening of individuals based on their philosophy of education and on evidence of its practice. The prominent characteristics of educators must be caring, compassion, and empathy. They must be individuals who see their task "first and foremost as nurturing the skills, attitudes, and values necessary for democratic life."[72] In addition, more professional development is needed to expose teachers to the

---

65   "The Quiet Revolution," *supra* note 49 at 9.

66   Robert Garmston & Bruce Wellman, "Adaptive Schools In a Quantum Universe" (1995) 52:7 Educational Leadership 6 at 8. This is the same wording used by Gilligan when she describes the ethic of care as a web of connectedness.

67   *Ibid.* at 12.

68   "Reframing the School Reform Agenda," *supra* note 40.

69   *Ibid.* at 755.

70   Gaskell, *supra* note 61 at 182.

71   *Ibid.*

72   George H. Wood, "Teaching for Democracy" (1990) 48:3 Educational Leadership 32 at 33.

new and challenging obligations found under the *Charter* and other human rights documents.

The design of schools and class size are important factors to consider in promoting a democratic educational environment. Pedagogy must also be reshaped to reflect democratic values and principles. It must be reconstructed from the "standpoint of the least advantaged."[73] The development of curriculum must include the experiences of women as well as men, the experiences of Aboriginal people and other racialized groups, and the experiences of the poor. As Wayne MacKay noted, "There is a symbiotic relationship between education and equality that must permeate pedagogical theory."[74]

Democratic education means that direction from students in decision-making and curriculum planning is something to be valued. Education decision-makers need to ferret out all barriers that hinder students' right to learn. Doing otherwise leads to institutionalized inequality and the truncation of democratic rights.

On the Government and Community

The young need to be exposed to the workings, advantages, and disadvantages of democracy. They, too, are its citizens and our neighbours. For the public education system to systemically adjust itself so as to better foster the development of a civic- and community-minded citizenry, public support, financial support, emulation, and legislative changes are required.

Hillary Clinton chose the title to her book *It Takes a Village* from an African saying: "It takes a village to raise a child." She said she chose it because it is "a timeless reminder that children will thrive only if their families thrive and if the whole of society cares enough to provide for them."[75]

Conclusion

In 1932, educational philosopher George Counts implored teachers to take a stand and fashion curricula and school procedures to positively influence the social attitudes, ideals, and behaviour of the coming generation. He urged teachers and administrators to build a new social order, one that would challenge the forces of conservatism epitomized in capitalism, "with its deification of the principle of selfishness, its exaltation of the profit motive, its reliance upon the forces of competition, and its placing of property above human rights."[76] Counts's

---

73 R.W. Connell, *Schools and Social Justice* (Montreal: Our Schools Our Selves, 1993) c. 4.

74 A. Wayne MacKay & Vincent C Kazmierski, "And on the Eighth Day, God Gave Us . . . Equality in Education: *Eaton v. Brant (County) Board of Education* and Inclusive Education" (1996) 7 National Journal of Constitutional Law 1 at 20.

75 Hillary Rodham Clinton, *It Takes a Village and Other Lessons That Children Teach Us* (Toronto: Simon & Schuster, 1996) at 12.

76 George S. Counts, *Dare the School Build a New Social Order?* (New York: Arno, 1969) at 47.

vision included the development of a democratic society that would

> combat all forces tending to produce social distinctions and classes; repress every
> form of privilege and economic parasitism; manifest a tender regard for the weak,
> the ignorant and the unfortunate; . . . transform or destroy all conventions,
> institutions, and special groups inimical to the underlying principles of democracy;
> and finally be prepared . . . to follow the method of revolution.[77]

I would direct students, parents, and their advocates to Counts's manifesto. I would encourage them to insist on democratic participation, to repress every form of educational privilege used by educators to maintain their control and power, and to fashion a new school order imbued with the values and principles of a democratic society. At the same time, I would challenge educational professionals to dismantle the forces of authoritarianism in education and to transform educational design from a bureaucracy to a web of interconnectedness,[78] a place of community.

MacKay wrote:

> I think it would be reasonable for a student to say that the system whereby adults,
> and largely white male adults, have defined the best interests for students and for
> everybody else in society has not worked well. And perhaps if we give more rights
> to students, if we give more recognition to women in society, if we give more
> recognition to minorities, homosexuals, or others, we are going to produce a different
> kind of society, one that will make more rational decisions for adults, as well as for
> students.[79]

Counts's new school order, MacKay's vision of a different kind of society, and Dewey's charge to educators to move forward will be advanced through the selection of caring, compassionate educators who walk in the talk of democracy, recognize completely the inherent dignity of students, and fulfil absolutely their obligations to them. With a "critical mass" of professionals such as these, there is a good chance of change and of moving schools forward in step with our democratic society: "Failing in this, the schools cannot give democracy the intelligent direction of its forces which it needs to continue in existence."[80]

---

77 *Ibid.* at 41–42.
78 Gilligan, *supra* note 41; Kathy E. Ferguson, *The Feminist Case Against Bureaucracy* (Philadelphia: Temple University Press, 1984); Charol Shakeshaft, *Women in Educational Administration* (Newbury Park: Sage, 1989).
79 A. Wayne MacKay, "The Judicial Role in Educational Policy-Making: Promise of Threat?" (1988–1989) 1 Education Law Journal 127 at 147.
80 Dewey, *supra* note 45.

Appendix ■

Canadian Charter of Rights and Freedoms

Schedule B
Constitution Act, 1982 (79)
Enacted as Schedule B to the Canada Act 1982 (U.K.) 1982, c. 11, which came into force on April 17, 1982

PART I
Canadian charter of rights and freedoms

Whereas Canada is founded upon principles that recognize the supremacy of God and the rule of law:

Guarantee of Rights and Freedoms

1. The *Canadian Charter of Rights and Freedoms* guarantees the rights and freedoms set out in it subject only to such reasonable limits prescribed by law as can be demonstrably justified in a free and democratic society.

Fundamental Freedoms

2. Everyone has the following fundamental freedoms:
a) freedom of conscience and religion;
b) freedom of thought, belief, opinion and expression, including freedom of the press and other media of communication;
c) freedom of peaceful assembly; and
d) freedom of association.

Democratic Rights

3. Every citizen of Canada has the right to vote in an election of members of the House of Commons or of a legislative assembly and to be qualified for membership therein.

4. (1) No House of Commons and no legislative assembly shall continue for longer than five years from the date fixed for the return of the writs of a general election of its members.

(2) In time of real or apprehended war, invasion or insurrection, a House of Commons may be continued by Parliament and a legislative assembly may be continued by the legislature beyond five years if such continuation is not opposed by the votes of more than one-third of the members of the House of Commons or the legislative assembly, as the case may be.

5. There shall be a sitting of Parliament and of each legislature at least once every twelve months.

Appendix

Mobility Rights

6. (1) Every citizen of Canada has the right to enter, remain in and leave Canada.

(2) Every citizen of Canada and every person who has the status of a permanent resident of Canada has the right
a) to move to and take up residence in any province; and
b) to pursue the gaining of a livelihood in any province.

(3) The rights specified in subsection (2) are subject to
a) any laws or practices of general application in force in a province other than those that discriminate among persons primarily on the basis of province of present or previous residence; and
b) any laws providing for reasonable residency requirements as a qualification for the receipt of publicly provided social services.

(4) Subsections (2) and (3) do not preclude any law, program or activity that has as its object the amelioration in a province of conditions of individuals in that province who are socially or economically disadvantaged if the rate of employment in that province is below the rate of employment in Canada.

Legal Rights

7. Everyone has the right to life, liberty and security of the person and the right not to be deprived thereof except in accordance with the principles of fundamental justice.

8. Everyone has the right to be secure against unreasonable search or seizure.

9. Everyone has the right not to be arbitrarily detained or imprisoned.

10. Everyone has the right on arrest or detention
a) to be informed promptly of the reasons therefor;
b) to retain and instruct counsel without delay and to be informed of that right; and
c) to have the validity of the detention determined by way of habeas corpus and to be released if the detention is not lawful.

11. Any person charged with an offence has the right
a) to be informed without unreasonable delay of the specific offence;
b) to be tried within a reasonable time;
c) not to be compelled to be a witness in proceedings against that person in respect of the offence;
d) to be presumed innocent until proven guilty according to law in a fair and public hearing by an independent and impartial tribunal;
e) not to be denied reasonable bail without just cause;
f) except in the case of an offence under military law tried before a military tribunal, to the benefit of trial by jury where the maximum punishment for the offence is imprisonment for five years or a more severe punishment;
g) not to be found guilty on account of any act or omission unless, at the time of the act or

omission, it constituted an offence under Canadian or international law or was criminal according to the general principles of law recognized by the community of nations;
h) if finally acquitted of the offence, not to be tried for it again and, if finally found guilty and punished for the offence, not to be tried or punished for it again; and
i) if found guilty of the offence and if the punishment for the offence has been varied between the time of commission and the time of sentencing, to the benefit of the lesser punishment.

12. Everyone has the right not to be subjected to any cruel and unusual treatment or punishment.

13. A witness who testifies in any proceedings has the right not to have any incriminating evidence so given used to incriminate that witness in any other proceedings, except in a prosecution for perjury or for the giving of contradictory evidence.

14. A party or witness in any proceedings who does not understand or speak the language in which the proceedings are conducted or who is deaf has the right to the assistance of an interpreter.

Equality Rights

15. (1) Every individual is equal before and under the law and has the right to the equal protection and equal benefit of the law without discrimination and, in particular, without discrimination based on race, national or ethnic origin, colour, religion, sex, age or mental or physical disability.

(2) Subsection (1) does not preclude any law, program or activity that has as its object the amelioration of conditions of disadvantaged individuals or groups including those that are disadvantaged because of race, national or ethnic origin, colour, religion, sex, age or mental or physical disability.

Official Languages of Canada

16. (1) English and French are the official languages of Canada and have equality of status and equal rights and privileges as to their use in all institutions of the Parliament and government of Canada.

(2) English and French are the official languages of New Brunswick and have equality of status and equal rights and privileges as to their use in all institutions of the legislature and government of New Brunswick.

(3) Nothing in this Charter limits the authority of Parliament or a legislature to advance the equality of status or use of English and French.

16.1. (1) The English linguistic community and the French linguistic community in New Brunswick have equality of status and equal rights and privileges, including the right to distinct educational institutions and such distinct cultural institutions as are necessary for the preservation and promotion of those communities.

(2) The role of the legislature and government of New Brunswick to preserve and promote the status, rights and privileges referred to in subsection (1) is affirmed.

17. (1) Everyone has the right to use English or French in any debates and other proceedings of Parliament.

(2) Everyone has the right to use English or French in any debates and other proceedings of the legislature of New Brunswick.

18. (1) The statutes, records and journals of Parliament shall be printed and published in English and French and both language versions are equally authoritative.

(2) The statutes, records and journals of the legislature of New Brunswick shall be printed and published in English and French and both language versions are equally authoritative.

19. (1) Either English or French may be used by any person in, or in any pleading in or process issuing from, any court established by Parliament.

(2) Either English or French may be used by any person in, or in any pleading in or process issuing from, any court of New Brunswick.

20. (1) Any member of the public in Canada has the right to communicate with, and to receive available services from, any head or central office of an institution of the Parliament or government of Canada in English or French, and has the same right with respect to any other office of any such institution where
a) there is a significant demand for communications with and services from that office in such language; or
b) due to the nature of the office, it is reasonable that communications with and services from that office be available in both English and French.

(2) Any member of the public in New Brunswick has the right to communicate with, and to receive available services from, any office of an institution of the legislature or government of New Brunswick in English or French.

21. Nothing in sections 16 to 20 abrogates or derogates from any right, privilege or obligation with respect to the English and French languages, or either of them, that exists or is continued by virtue of any other provision of the Constitution of Canada.

22. Nothing in sections 16 to 20 abrogates or derogates from any legal or customary right or privilege acquired or enjoyed either before or after the coming into force of this Charter with respect to any language that is not English or French.

Minority Language Educational Rights

23. (1) Citizens of Canada
a) whose first language learned and still understood is that of the English or French

linguistic minority population of the province in which they reside, or

b) who have received their primary school instruction in Canada in English or French and reside in a province where the language in which they received that instruction is the language of the English or French linguistic minority population of the province, have the right to have their children receive primary and secondary school instruction in that language in that province.

(2) Citizens of Canada of whom any child has received or is receiving primary or secondary school instruction in English or French in Canada, have the right to have all their children receive primary and secondary school instruction in the same language.

(3) The right of citizens of Canada under subsections (1) and (2) to have their children receive primary and secondary school instruction in the language of the English or French linguistic minority population of a province

a) applies wherever in the province the number of children of citizens who have such a right is sufficient to warrant the provision to them out of public funds of minority language instruction; and

b) includes, where the number of those children so warrants, the right to have them receive that instruction in minority language educational facilities provided out of public funds.

Enforcement

24. (1) Anyone whose rights or freedoms, as guaranteed by this Charter, have been infringed or denied may apply to a court of competent jurisdiction to obtain such remedy as the court considers appropriate and just in the circumstances.

(2) Where, in proceedings under subsection (1), a court concludes that evidence was obtained in a manner that infringed or denied any rights or freedoms guaranteed by this Charter, the evidence shall be excluded if it is established that, having regard to all the circumstances, the admission of it in the proceedings would bring the administration of justice into disrepute.

General

25. The guarantee in this Charter of certain rights and freedoms shall not be construed so as to abrogate or derogate from any aboriginal, treaty or other rights or freedoms that pertain to the aboriginal peoples of Canada including

a) any rights or freedoms that have been recognized by the Royal Proclamation of October 7, 1763; and

b) any rights or freedoms that now exist by way of land claims agreements or may be so acquired.

26. The guarantee in this Charter of certain rights and freedoms shall not be construed as denying the existence of any other rights or freedoms that exist in Canada.

27. This Charter shall be interpreted in a manner consistent with the preservation and enhancement of the multicultural heritage of Canadians.

28. Notwithstanding anything in this Charter, the rights and freedoms referred to in it are guaranteed equally to male and female persons.

29. Nothing in this Charter abrogates or derogates from any rights or privileges guaranteed by or under the Constitution of Canada in respect of denominational, separate or dissentient schools.

30. A reference in this Charter to a Province or to the legislative assembly or legislature of a province shall be deemed to include a reference to the Yukon Territory and the Northwest Territories, or to the appropriate legislative authority thereof, as the case may be.

31. Nothing in this Charter extends the legislative powers of any body or authority.

Application of Charter

32. (1)This Charter applies
a) to the Parliament and government of Canada in respect of all matters within the authority of Parliament including all matters relating to the Yukon Territory and Northwest Territories; and
b) to the legislature and government of each province in respect of all matters within the authority of the legislature of each province.

(2) Notwithstanding subsection (1), section 15 shall not have effect until three years after this section comes into force.

33. (1) Parliament or the legislature of a province may expressly declare in an Act of Parliament or of the legislature, as the case may be, that the Act or a provision thereof shall operate notwithstanding a provision included in section 2 or sections 7 to 15 of this Charter.

(2) An Act or a provision of an Act in respect of which a declaration made under this section is in effect shall have such operation as it would have but for the provision of this Charter referred to in the declaration.

(3) A declaration made under subsection (1) shall cease to have effect five years after it comes into force or on such earlier date as may be specified in the declaration.

(4) Parliament or the legislature of a province may re-enact a declaration made under subsection (1).

(5) Subsection (3) applies in respect of a re-enactment made under subsection (4).

Citation

34. This Part may be cited as the *Canadian Charter of Rights and Freedoms.*

Index